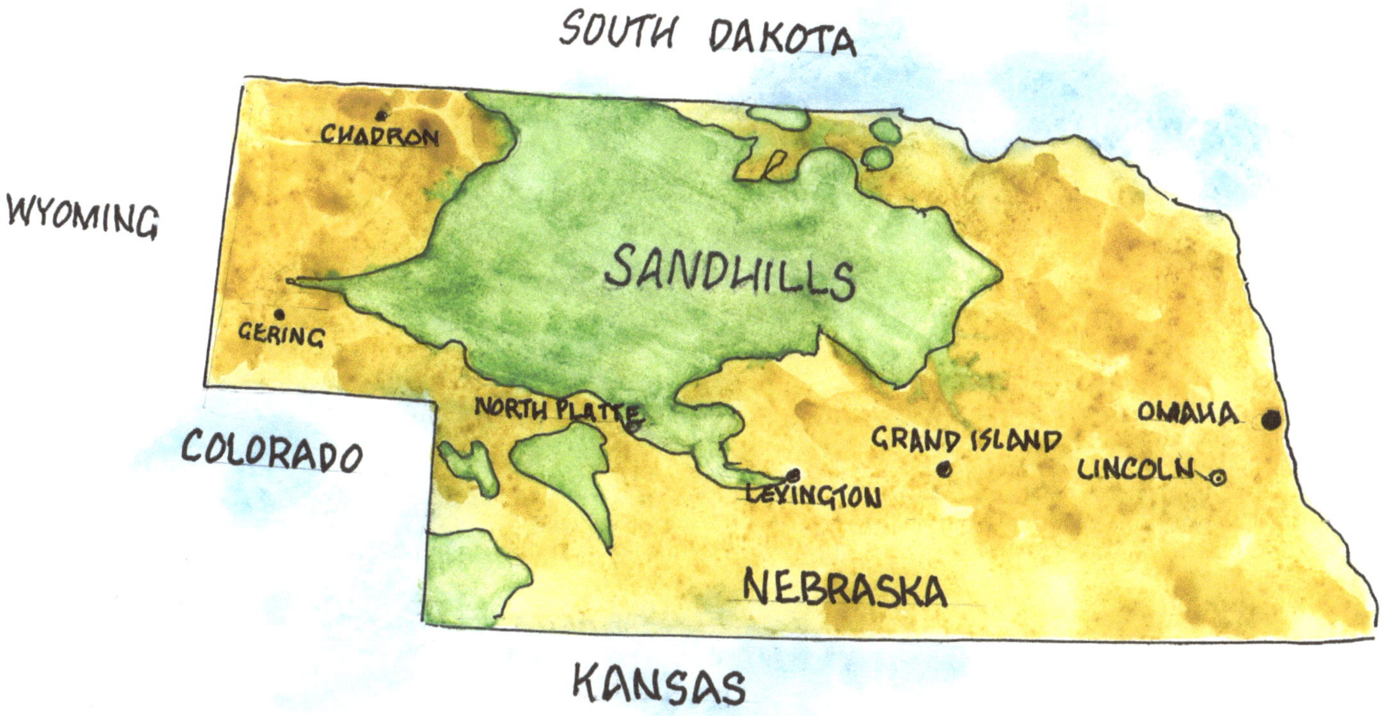

Other Books by Richard Schilling

Watercolor Journeys

Portraits of the Prairies: The Land That Inspired Willa Cather

The Forgotten Edge of Russia

Passport to Painting

A European Odyssey

An African Journal

Drawing on The Ancient Ones

Portraits *of the* Sandhills
in words and watercolors

RICHARD SCHILLING

▶▶CHINOOK WIND▶▶
B O O K S

LOVELAND, COLORADO

©2018 Richard Schilling

All rights reserved. No part of this book may be used or reproduced by any means, graphic, electronic, or mechanical, including photocopying, recording, taping or by any information storage retrieval system without the written permission of the publisher except in the case of brief quotations embodied in critical articles and reviews.

PAPERBACK: 978-1-7325382-1-4
HARDCOVER: 978-1-7325382-2-1
LCCN: 2018950692

Cataloging in Publication data on file with the publisher.

Chinook Wind Books: www.worldwidewatercolorist.com

Because of the dynamic nature of the Internet, any web addresses or links contained in this book may have changed since publication and may no longer be valid. Excerpts and stories have been reprinted with permission where required and include a citation of the origin of the piece.

Publishing and Production services provided by Concierge Marketing Inc.

Printed in the United States of America
First Printing 2018

10 9 8 7 6 5 4 3 2 1

Dedication

In memory of those stalwart pioneers and

settlers who endured, and their progeny

who now inhabit the land that is theirs for a little while.

About the Author and Artist

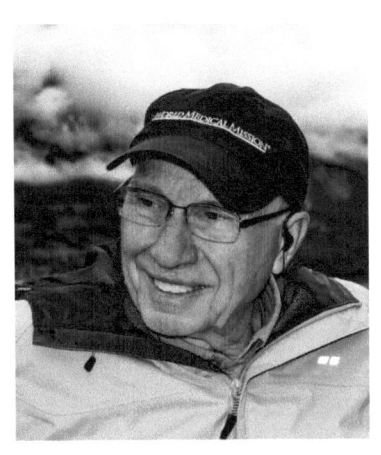

Richard Schilling was born and raised in Lincoln. He's a graduate of the University of Nebraska Lincoln. His passion for painting began at the age of twelve when he was invited to take lessons in watercolor at the University of Nebraska. Since then he has established his own style and reputation through his decades of experience and several hundred paintings.

For many years Schilling was a missionary dentist abroad and a part-time officer for Holland America Cruise Line. These rich experiences provided opportunities to paint scenes on six continents. He is the author of eight art books. His adventures abroad are chronicled in his best-selling book, *Watercolor Journeys*. Recent books are *Portraits of the Prairie: The Land That Inspired Willa Cather* (University of Nebraska Press), *The Forgotten Edge of Russia* (WestBow Press), and *Portraits of the Sandhills In Words and Watercolors* (Chinook Wind Books).

Today, he paints most every day, and oversees the Smiles Without Borders Foundation that he and two others created to provide free dental care for needy children.

WATERCOLORS

For information on purchasing Richard Schilling's work, please contact the artist at wwwatercolorist@comcast.net.

i	Map of Nebraska	23	A Road Less-Traveled
3	Morning After a Spring Storm SIOUX COUNTY	25	Mills Valley in Logan County JUDKIN'S HILL, ARNOLD, NEBRASKA
5	After a Winter Storm MCPHERSON COUNTY	27	Middle Loup River THEDFORD, NEBRASKA
6	Colors of Winter SIOUX COUNTY	29	Jules Sandoz's Grave Marker ALLIANCE, NEBRASKA
9	No Parking Meters Here ASHBY, NEBRASKA	30	Lake Minatare SCOTTSBLUFF COUNTY
11	The Old Potash Plant ANTIOCH, SHERIDAN COUNTY	32	Sentinels of the Prairie C. R. WATSON PLACE SIOUX COUNTY
13	Glorious Evening in Garden County GARDEN COUNTY	35	A Lazy Summer Day SHERIDAN COUNTY
15	Pintails Rising to the Wind HOOKER COUNTY	37	Road to Nowhere
16	White Pelicans SIOUX COUNTY	39	Rural Mail Boxes GRANT COUNTY
19	A Caucus of Cowboys SHERIDAN COUNTY	40	Mail Boxes in Brown County
21	Branding on the Burford Ranch SHERIDAN COUNTY	43	School Before a Storm DISTRICT #71 SCHOOL, SIOUX COUNTY

45	Pasture Gate GRANT COUNTY	68	Autumn Clouds
47	The Flaherty Place SIOUX COUNTY	70	Blow Out LOGAN COUNTY
48	Sunrise on the Calamus River LOUP COUNTY	73	A Lazy Afternoon in Spring SHERIDAN COUNTY
50	The Farmer's Co-Op HEMINGFORD, BOX BUTTE COUNTY	75	Memories of Better Days BROWN COUNTY
51	Buddies on the Range SIOUX COUNTY	76	Misty Morning in Sheridan County
55	Night Train	79	Return to Sender GRANT COUNTY
57	Abandon Home SIOUX COUNTY	81	Approaching Dust Storm
59	The Dismal River THOMAS COUNTY	82	The Lazy North Loup River BLAINE COUNTY
60	Hay Bales in Logan County	85	Springtime in the Wamaduze Valley
63	Window in the Old Jail ARTHUR COUNTY JAIL	88	Golden Bluffs in March SIOUX COUNTY
65	A Blow-Out in Cherry County	89	Trumpeter Swan and Cygnet
67	Small Beginnings of a Great River NIOBRARA RIVER, SIOUX COUNTY	91	Cherry County Spring

93 An Evening in Spring
SHERIDAN COUNTY

95 The Bohemian Hall
BOX BUTTE COUNTY

97 Summer Sunflowers in Brown County

101 The Sandoz Orchard
SHERIDAN COUNTY

102 Canada Geese Rising
GRANT COUNTY

104 Longbill Curlew
CRESCENT LAKE, GARDEN COUNTY

105 Spring Song
THOMAS COUNTY

109 Counting New Calves
SIOUX COUNTY

112 Prairie Clouds

113 Summertime in Logan County

117 Sandhill Cranes Grazing at Dawn

120 Gathering Storm Clouds in the Sandhills

125 Homecoming

ACKNOWLEDGMENTS

Creating a book is a journey. Like most journeys, it requires good preparation and a desire to explore. This can be tiresome work; but for me, it is never boring. I am always eager to discover what I might see from the next hilltop. My memorable experiences in the Sandhills are exceeded only by the friendships of ranchers and residents that welcomed me and pointed me in the direction of a good story.

I was a sojourner in this land but I found my "newest best friends" willing to help me along the way. Laura Ramirez started me on this journey by providing suggestions and contacts for people to meet. I wish to thank ranchers Ed and Delilah Flaherty who graciously invited me into their home for stories told over cups of coffee at the kitchen table. Becci Thomas, Director of the Knight Museum in Alliance, reminisced of family tales and local history, sending me along to more way-points of interest. I am very grateful to Glenna Abbott of Long Pine who taught me the basics of pasture management and the identification of prairie grasses. There are many others who I am unable to personally thank. You will read their stories in the following pages. They may bring a tear to the eye, or a smile to one's face. . . all are endearing.

A special thanks to Lisa Pelto and the Concierge Marketing team. It could have been an arduous process to develop this book if it were not for their skill and experience. Olivia Nixon brought the book to life with her graphic and design talents.

. . . then I will send rain on your land in its season, both autumn and spring rains, so that you may gather in your grain, new wine and olive oil. I will provide grass in the fields for your cattle, and you will eat and be satisfied.

—DEUTERONOMY 11: 14,15
[New International Version]

INTRODUCTION

Billions of years ago, cosmic storms raged, and with the help of gravity, organized and concentrated large particles into the third planet from the sun. Frigid aeolian winds swirled around both poles of the planet depositing ice crystals that formed massive glaciers. The coalesced particles and rocky elements became what we now call Earth.

Later in the evolution, a tug-of-war occurred between tectonic plates that slowly moved over a more fluid mantle beneath the crust. As the continental plates squeezed together, tension pushed the pacific plate to rise and form a long chain of mountains.

The formation of the Sandhills may have begun as recently as 8,000 years ago. The Pleistocene was a geological epoch of repeated glaciation. At the end of this era the retreating glaciers left behind sand and debris that large rivers carried and deposited, creating a substructure for less dense sand that would follow. It is believed that during the formation of the Rocky Mountains sand and dust were blown eastward with strong winds from what are now Wyoming and Colorado.

Beneath these hills of sand reside permeable layers of saturated gravel that contain an immense underground sea of water. It is known today as

> "...gentle rolling hills of green or tan depending upon the season."

the Ogallala Aquifer and supplies water to a thirsty 170,000 square miles of ranchland and farmland above.

This region of sand dunes comprises the largest area of dunes in the Western Hemisphere. If you were to view a computerized geographic information system map (GIS) the Sandhills might appear as a giant right-handed glove with fingers extended eastward. This area comprises more than twenty-five percent of the State of Nebraska with additional small extensions into Colorado, Kansas and South Dakota.

Some who have viewed my paintings of the Sandhills question, "Where are the sand dunes?" The dunes are uniquely covered with stabilizing vegetation which accounts for gentle rolling hills of green or tan depending upon the season. The exceptions are "blow outs" that occasionally occur on the leeward sides of dunes, often facing southeast. They result from gradual eroding of the surface vegetation, exposing very fine sand beneath. To a golfer, they conjure nightmarish visions of giant sandtraps.

I have compressed millions of years of geological development into a few words. I refer the reader to Paul A. Johnsgard's excellent book *This Fragile Land* (University of Nebraska Press) for a comprehensive explanation. The stories and testimonies in this book may conjure memories of your own. For others, it may introduce a magical land that lies just north of a ribbon of concrete and asphalt that carries thousands of travelers each day. It is also a testament to the hardy families who like the prairie grasses that stabilize the dunes, who are anchored to the land. I ask my reader to retreat from a busy world and discover mysteries that sometimes lie just beneath our feet. Mr. Johnsgard provides good advice:

> ...The Nebraska Sandhills are a very special place that have obviously been patiently shaped by water, wind, and time. One is well advised not to try to analyze the probable type of every dune or to identify the species of every plant. Rather, visiting the Sandhills should always partly be an exercise in visual aesthetics. What is present today is a fragile land, a land of no straight lines, where wind becomes artist and sand has metamorphosed into art. The Sandhills are a place of endless grass and countless hills, of unbroken horizons and broken hearts, of astonishing beauty and unimagined hardships, of abundant life and unexpected death. They are a region to be visited and revisited, to be long remembered and forever treasured.

"where wind becomes artist and sand has metamorphosed into art."

My Sandhills Safari

...began on an extremely windy day early in March. I first wanted to visit Lake Minatare which is located on the southern fringe of sandy hills in Scottsbluff County. I parked at a lonely lakeside campground and pushed the car door open against a driving gale. The beach was deserted except for a giant Cottonwood tree which had been decapitated by a recent storm. It was an ugly reminder that weather can change without warning. I quickly took several photographic studies and returned to my car.

The weather conditions began to deteriorate and soon I was driving in a snowstorm that pulled a white curtain over the land and obliterated the road ahead. It was late in the day and I turned back to Scottsbluff to spend the night before attempting another run to Hemingford. That night in my motel, I painted the beach scene (page 30). I shivered, still feeling the effects of the cold March wind.

The next morning dawned gloriously as the sun rose over the eastern prairie, and soon the cloudless sky was draped in cobalt blue. The prairie bluffs reflected gold in early morning light and purple shadows separated each sandstone cliff. A light dusting of snow covered the prairie, leaving sage and native grasses exposed in contrasting shades of tawny brown and ochre. The altimeter readings on my dashboard were increasing with each mile until a height of 4,800 feet above sea level was reached—only 400 feet short of a mile high. I should not have been surprised for these are the High Plains where winters can be severe but often short, and summer days bake but cool in the evenings.

I thought I had never seen such extraordinary beauty.

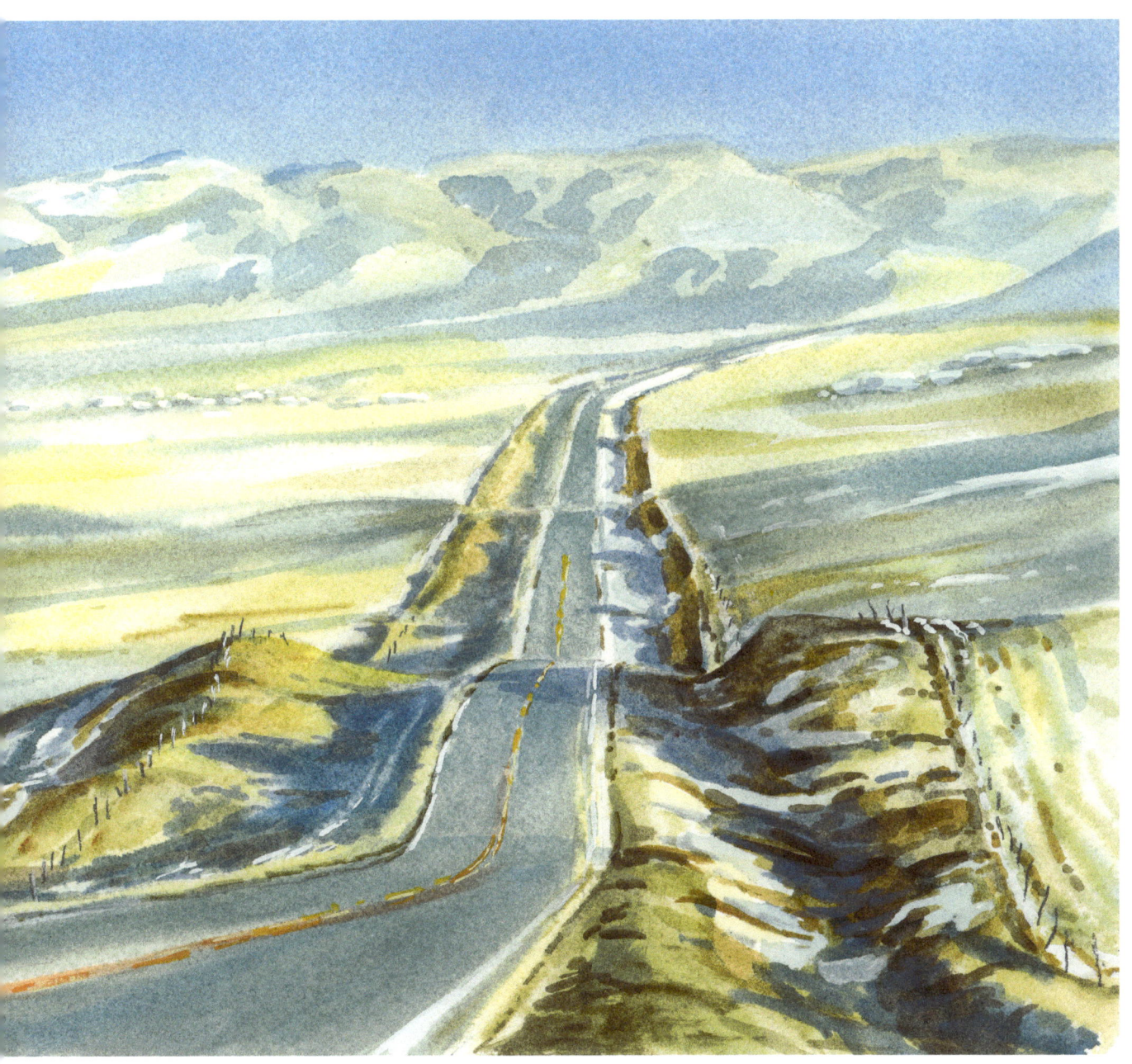

Blizzards and Storms

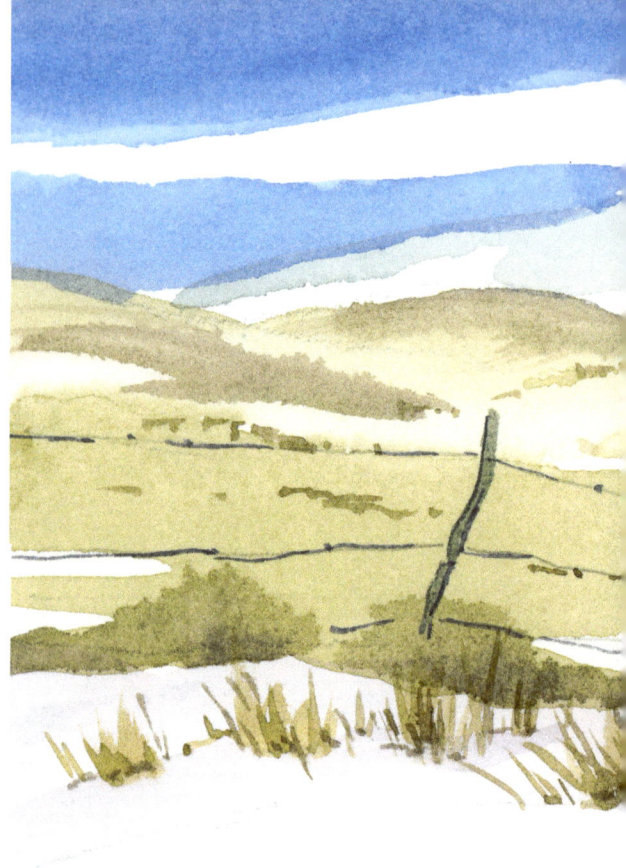

In 1949, I was in high school living in Lincoln, Nebraska. I was a "city boy," but always wanted to go deer hunting. I asked my uncle in Chadron if he would take me hunting over the Christmas holidays. Heavy snows were falling when I went to the train depot in Lincoln. Soon, travelers were notified that there would be no service that night. The route to Chadron through the Sandhills was peppered with many cuts through the hills. They had filled with snow drifts and would not be passable until cleared by engines with large rotary plows. I spent the night sleeping on the cement floor of the station—no big deal except for the lack of food for a hungry teenager. Eventually I arrived in Chadron. County roads were impassable making hunting almost impossible. My uncle arranged with the local butcher to fly me in a Piper Cub to an area where I might see some deer. I got my four-point mule deer and the trip ended successfully.

> "My uncle arranged with the local butcher to fly me in a Piper Cub to an area where I might see some deer."

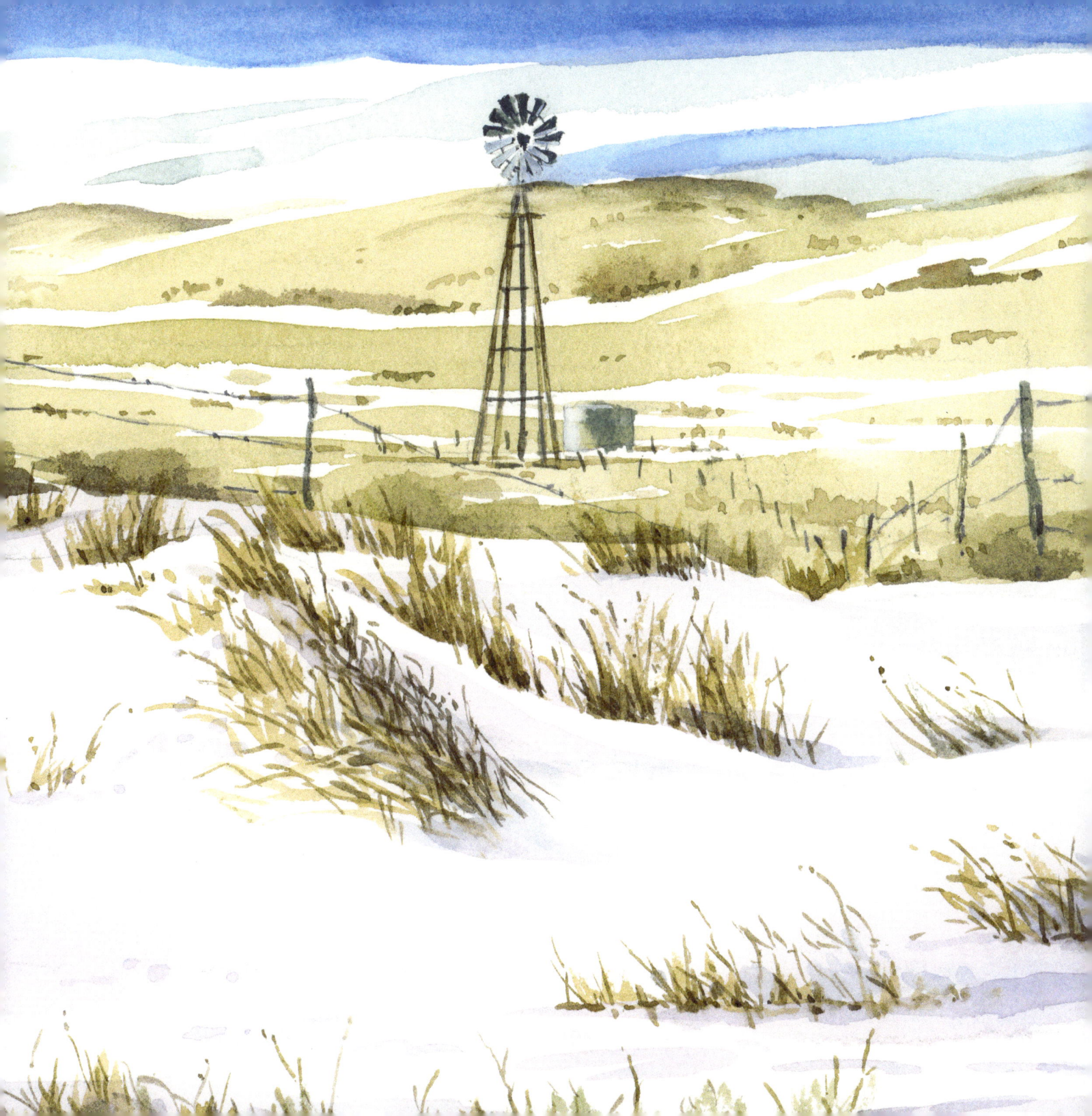

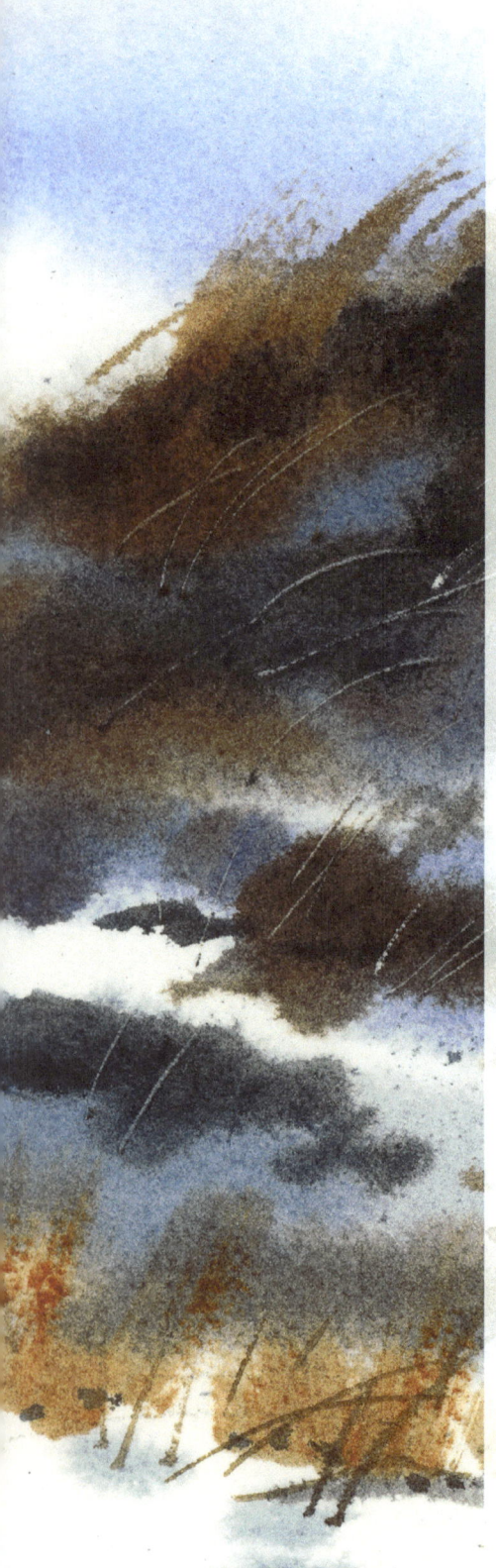

Four Seasons

I am reminded of the blizzards we had back in the days of 1949. My twin sisters were born January 25, 1949. Mom was flown into the hospital as we lived seventeen miles south of Long Pine. Mom stayed at a boarding house a month before the girls were born and they called dad and told him he had twins! They brought Mom and the babies, twenty miles in a six-wheel-drive road grader. My Uncle, Dad and myself went seven miles with a car and either two or four horses pulling it to meet them and bring them back home. Even then we had to scoop some of the drifts to get the horse and car through. Anyone needing hay, food or anything was to write it in the snow and planes would air-drop it.

–DON ATEN, LONG PINE

After a Spring Snow Storm

By the time we were on the hill half a mile from home, the sun shimmered on the endless field of spotless white. Mother had dug the cow out; her blackish hulk lay free in the glare. Over the ridge of hills toward the south the trail was blown clearer; here and there a track was visible, the crusted snow carved into fantastic sculpture or trailing white behind the soapweeds. We found several range cows, thin and exhausted, lying flat, and one of our calves, only his starred forehead out of a drift, dead.

–MARI SANDOZ, *SANDHILL SUNDAYS*

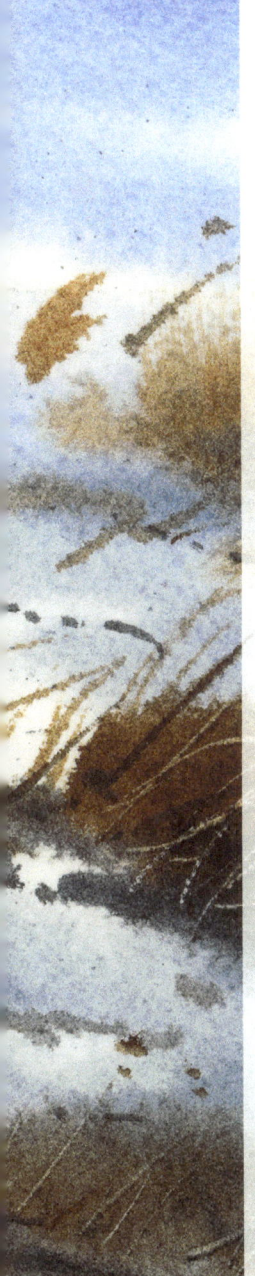

Blizzards

The most dreaded storm of the upper homestead region was and still is the blizzard. The first one to kill many people was the Buffalo Hunter's Storm of the 1870's, although the School Children's Blizzard of 1888 is sadly remembered, and even the one of 1949. Most of the people who died in blizzards died through some foolishness, some stupidity, and a few years later would have known better. There are always signs before the worst storms: unseasonal warmth, calm, and stillness, as on January 12, 1888, and old timers were ready with warnings of what to do if caught in a blizzard. "If lost in the Sandhills, any blowout will give the directions. The wind cuts the hollows from the northwest and moves the sand out southeastward... Practically anyone with a little sense and a little luck can outlast a blizzard."

–MARI SANDOZ, *OLD JULES COUNTRY*

Winter in the Sandhills

"I think it was two years ago last winter and it was a really bad snow storm. A lot of people lost a lot of cattle. They followed the fence line and then got drifted over and died. I don't think we lost that many. It was pretty nerve-racking. When we get snowed in we have snowmobiles that we can drive over the pastures. The roads are pretty good most of the time.

"There was one snowstorm this year, but we knew it was coming. Our basketball coach said, 'we will practice tonight, practice in the morning, no school tomorrow, so go home for the weekend and don't worry about it.'"

–MADDIE MEIDELL, SIOUX COUNTY

A Pot Shop That Puffs Only Colors And Clay

It is a little white building about the size of a two-car garage, but inside bursts with energy and beauty. Linda Smith greeted me at the door. She was quick to clear the smoke of false impressions. "We sell and create pots, not pot." CaLinda's Pot Shop and Art Gallery resides not in some snooty art district, but alone in a most unpretentious town of Ashby, population 150.

You can find Linda and Ashby after leaving the Sandhills Journey Scenic Byway (2) and crossing over the busy Burlington Northern railroad tracks. There are no paved streets and only a couple of viable businesses. Still, it is a pleasant little village. Linda hosts a group in her gallery and studio called "Sip and Stroke" where women from ranches and far out places come to sip wine, laugh and paint on canvas.

When asked the big question, "What keeps you here in the Sandhills?" Linda said it was a generational thing. "My father came to America with a Swiss aunt and uncle when he was only five to homestead near Columbus. Without parents, Ellis Island officials were baffled not knowing what to do with an infant without proper papers. They told the elders either they would have to adopt him or he would be sent back. When his parents were finally located in Switzerland they said, 'You can keep him. We have more.'"

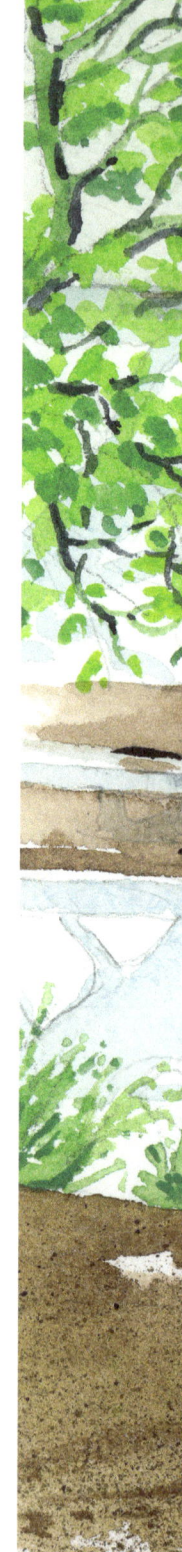

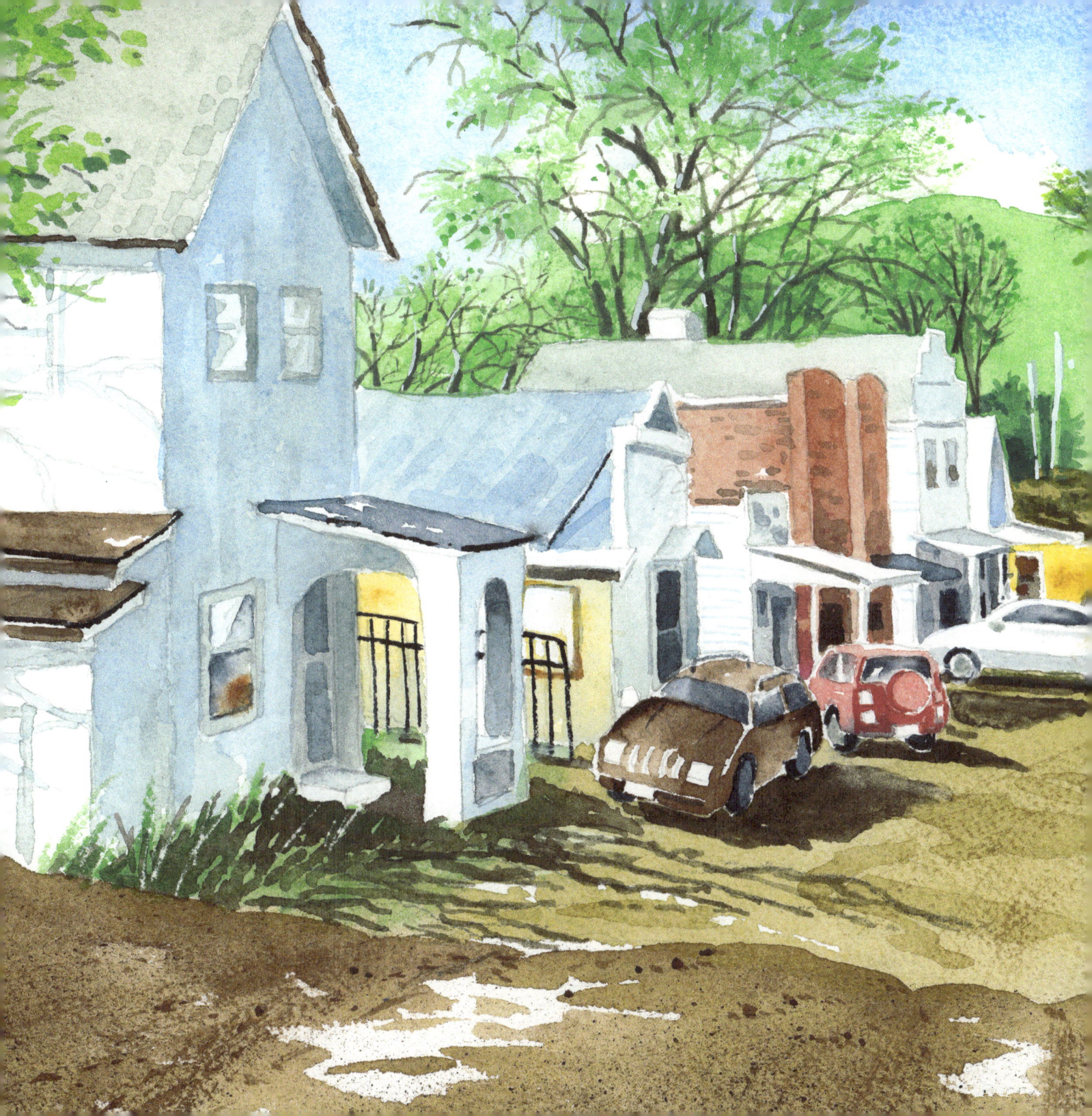

Antioch: Potash Boom-Town

Not far from the village of Antioch, on Highway 2 and just north of the railroad, stands a remnant of better times. Today, it resembles the remains of a World War concrete fortress. The afternoon sunlight reflects on a few thick remaining walls that no longer support a roof. A few twisted rebars hang from above. The only sounds are the wind whistling through empty rooms and the snapping of grasshoppers aroused by my footsteps. A nearby Nebraska Historical Marker provides the history.

For a few years, the Antioch vicinity was one of the most important potash-producing regions in the nation. Antioch grew from a small village to a town of about 2,000. When the First World War broke out, the United States was cut off from European sources of potash, which was a component of fertilizer used in the cotton belt. Two University of Nebraska graduates in chemistry developed a method for separating potash from the alkaline lakes of the Nebraska Sandhills. Large-scale production began in 1916.

The potash-producing brine was pumped from the lakes to reduction plants near the railroads. By the spring of 1918, five plants were in operation in this vicinity. Nebraska potash was used in the manufacture of fertilizer, Epsom salts, soda, and other products.

With the end of the war, importation of foreign potash resumed. Because French and German potash could be produced more cheaply than the Nebraska product, the Nebraska potash boom collapsed. The last Antioch plant closed in 1921. Today, the ruins of reduction plants and pumping stations bear mute testimony to the activity which once made Antioch a major potash production center.

–SHERIDAN COUNTY HISTORICAL SOCIETY AND
NEBRASKA STATE HISTORICAL SOCIETY

"The only sounds are the wind whistling through empty rooms and the snapping of grasshoppers aroused by my footsteps."

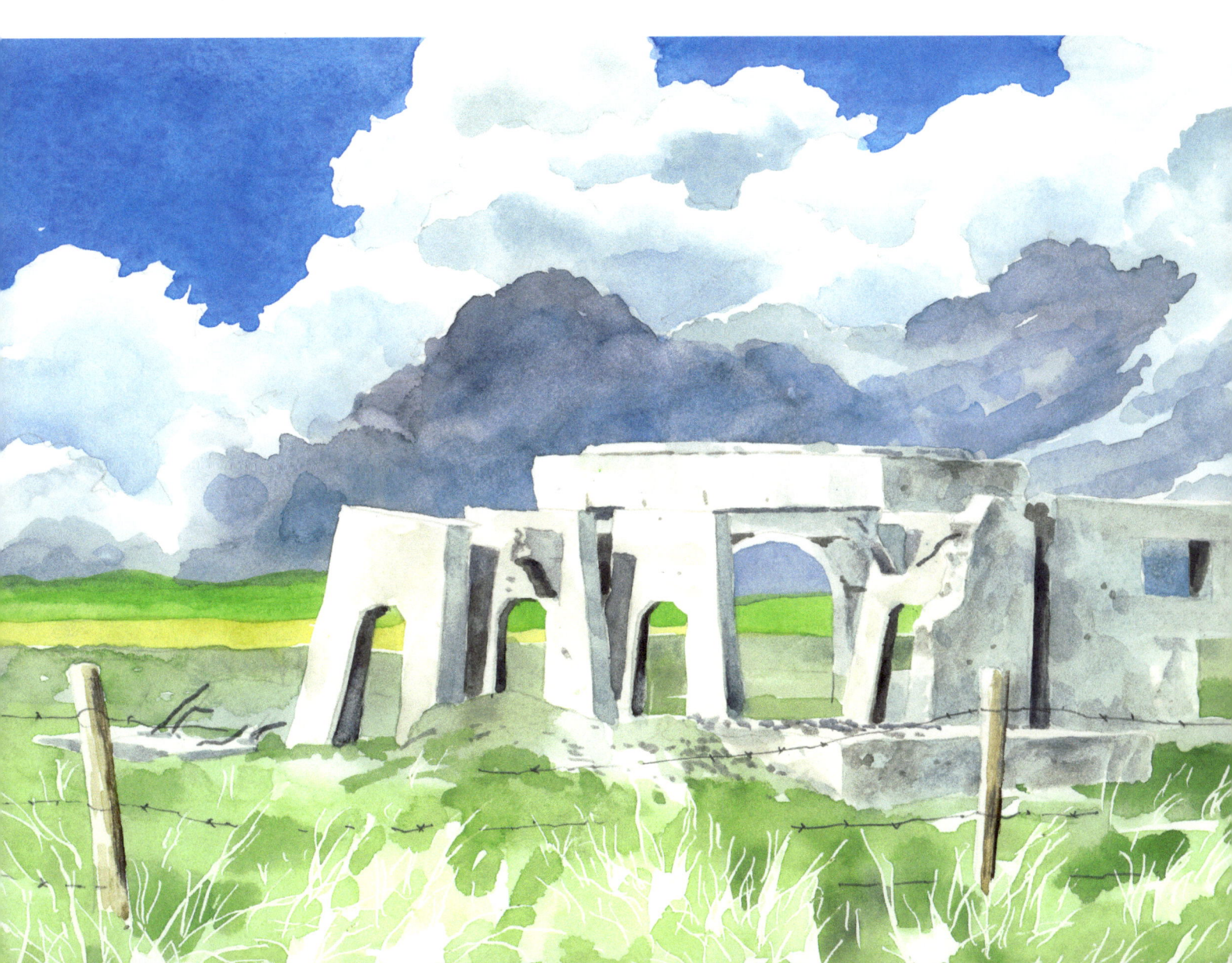

"Cool, Clear, Water...*water, water*"

Parts of the West are often parched and suffer from lack of rain, but the Sandhills enjoy an abundance of underground water. Twenty-five percent of Nebraska and smaller acreage in portions of Colorado and Kansas contain vegetated sand dunes that hold a virtual ocean in the sand and gravel beneath. This is called the Ogallala Aquifer.

> *"...a virtual ocean in the sand and gravel beneath."*

Rain and snowmelt nourish the prairie grasses before percolating into the subsoil. Very little runs off. Here and there small springs burst forth on the prairie and become the genesis of hundreds of small streams. The water table in certain areas may be higher than the surrounding prairie creating standing water, hundreds of lakes, and shallow marshes that invite millions of visiting waterfowl. Each spring the ponds are alive with geese, ducks, curlews, pelicans, and swans that visit these potholes to breed.

You will not find mud in these hills...only sand. It brushes off boots and jeans easily, but can be an annoyance in your sandals. After a rain, people in some places may contend with slippery, muddy roads, but here, ranch roads are passable and less dangerous than when dry, loose sand can send a speeding vehicle into the ditch.

The Ogallala Aquifer is not without threats. Changing weather patterns and increased usage may lower the water level faster than it can be replaced. Other areas of the country are looking to the Sandhills to satiate their thirst. Questions arise whether or not this water should be transported to more arid states for irrigation of crops. Individual ranchers and growers face a dilemma: whether to continue to draw water for temporal needs knowing that they are depleting reserves, or preserve the heritage of water for future generations. It is an ethical issue that must be reconciled. Pogo got it right: "We have met the enemy and he is us."

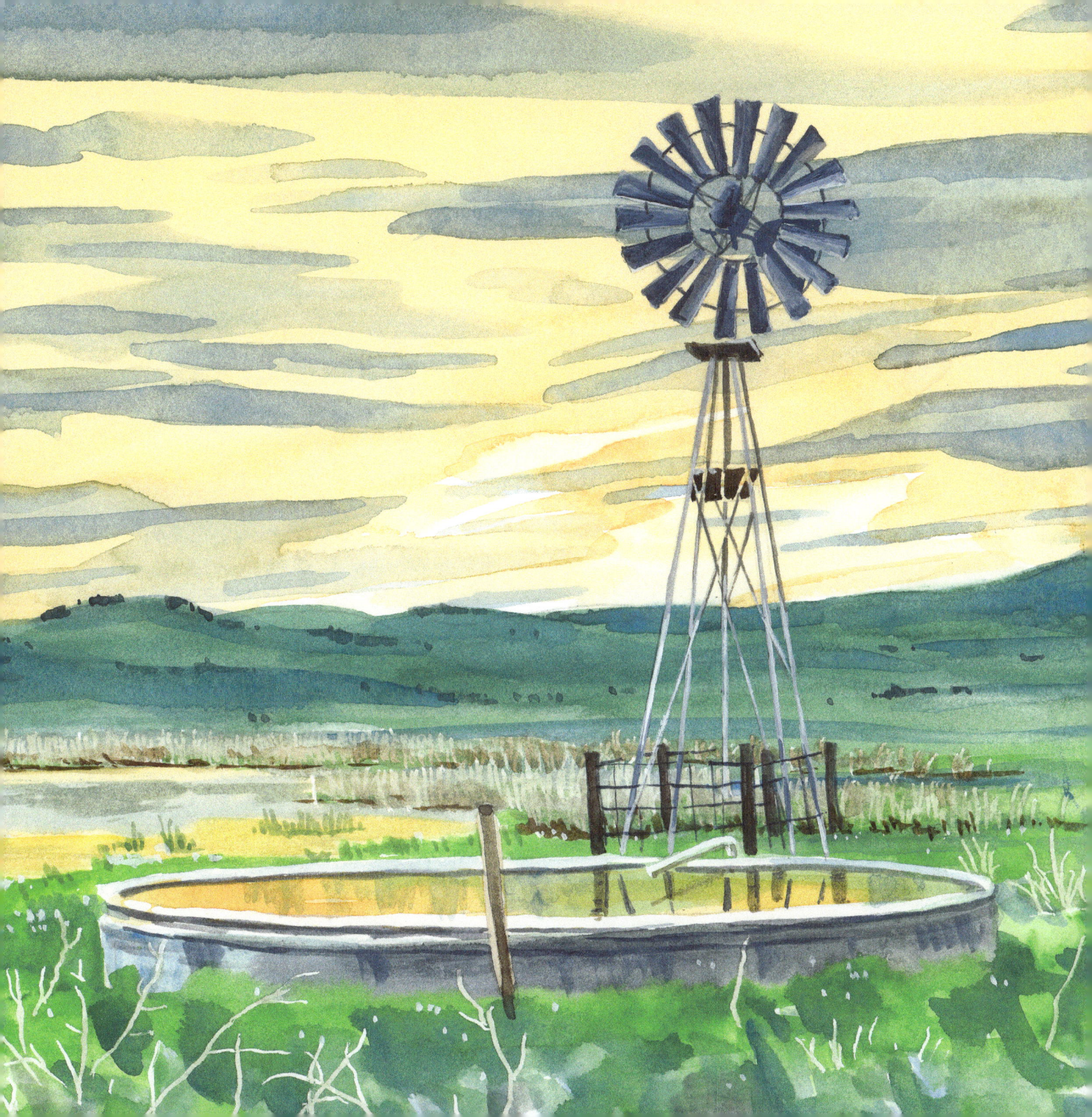

Lakes and Marshes

Most "lakes" in the Sandhills are marshes. At least in an ecological sense, few wetlands there qualify as real lakes, being too shallow to develop much thermal stratification in summer and too small to have the barren shorelines that lakes usually produce through wave action. The larger wetlands are concentrated in the western and north-western parts of the region, beyond the upper limits of the Loup and Calamus drainage system in the northern and central Sandhills, and similarly beyond the limits of Blue and Birdwood Creeks in the western Sandhills.

–PAUL A. JOHNSGARD,
THIS FRAGILE LAND

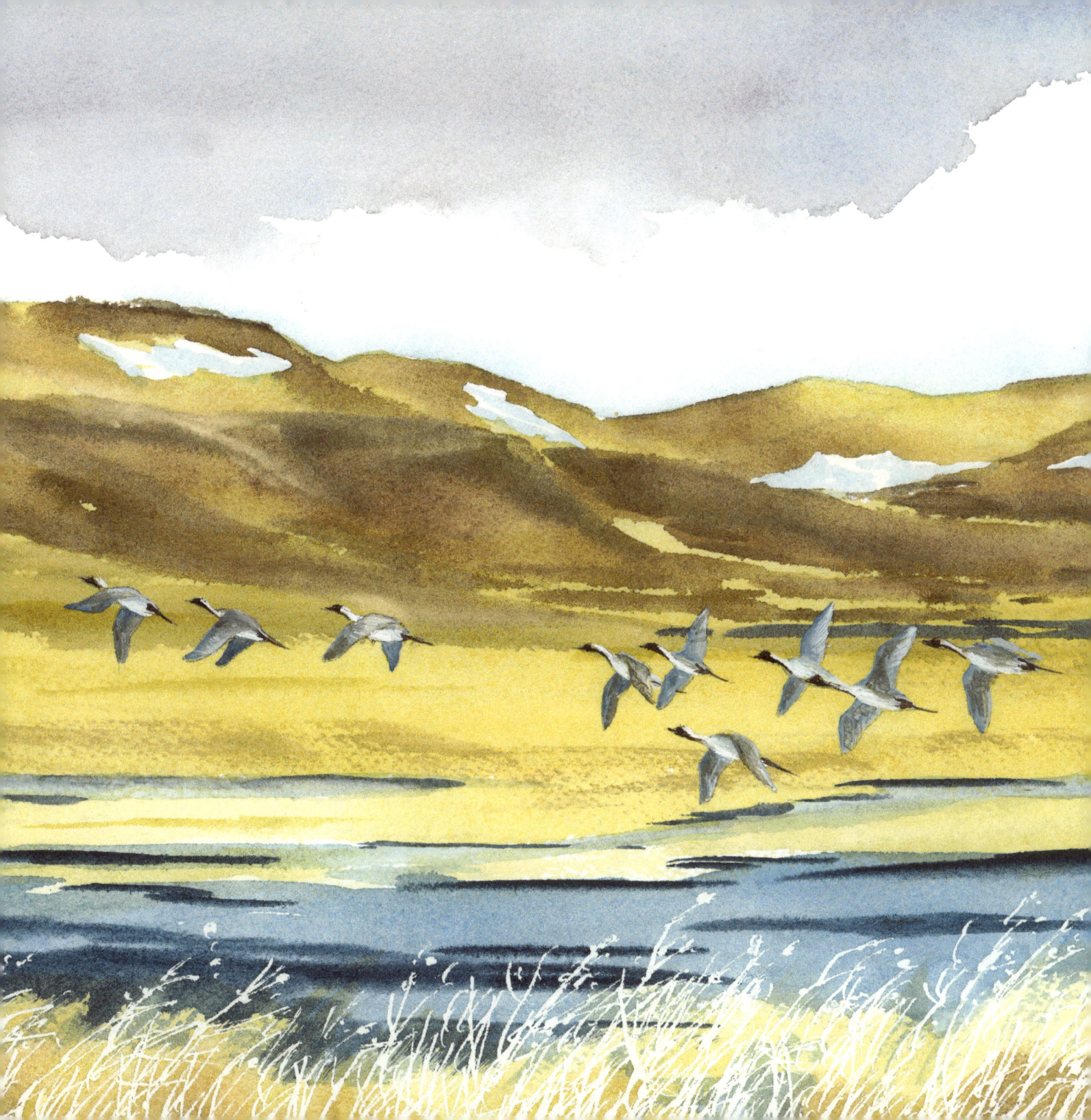

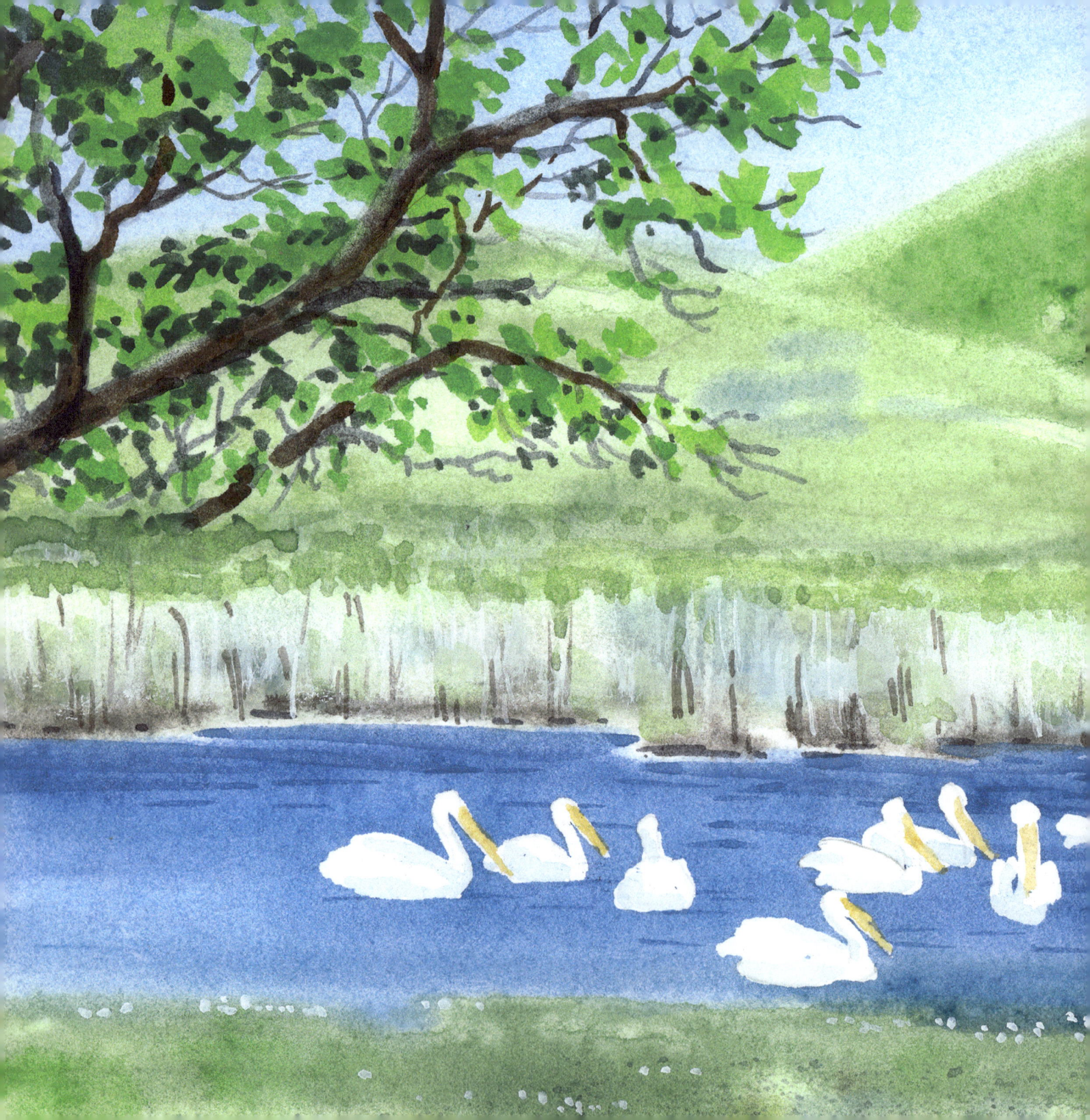

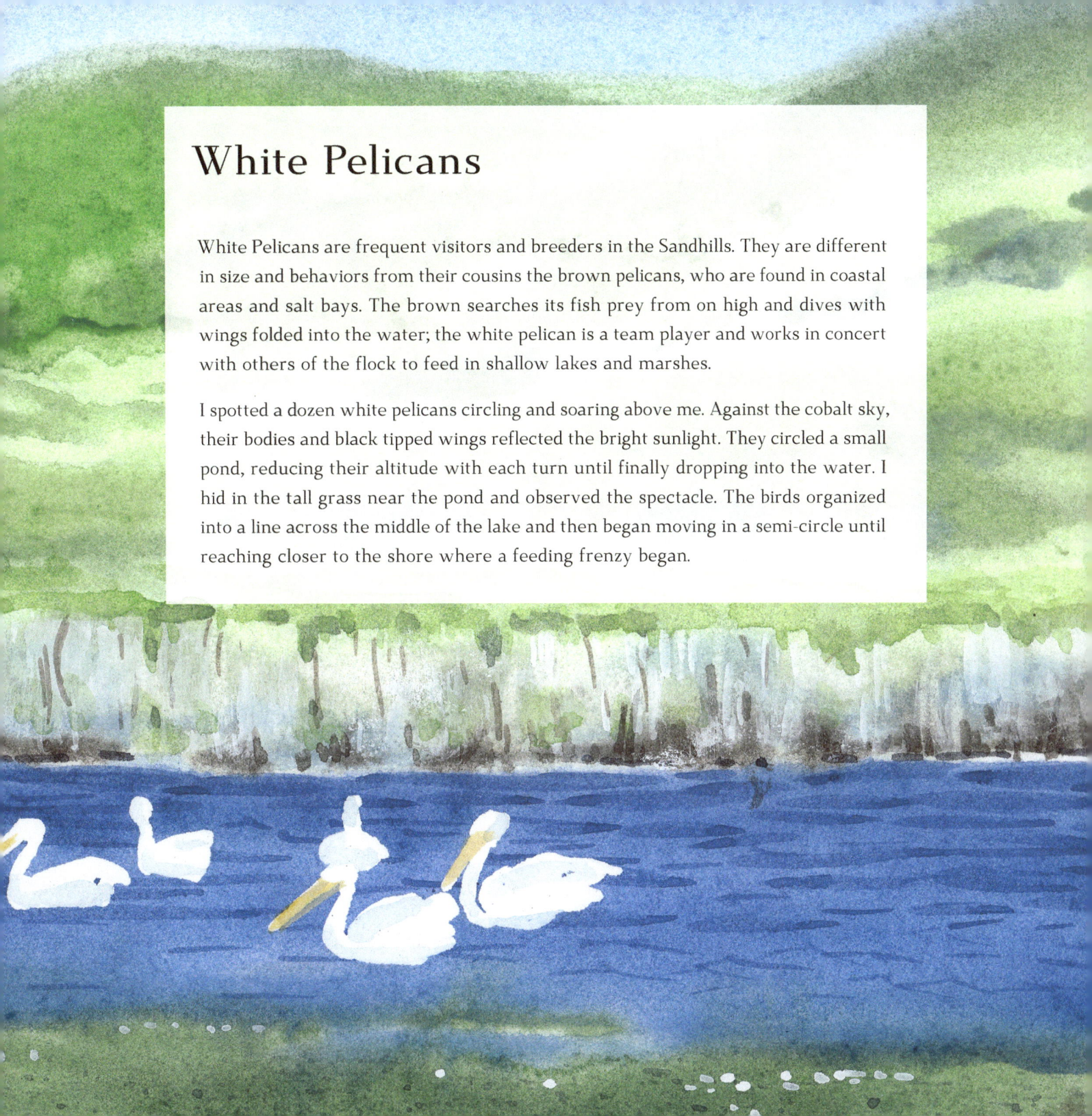

White Pelicans

White Pelicans are frequent visitors and breeders in the Sandhills. They are different in size and behaviors from their cousins the brown pelicans, who are found in coastal areas and salt bays. The brown searches its fish prey from on high and dives with wings folded into the water; the white pelican is a team player and works in concert with others of the flock to feed in shallow lakes and marshes.

I spotted a dozen white pelicans circling and soaring above me. Against the cobalt sky, their bodies and black tipped wings reflected the bright sunlight. They circled a small pond, reducing their altitude with each turn until finally dropping into the water. I hid in the tall grass near the pond and observed the spectacle. The birds organized into a line across the middle of the lake and then began moving in a semi-circle until reaching closer to the shore where a feeding frenzy began.

A Caucus of Cowboys

The ranch road wandered over grassy hillocks and through swales as if uncertain of its purpose. Ahead, small sandstorms chased two long horse trailers travelling to the ranch headquarters. The road, tired of roaming, ended on a hillside where many other horse trailers were already parked.

Upon leaving the vehicle, our senses were assailed with the smell of burning hair, bawling cattle, and the heat of an intense sun. The operation was well-organized, with each rancher knowing his or her task. Teenagers and even children entered into the activities. Boys mounted on horses mimicked their older brothers and other cowboys, dreaming of the day they could help their elders. Two cowboys worked the propane burners, keeping the branding irons red-hot and ready.

In holding pens, the calves were roped and dragged into the branding area where they were jumped by two individuals; one sat on the head of the calf and the other splaying the legs of those males to be castrated. At the same time, three more designated men quickly branded, gave shots and castrated the males. When released, the calves jumped to their feet, no worse for wear. Later, when all were branded and treated, the calves were released again to pair with their mothers.

When the work was done, everyone gathered in the barn for a grand, ranch-style banquet of Bar-B-Qued beef, potato salad, baked beans, and cake, all of which were slaked with cold beer or other refreshments. Ranchers spent the remaining afternoon relaxing and catching up on news of each other's families before heading home to nurse their aching muscles.

"Boys mounted on horses mimicked their older brothers and other cowboys, dreaming of the day they could help their elders."

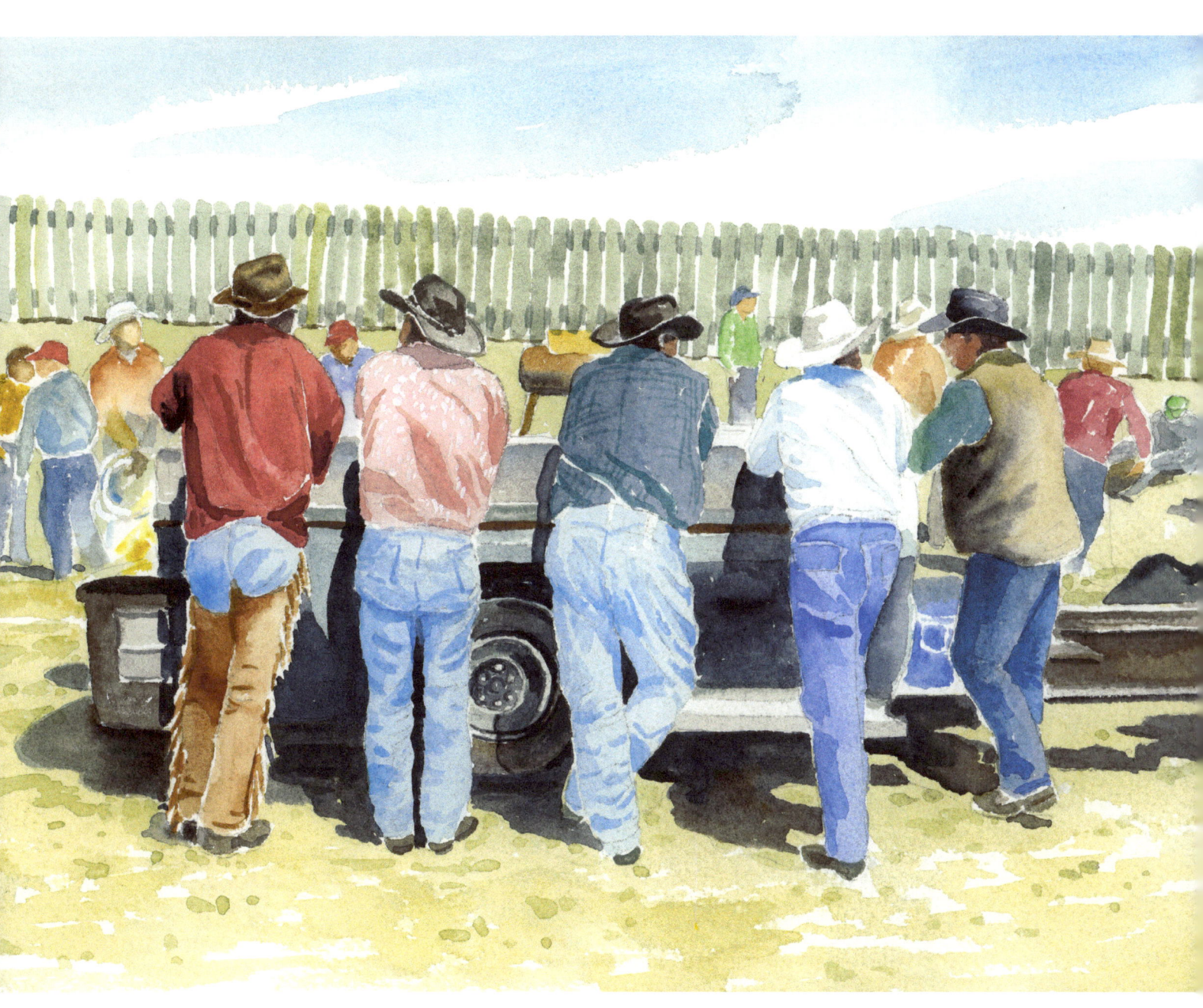

The Girl in the Yellow Shirt

Young women take part in branding along with men. I asked Maddie Meidell, a high school senior, what she liked about living in the Sandhills. "They can't find me here." Her quick reply startled me. However, her self-confidence told me she was no shrinking violet. It was the peace and quiet of the hills she liked. Besides bulldogging calves for branding, Maddie plays basketball and just won a giant silver buckle for winning the Cutting Event at the annual High School Rodeo in Thedford. I asked her to tell me about her job at the branding.

When the calf is roped and dragged out [from the holding pen by cowboys] I grab the tail. You get in sync with the person holding the rope. When he pulls up on the rope, I pull down on the tail and it flips the calf over. I'm the "header," so I then sit on the head.

–MADDIE MEIDELL, SIOUX COUNTY

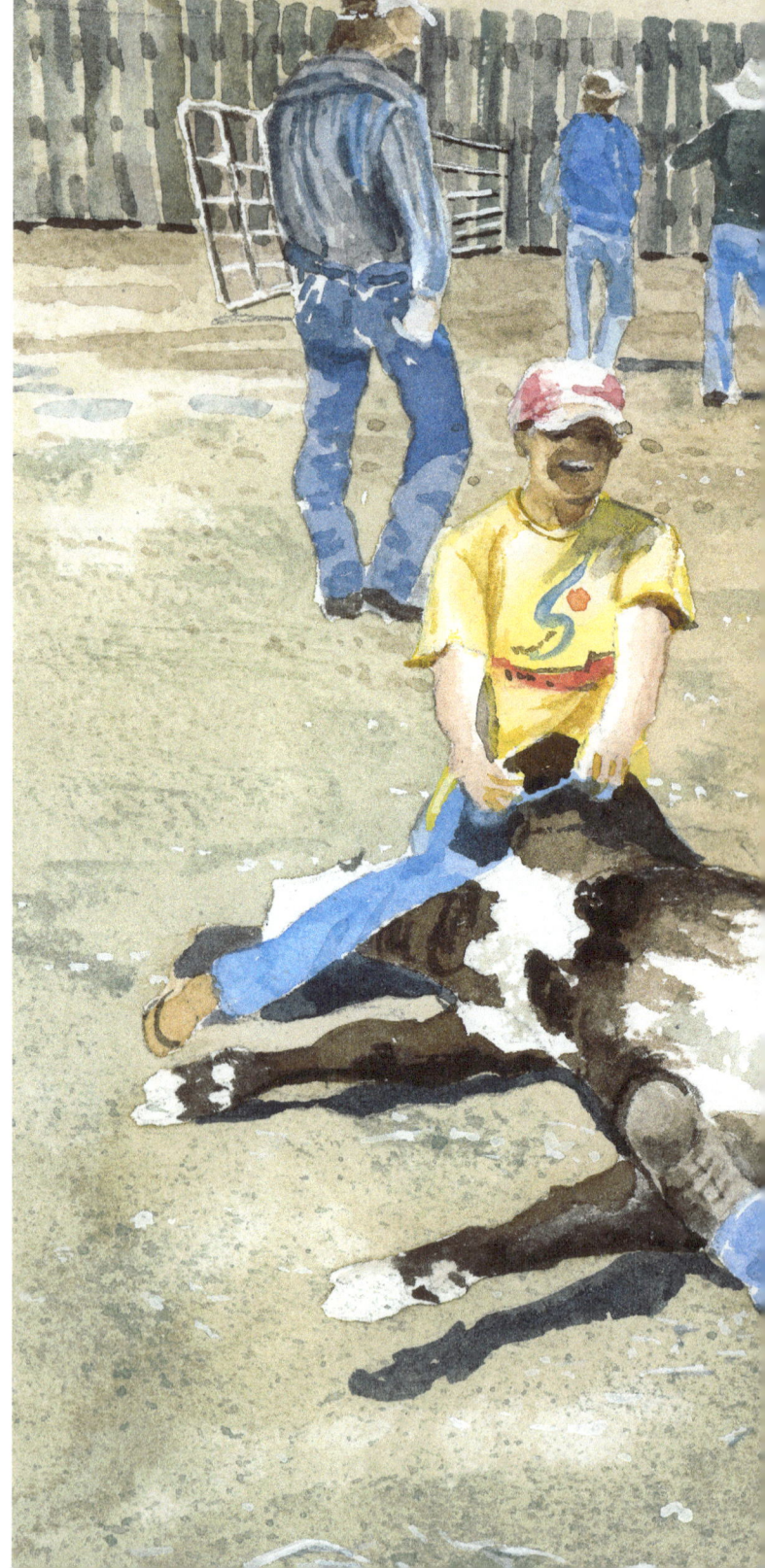

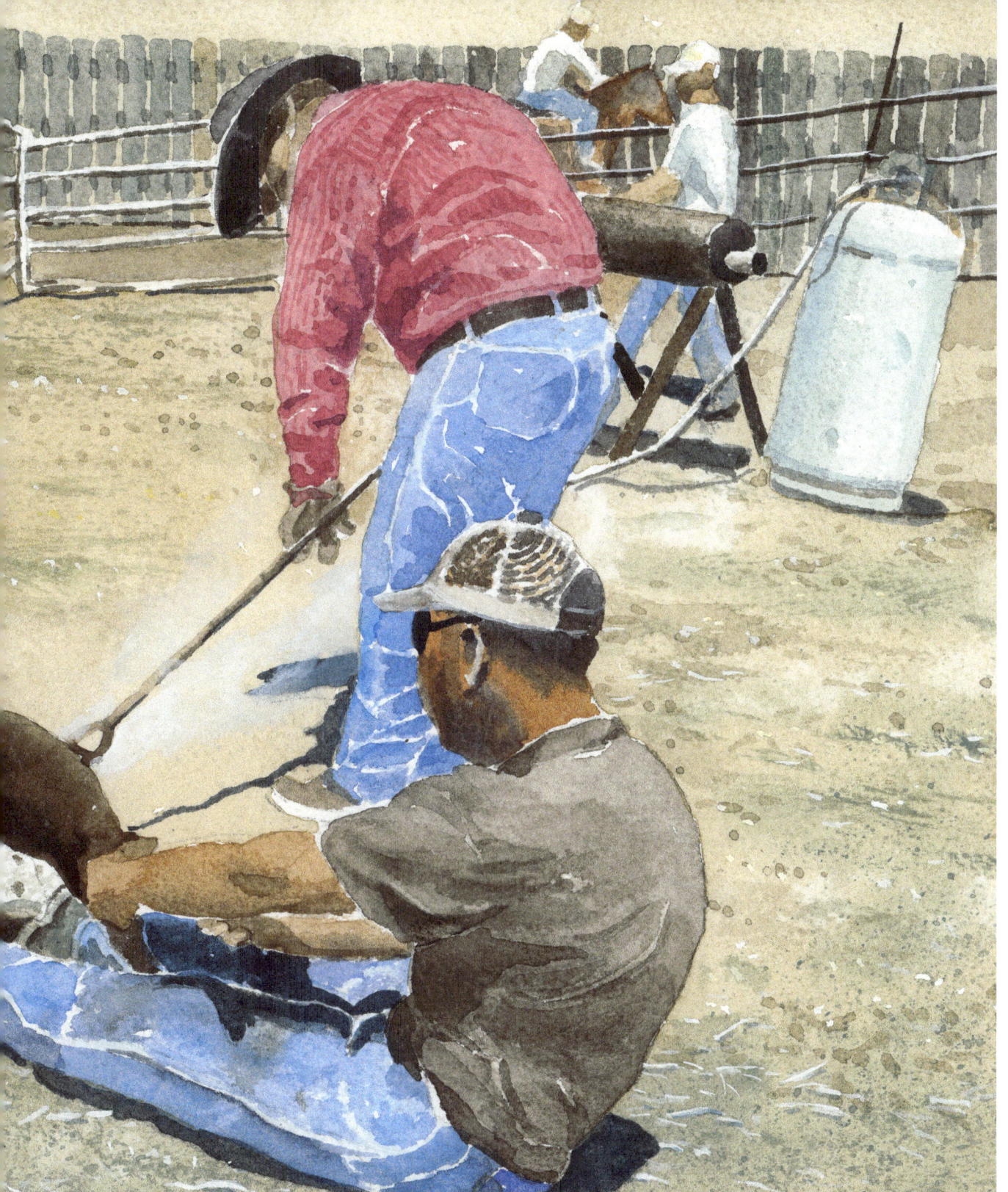

Thedford Chronicles

Late in the day, I checked into a motel on the edge of Thedford and placed a call to a lady I was told might help me write about her town. She told me to visit the Life Center next to the Thedford Post Office at 9 in the morning and I would find some retirees who could tell stories.

I was the first to arrive; however the coffee had brewed and the pot was warm. I served myself a cup and sat down to await the arrival of the regulars. They soon began to enter, and as they did, I introduced myself. "Oh yes, we know who you are." I was startled by their remarks and asked, "How would you know me?" One of them said, "Well, there are no secrets in the Sandhills." Apparently, news of a stranger in town travels faster than Internet service.

"Apparently, news of a stranger in town travels faster than Internet service."

Thedford was founded in 1887 when the Chicago, Burlington and Quincy Railroad arrived. It not only brought railroad workers, but teachers to educate the ranchers' children. Most teachers were sent out into the hills to teach in small one-room schools, living with ranch families, sometimes sharing a room, or maybe a bed, with a child.

In town, there was an active social life: church gatherings, picnics, card parties, boating, and swimming in nearby lakes or the sandy bottom clear waters of the Dismal River.

Today, Thedford is a charming, quiet little village. Trains do not stop there, although twenty or thirty pulling a hundred cars each loaded with 100 tons of Wyoming coal speed through town to eastern cities. They return empty. I learned of the strong sense of community in Thedford and was told that if you were in need of help, friends, and even those not so friendly with you, would show up to assist. On the corner of the shady city park, I found a historical marker and a bronze sculpture commemorating two small children lost in the Sandhills. The historical marker reads as follows.

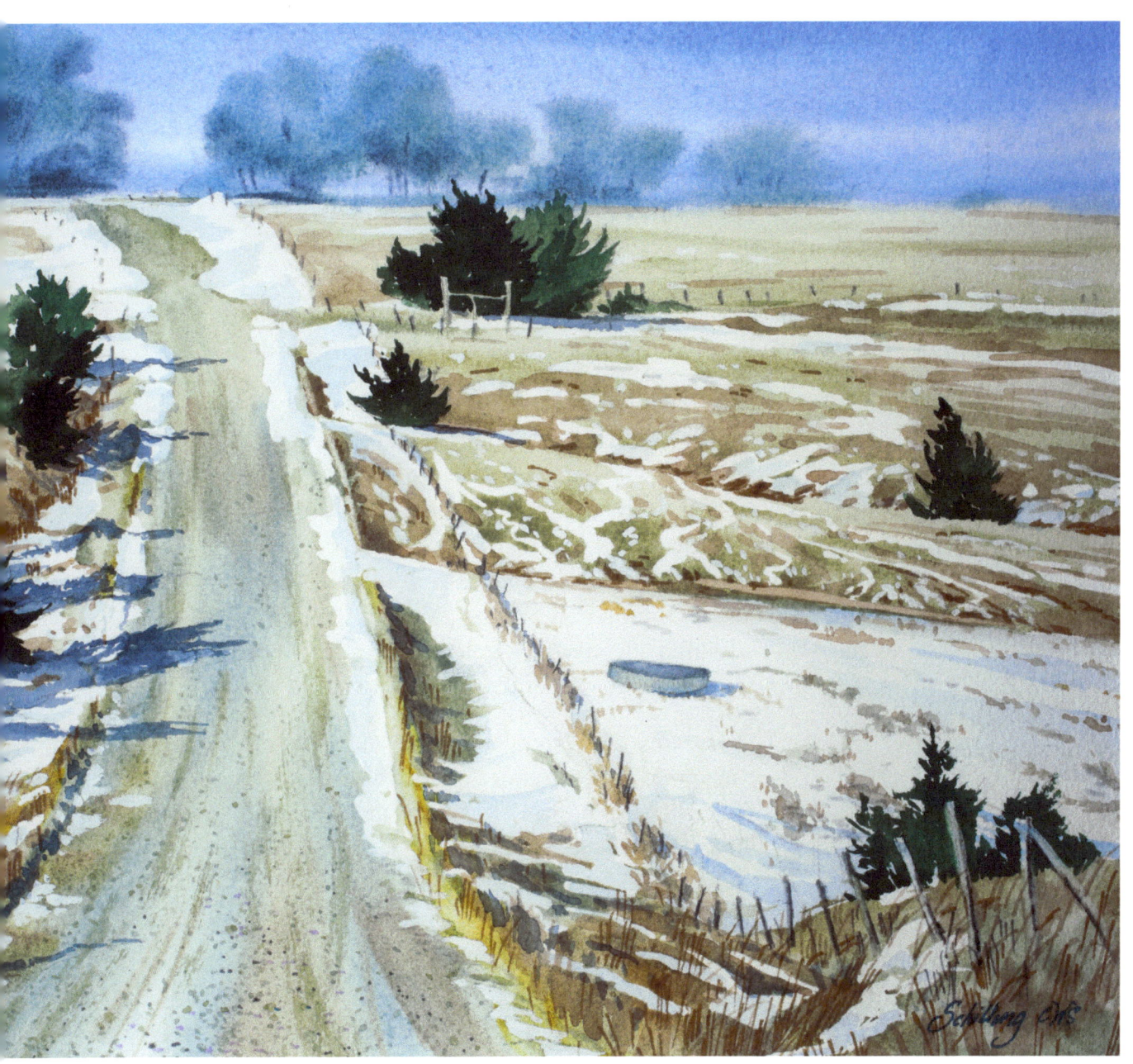

FROM THE HISTORICAL MARKER:

The Haumann Sisters Lost In The Sandhills

On May 10, 1891, eight-year-old Matilda (Tillie) Haumann and her four-year-old sister, Anna Henrietta (Retta), became lost in the Sandhills while returning home from visiting their sister who was helping a neighbor. Their parents, Carl and Henrietta Haumann were German immigrants who moved from Illinois to Thomas County, Nebraska, in March 1891, and homesteaded approximately five miles north of Thedford.

The parents reported the girls missing on May 11 and search parties were organized. Three days later, searchers found Retta alive some twenty-five miles east of her parents' house. Although suffering from dehydration and exposure, she recovered. Joined by scores of area residents, the search for Tillie continued until her lifeless body was discovered some seven miles from Dunning on Sunday, May 17. The child walked an estimated seventy-five miles before her death. She is buried in the Thedford Cemetery.

This tragedy reveals how neighbors and strangers can join together in times of need and validates the challenges new settlers faced in adapting to life in the treeless, roadless, and sparsely-settled Nebraska Sandhills.

–THOMAS COUNTY HISTORICAL SOCIETY, NEBRASKA STATE HISTORICAL SOCIETY, 2016, THOMAS COUNTY CITIZENS AND BUSINESSES

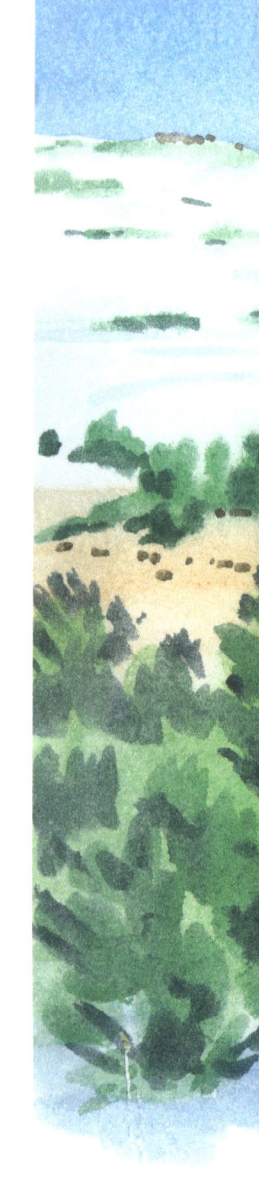

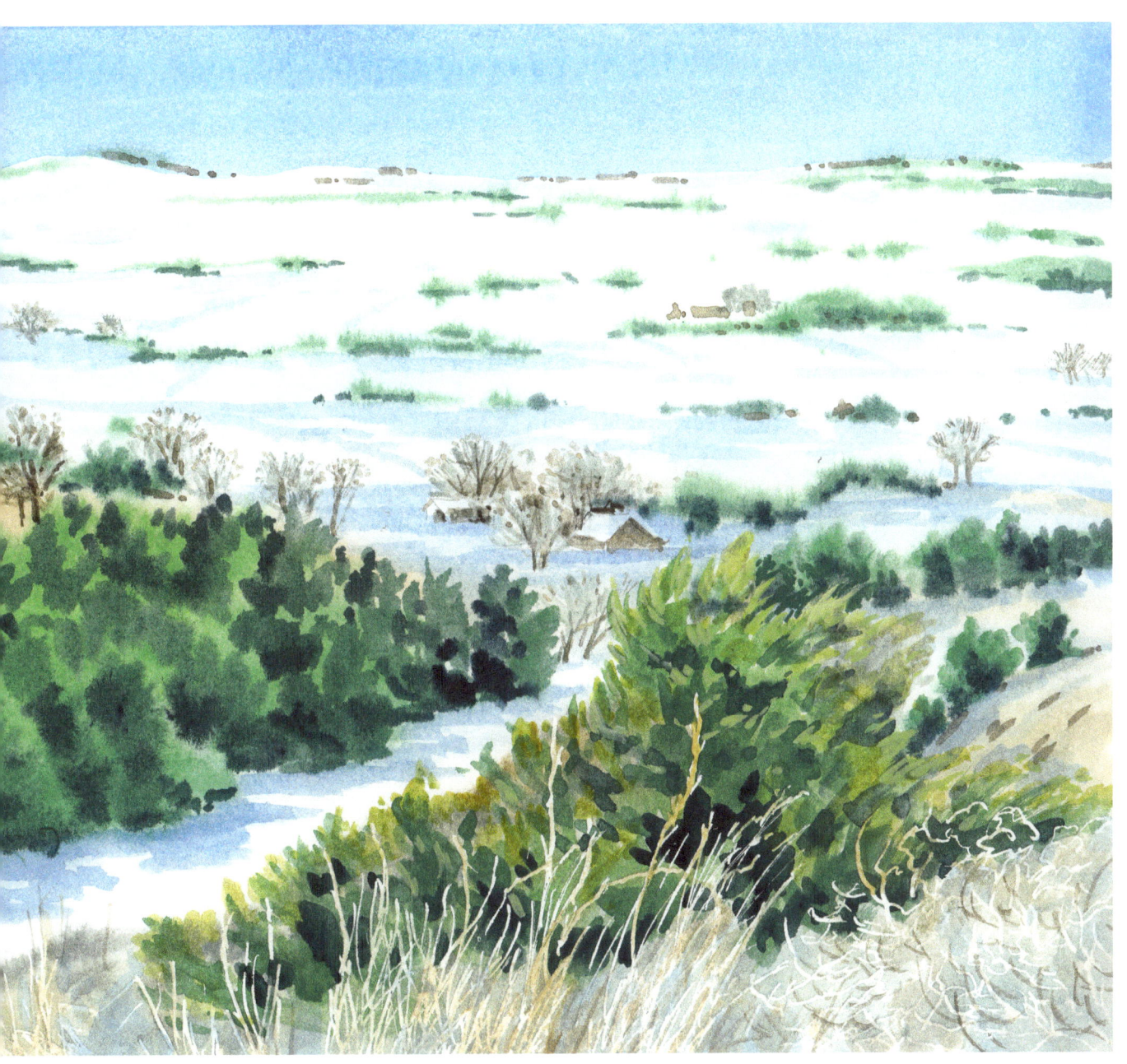

Just Part of the Job

A man lived alone west of town. His name was Kenny. Kenny broke his hip and called for an ambulance. Of course, I was responding with an ambulance and another EMT in order to get him to the hospital. On the way out there, we were talking about how we were going to package him and get him to the hospital. We have a bag that is filled with little Styrofoam balls that you pack around the patient to stabilize their bodies. It holds them stiff as a board. Kenny was always a practical joker. We were discussing how we would move him when somebody said, "I think we better get the body bag." Kenny rose up and said, "Well, I didn't think it was that bad." We all started to laugh which made Kenny hurt even more.

–SHERIFF GARY ENG,
THOMAS COUNTY

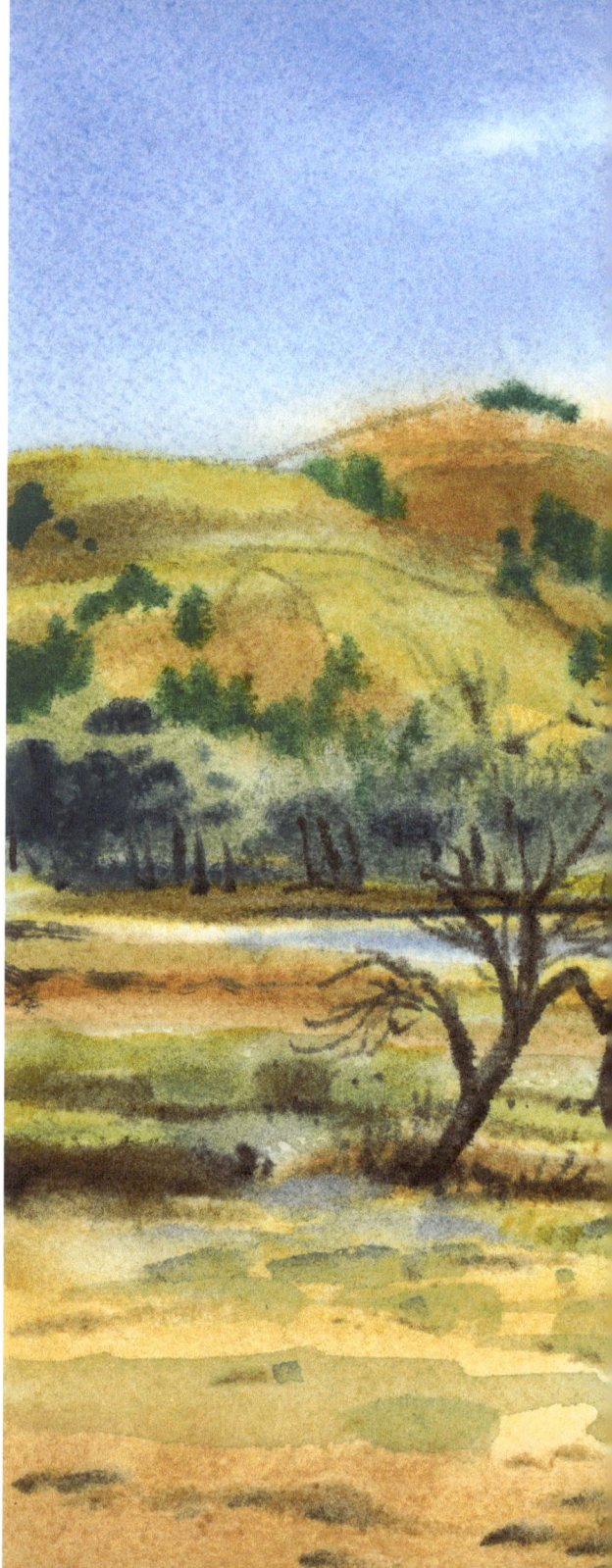

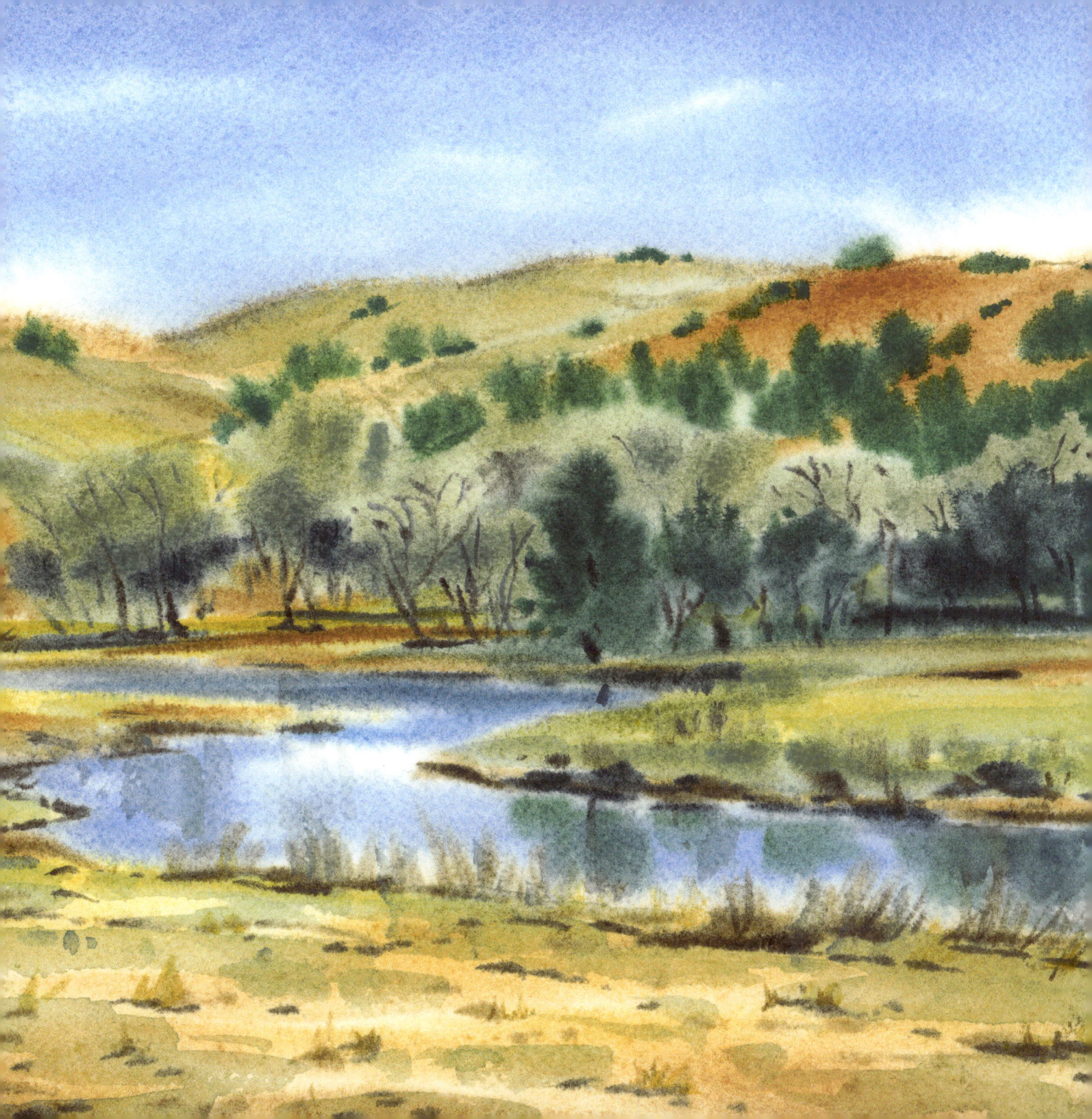

The Knight Museum and Sandhills Center

Becci Thomas is the Museum Director of the Knight Museum in Alliance, Nebraska. She is also the local historian. So, I went to call on her. She graciously invited me into her office. It was a small office in a museum where space was at a premium. It was not surprising that her desk was piled high with schedules and reports. Shelves an arm length away were stacked with museum catalogs and periodicals.

Becci pushed back in her desk chair and with a smile began telling me of the history of Box Butte County and the surrounding area. She was born in Alliance and educated in a one-room county school. There were fifty-four county schools at the time and one "skids school" that could be transported to different locations.

Becci directed me to the cemetery where Mari Sandoz's father, Jules, was buried along with his fourth wife, Mary Elizabeth. Jules was a cantankerous settler with a reputation for ruthless dispatching of lawless characters, yet with a passion for assisting newly arrived settlers.

"Jules was a cantankerous settler with a reputation for ruthless dispatching of lawless characters…"

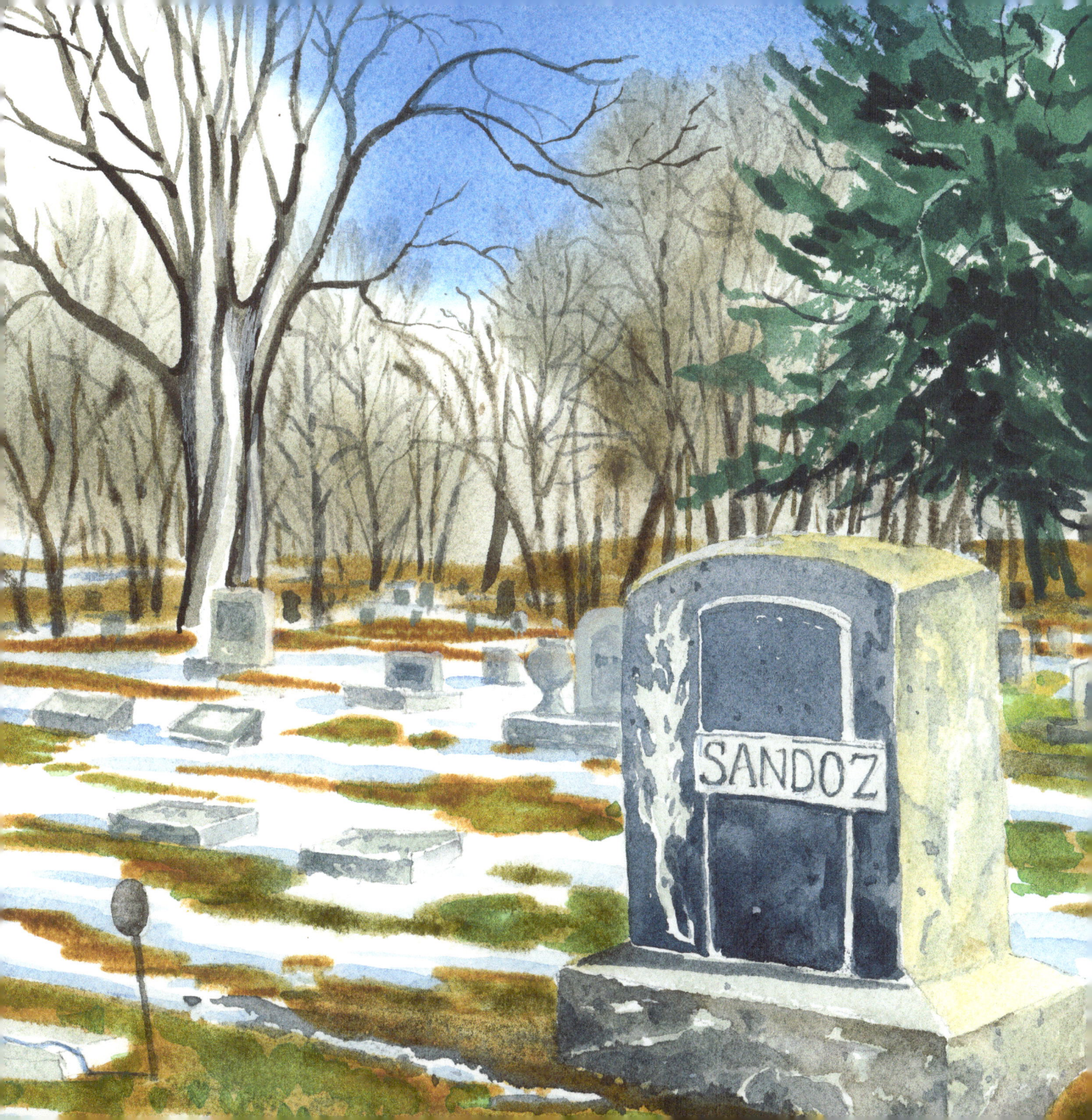

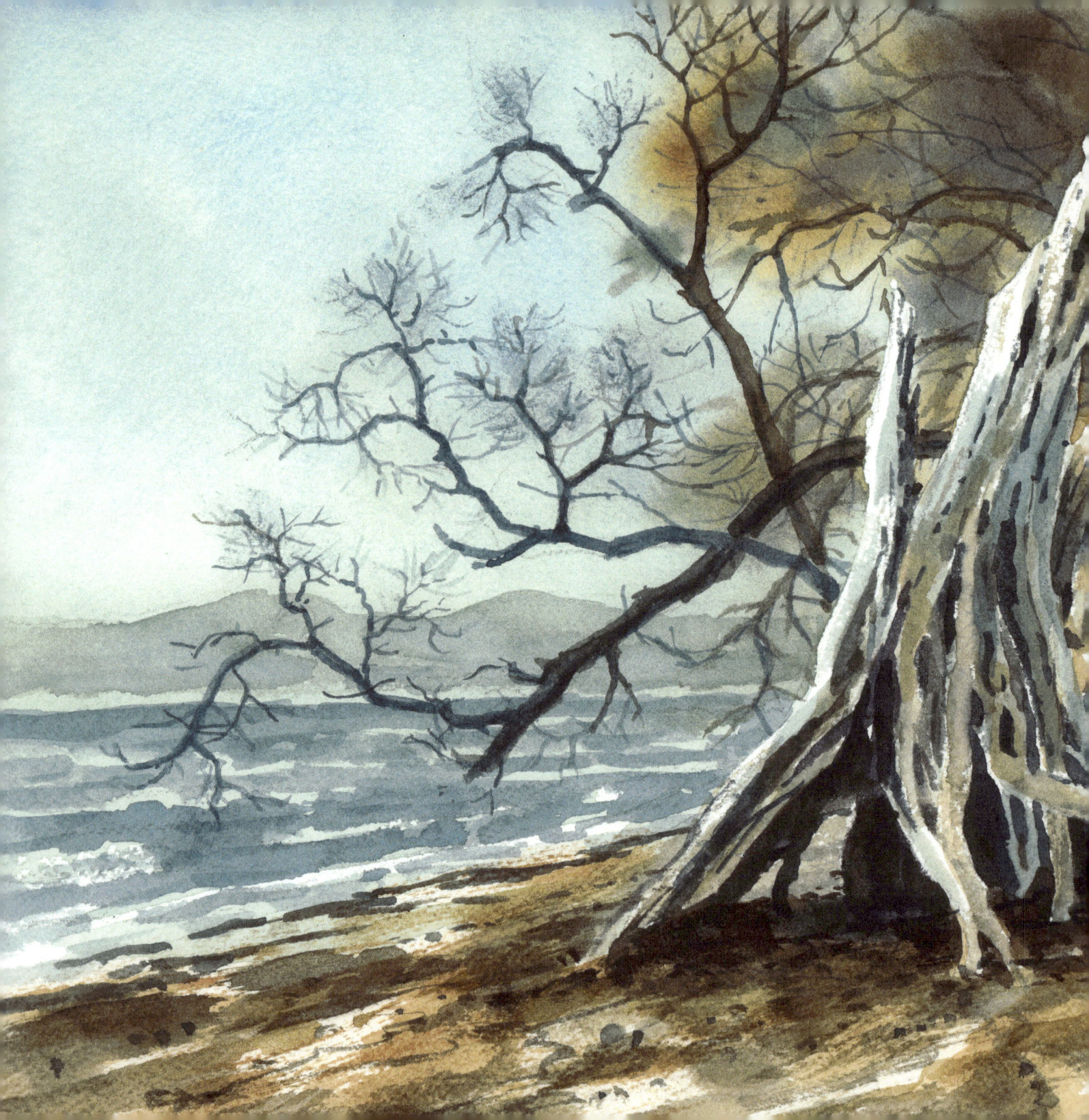

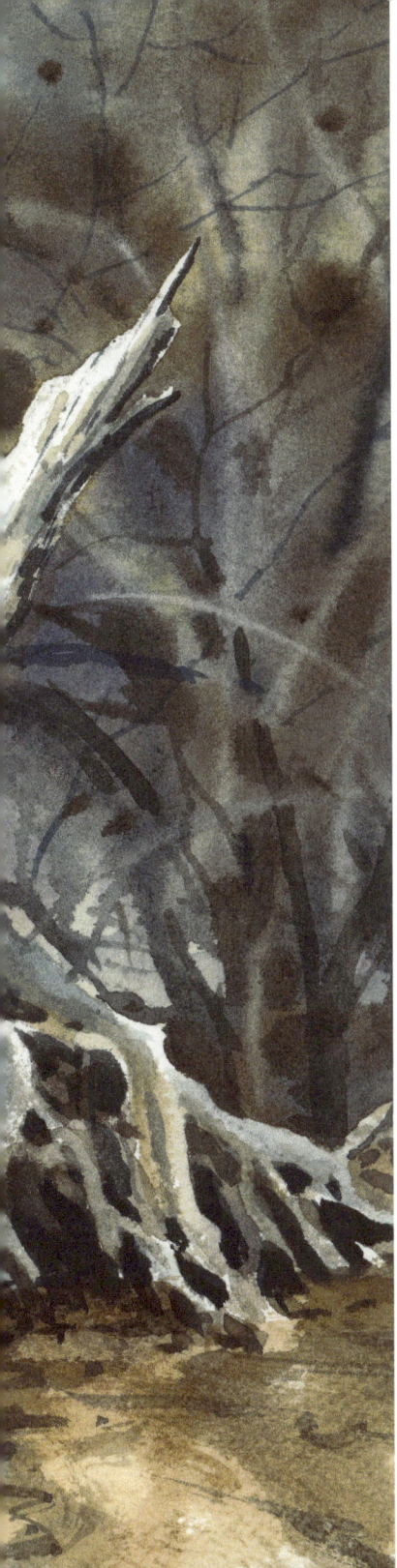

When Judge, Jury, and the Law Enforcement were One

We had a family reunion a few years back. My uncle and his older cousins were talking about a terrible drought we had for about three years in a row. They were bemoaning how the Sandhill lakes were just drying up. My mom's cousin said, "I hope it doesn't dry those lakes up or someone will be going to the 'pen'." And I said, "Why would that be?"

"Back in the days of great granddad, they lived a million miles from nowhere. It was hard to get anyplace. It was forty miles to the closest railroad to catch a ride into Alliance. They caught a couple of horse thieves, and they didn't know what to do with them. It was the dead of winter. So they just hung them and threw them in the lake out here. I guess if the lake ever dries up somebody will eventually find them.

"Well, that is what they had to do. They didn't really have a choice. Neighbors were chasing those rustlers and when they caught them no one could get away to haul them fifty miles to anyplace."

–BECCI J. THOMAS, DIRECTOR,
KNIGHT MUSEUM AND SANDHILLS
CENTER, ALLIANCE

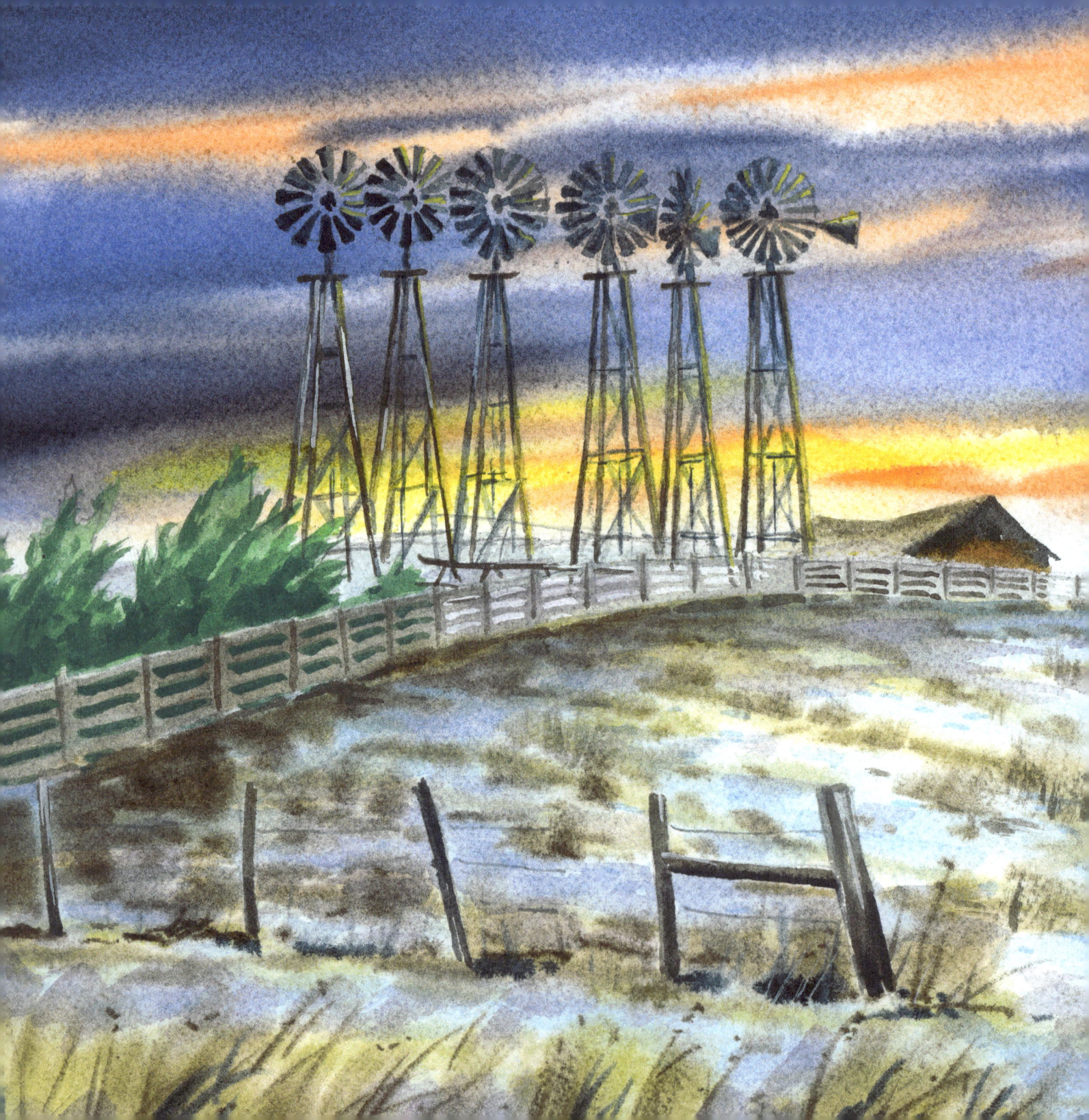

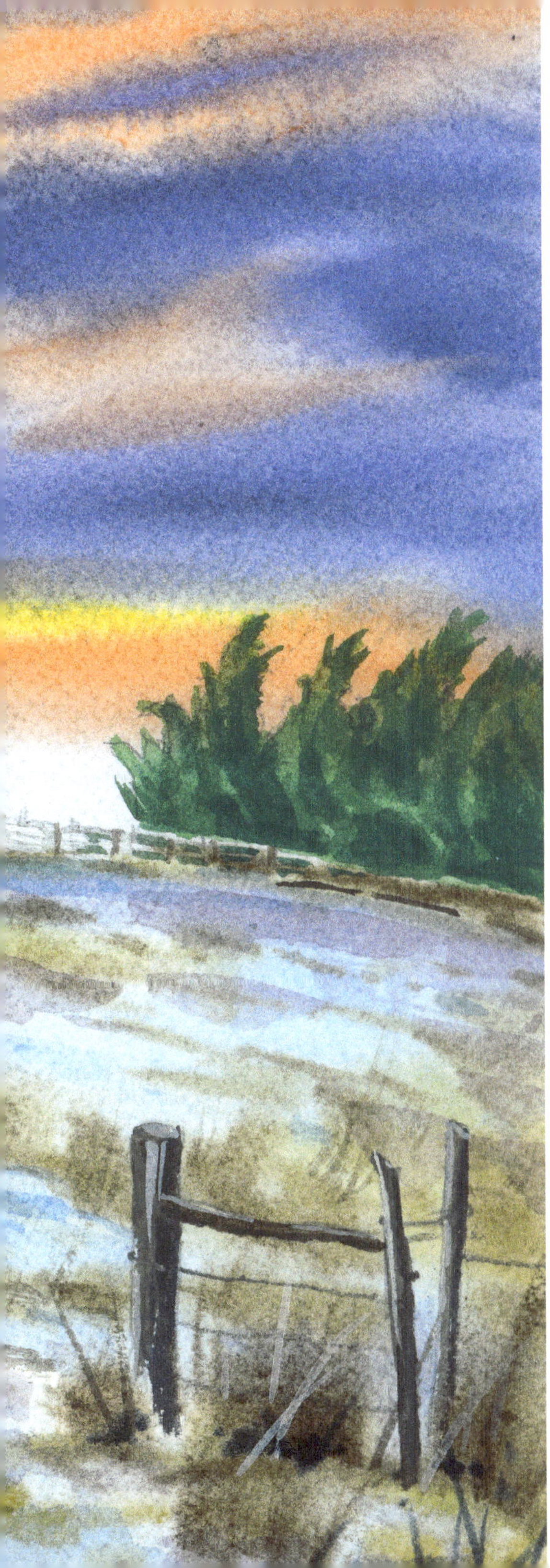

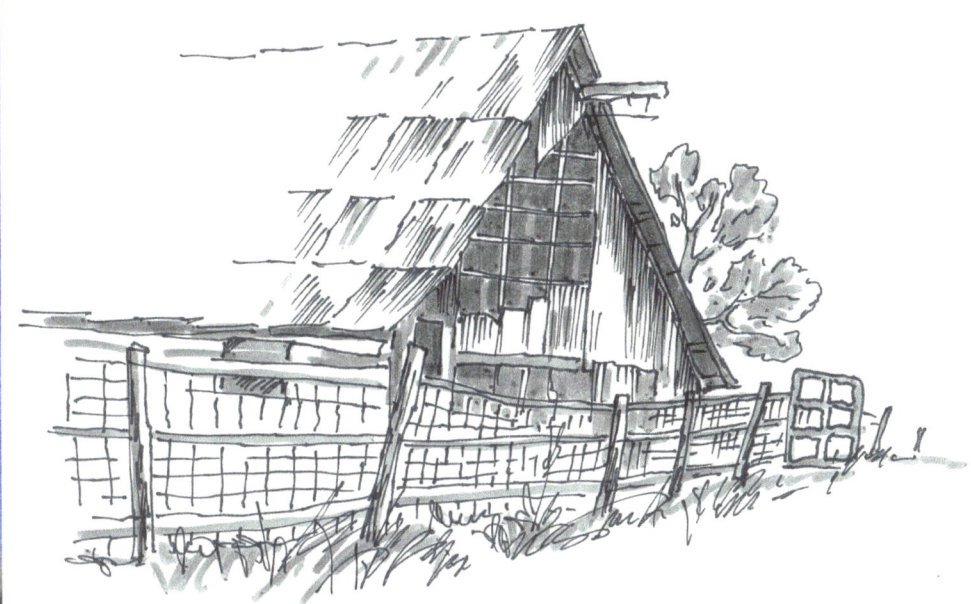

The Sun Behind the Hills

Probably the best visual treat of all in the Sandhills comes shortly before sundown. Then the shadows of the dunes play carelessly over their still-lighted slopes, creating endless yin-yang patterns to remind the viewer that light without darkness is incomplete, just as life and death are inextricably locked companions in the weft and warp of nature's rich tapestry.

–PAUL A. JOHNSGARD,
THIS FRAGILE LAND

The Best Place in the World

My name is Frances Gotschall Leighton. I was born the youngest of six children in an old farm home near Niobrara, Nebraska on March 1, 1936.

It was the time of the Great Depression. My parents were troubled as grasshoppers were beginning to come. There was no rain. My father told me that by late summer grasshoppers were so abundant they covered the fence posts. They ate the fields, so grass was scarce for the livestock. They ate the entire garden which provided the food for our family.

At that desperate time, a World War I Army buddy of my dad's and his brother phoned from his ranch in the Sandhills. He told them an elderly rancher nearby needed to sell his ranch. Dad and his brother, my Uncle Ray, traveled ninety-five miles in a Model T from Knox County—a long trip. They purchased the "Midwest Ranch" and we moved there when I was nine months old. It then became known as the Gotschall Brothers Ranch. It had an old ranch home, with no running water or bathroom facilities. It was located on a sandy trail twenty miles southwest of Atkinson, Nebraska.

My life was spent in the best place in the world. The environment was quiet, so peaceful, with only the sounds of nature. There was an abundance of wildlife, farm animals and poultry to care for and enjoy. The air was always clear and fresh. We had the best-tasting, coldest, most refreshing water in abundance. Our ranch had two faithful, sentinel windmills in our two big pastures that pumped life-giving

> *"The environment was quiet, so peaceful, with only the sounds of nature."*

water for the livestock. Wind propelled their blades to pump water into large metal stock tanks. Six flowing wells and a creek (Holt Creek) provided water to the remainder of the ranch. The creek and stock tanks were the source for our bathing as well. With our ranch located over the largest Ogallala Aquifer, our meadows were abundant with grass, as they were sub-irrigated. The high water table made it easy to drill flowing wells. A pipe was drilled into the ground and water gushed from it continuously year round—for over a hundred years now. It was the best place in the world.

—FRANCES GOTSCHALL LEIGHTON

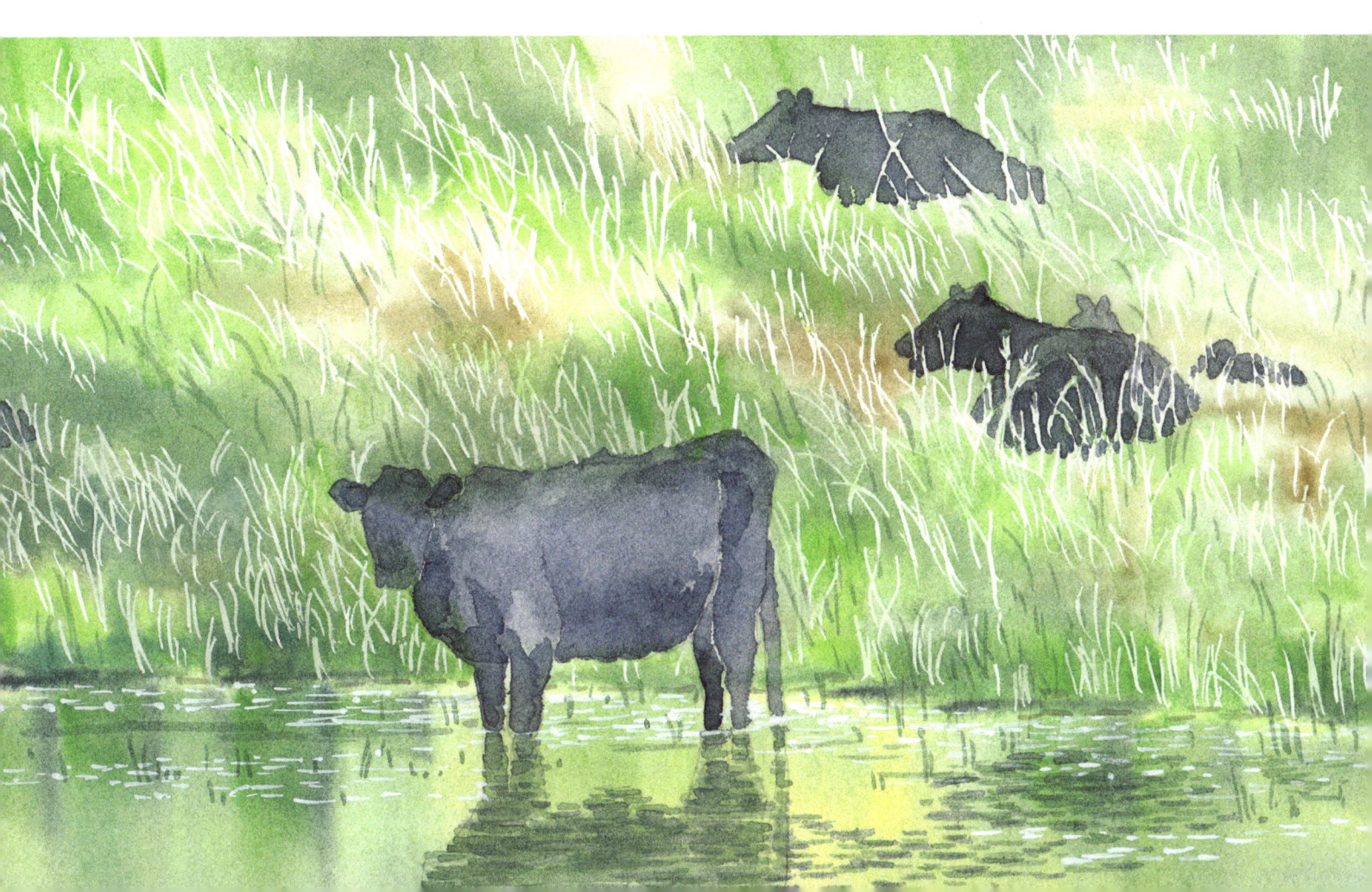

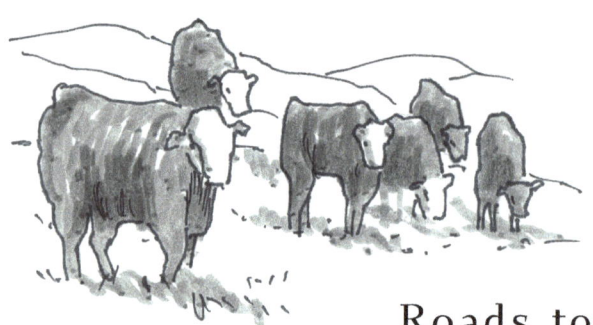

Roads to Nowhere

Most roads in the Sandhills lead nowhere. And that is one of their primary attractions. They tend to become more and more indecisive the farther one goes and finally disappear in sandy confusion, often at a fence or a rancher's gate.

—PAUL A. JOHNSGARD, *THIS FRAGILE LAND*

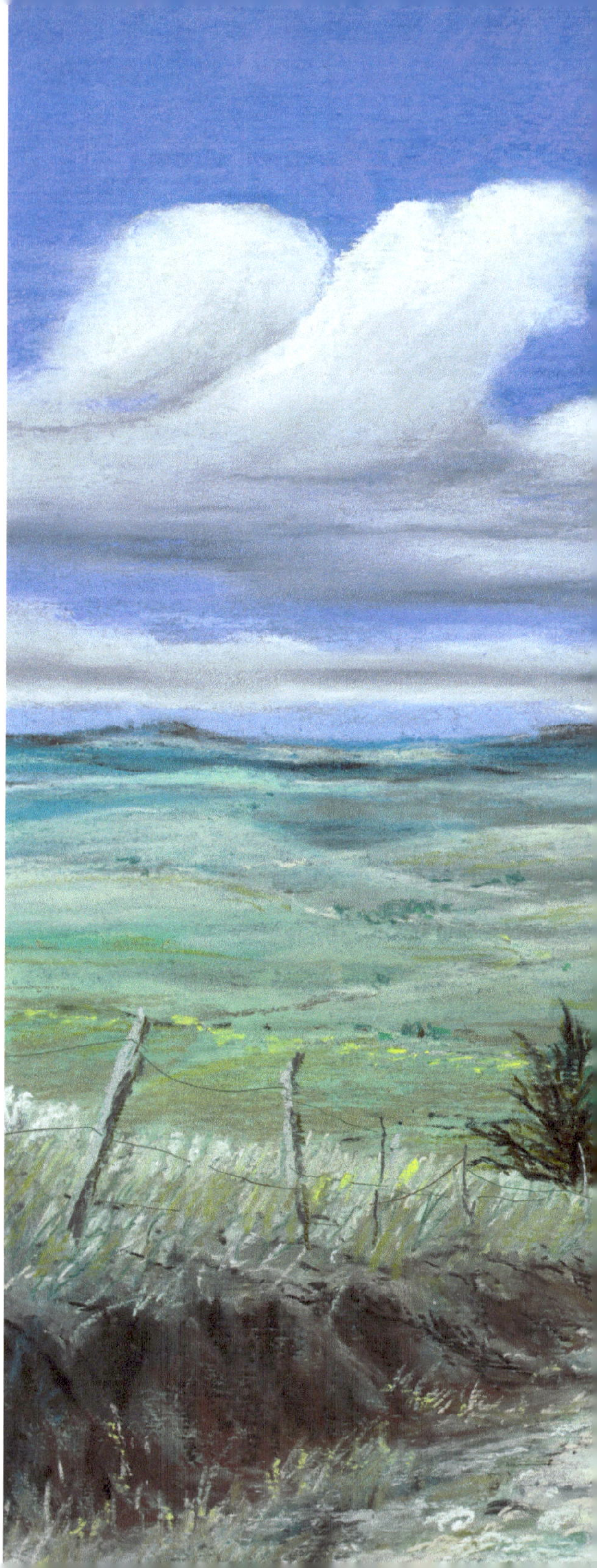

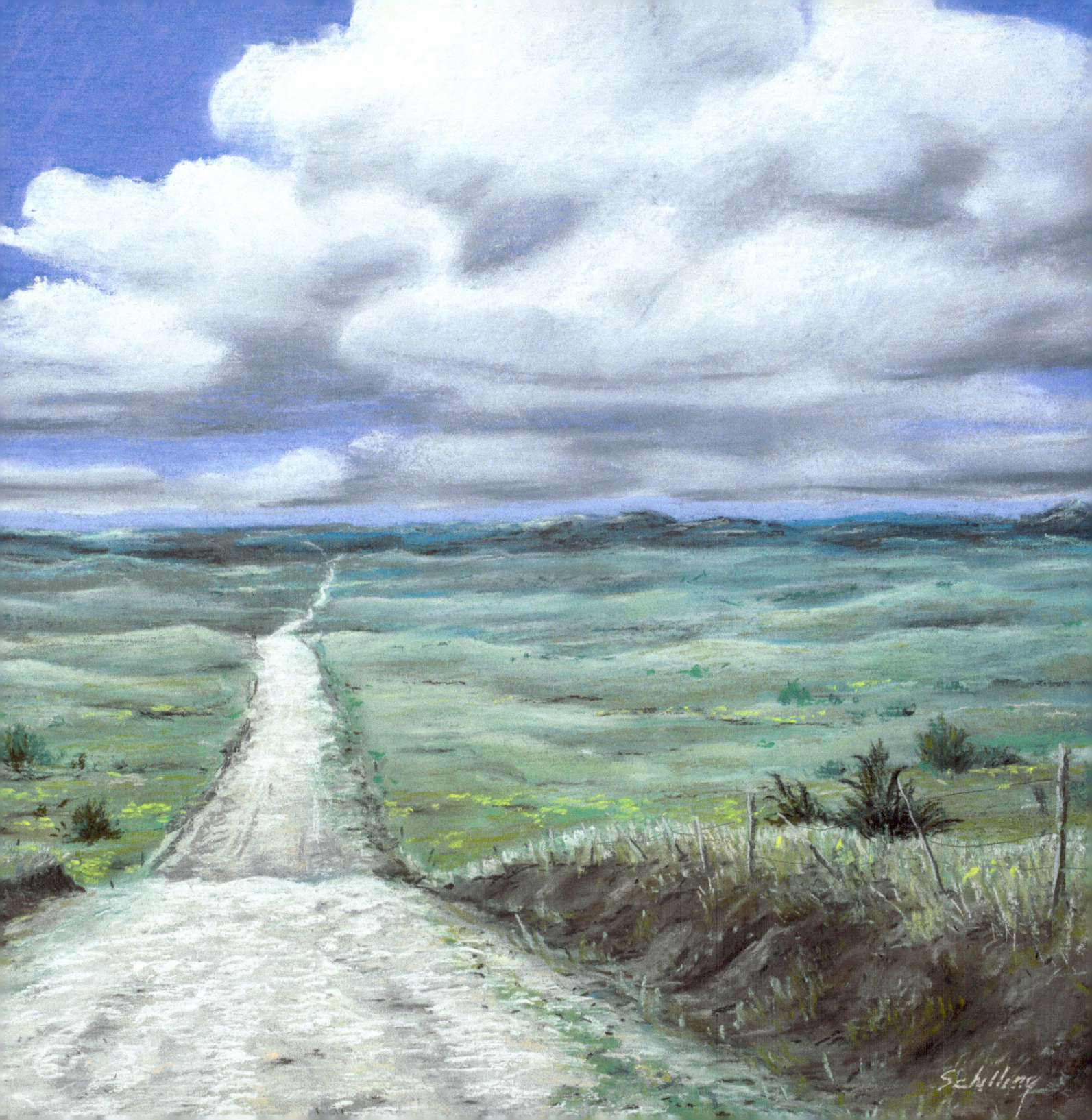

Rural Free Delivery

The Rural Free Delivery was established as an experiment on October 1, 1896. It was not until July 1, 1902, that Congress provided the service for all rural people. Farmers were happy and their wives were elated to order clothing and supplies by mail left in a box outside their homes. Not all were happy though. Critics thought the government's cost of operation was exorbitant. Some merchants in the towns were fearful the mail-order business would ruin their own. In the beginning, carriers of the mail provided their own transportation, which was usually by horse and wagon. By 1929 and with the improvement of roads, deliveries were almost always made by motor cars.

> In many rural communities the local mail carrier was an informal link among neighbors separated by miles rather than city blocks. The mail carrier was a friend of the family, a neighbor, and a certain constant in a changing world. Their comings and goings marked days and months and seasons. They delivered good news and bad; they were the bringers of tomorrow's surprise.
>
> My wife Deb grew up in northern Sheridan County, Nebraska. Their route was called The North Star Route. I like that even better than Rural route #1. North Star Route has a bit of an adventurous tone, perhaps even a bit of a romantic flare. Deb also remembers their mail carrier, Paul. She and her siblings would sometimes hide in the ditch until he had gone by or would stand by the roadside and wave. She remembers once when they picked sunflowers and spelled out "HI PAUL" with sunflower blossoms across the road.
>
> –TIMOTHY NOLTING, *WESTERN NEBRASKA OBSERVER*

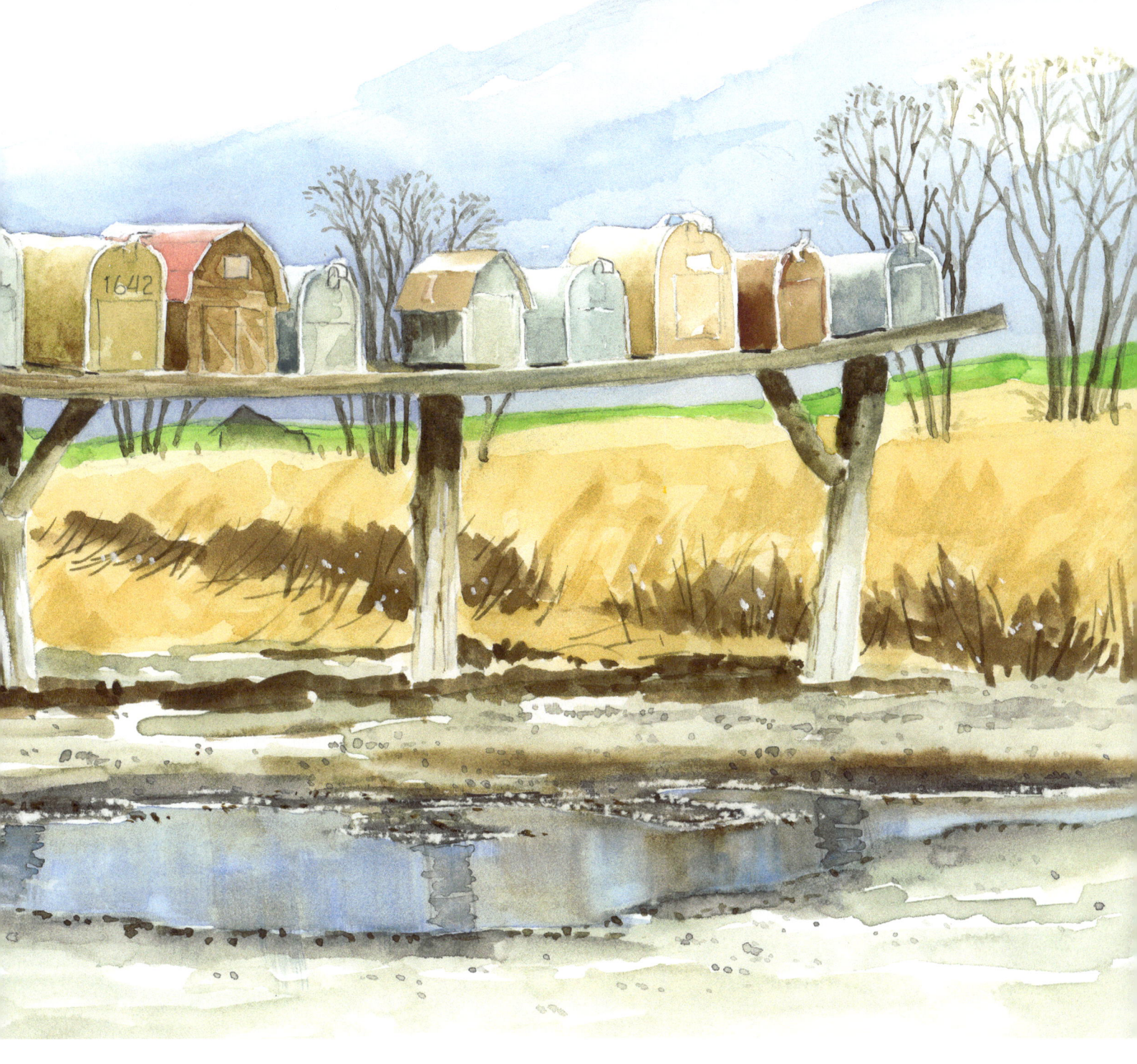

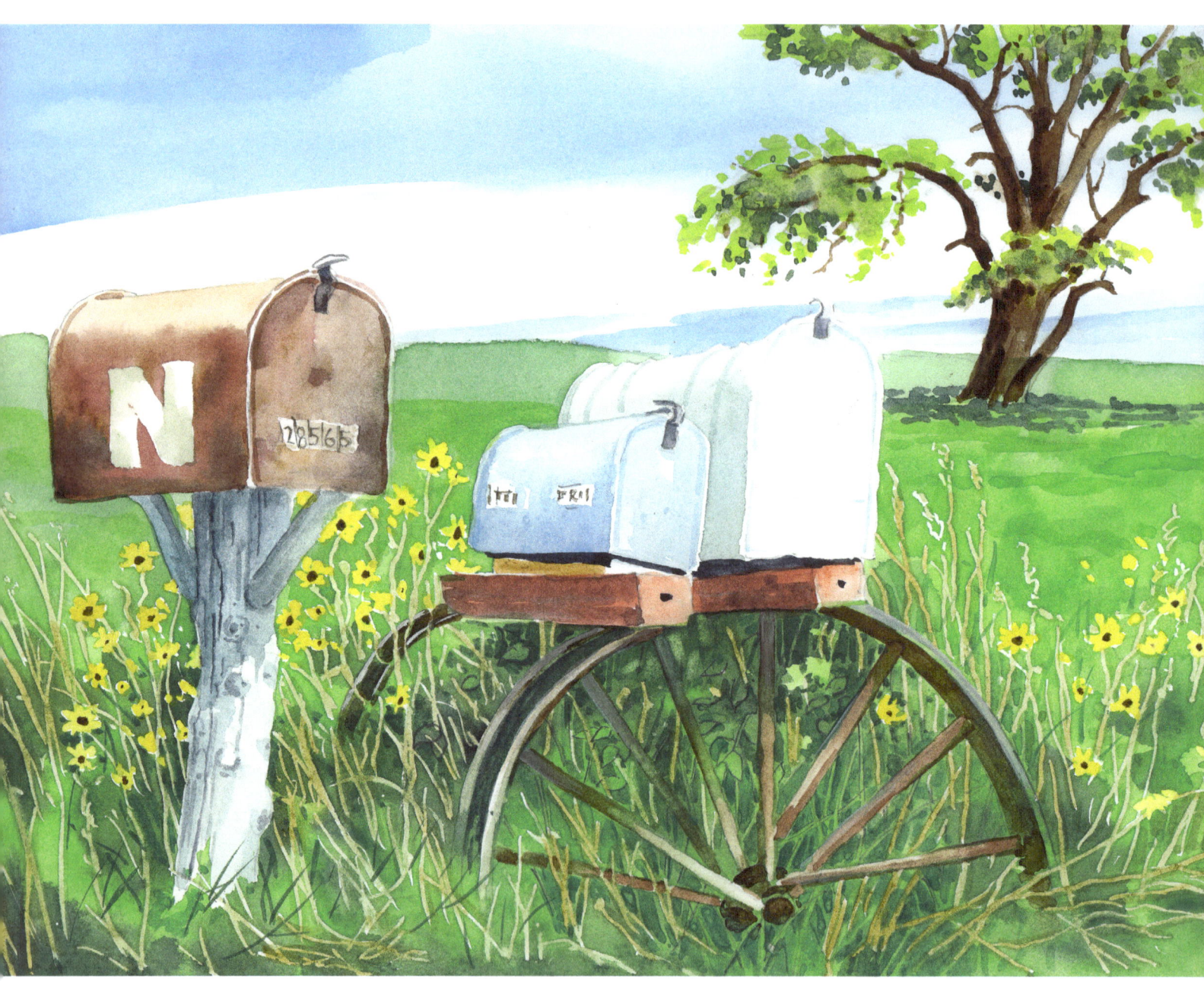

Rural Mail Boxes

They stand next to tire ruts in the sugary sand surrounded by cheery sunflower blossoms. Like ragtag militia volunteers, they wait for their "commanding officer." Only one seems to be officially appointed, bearing the stamped words "U.S. Mail" on the front drop-down cover. The rest of the boxes are expressions of the owner's creativity or, possibly their sense of utilitarianism. A rancher may use a re-purposed bread box, a retired doll house, a model wooden barn, or maybe, a mailbox purchased long ago at the Farm Supply in town, now brown and rusting. Occasionally a retired implement from the equipment grave yard was made into a support for a rancher's box.

Mail box design is an art form. Owners take pride in their uniqueness and often show a dry sense of humor. Some have address numbers attached, while others have nothing to show of ownership. No problem. Who else would they belong to? The postal carrier knows everyone in the county.

"It holds an untold story of lives once lived; of faded dreams and disappointments."

Down the road a piece a solitary RFD box is bent over, ravished by age and wind. It holds an untold story of lives once lived; of faded dreams and disappointments. The mail box connected immigrants to a world beyond. At times it held a milk check, a Sears and Roebuck catalog, a letter from a relative, or a rent due notice. Today, a cottonwood sapling struggles for survival in the midst of the ruins, just as earlier tenants did so many years ago.

Beyond the mailbox next to a broken down fence are sod-brick walls of a deserted home. Holes lost of their window frames stare out of the sagging walls that no longer support a roof.

Delilah Flaherty, Teacher Extraordinaire

In the late fall of 1935 when I was about nine months old, I became very ill. My parents took me from our rural Sioux County, Nebraska, home to the doctor in Crawford, Nebraska. He diagnosed me with spinal meningitis and told my parents that little could be done but to feed me jello or ice cream. This was the middle of the Great Depression and people were very poor. My dad said they had a cellar full of potatoes they had handpicked but couldn't trade the whole cellar-full for a quart of ice cream. However, Grandma had jello and happily I survived with no ill effects.

I taught in western-Nebraska, one-teacher rural schools for thirty-five years. Usually there were six or seven students and that many grades as well; however one year there was only one child. At one school the toilets were in the basement. One morning I discovered a large bull snake down there. A few days later, I noticed that two little boys were wetting their pants. They were afraid to go down to the basement. Eventually, I captured forty-five snakes down there ranging in size from three inches to three feet. We put them back in the pastures at the ranch. They are beneficial, you know. They kill rodents.

—DELILAH FLAHERTY,
SIOUX COUNTY

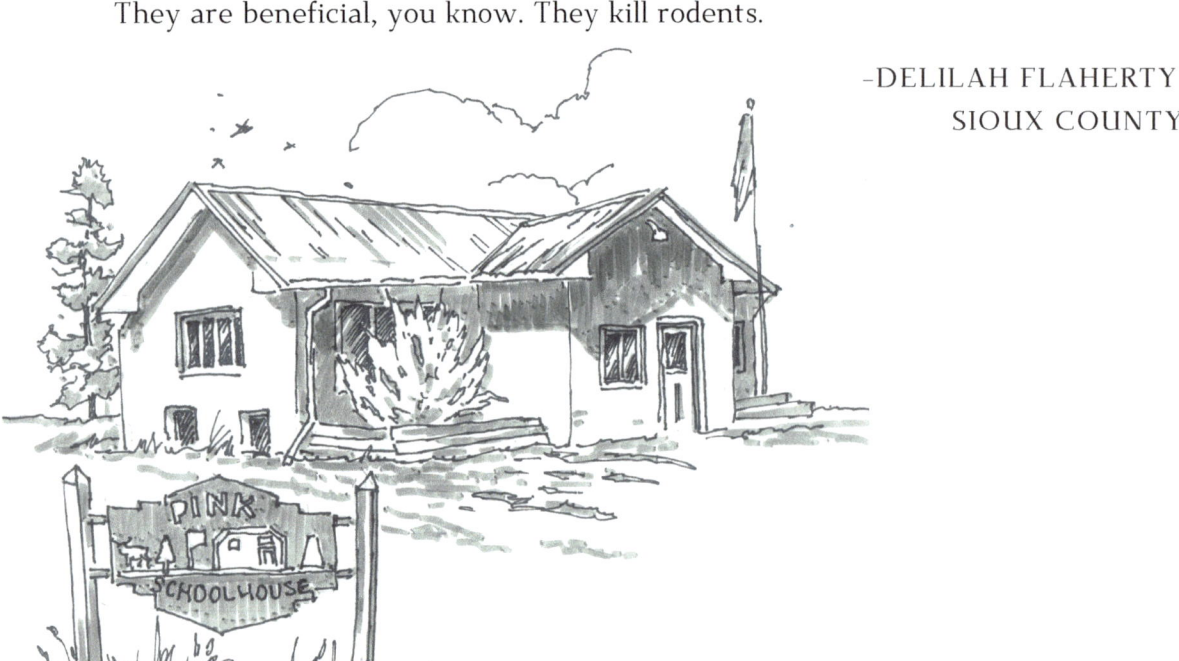

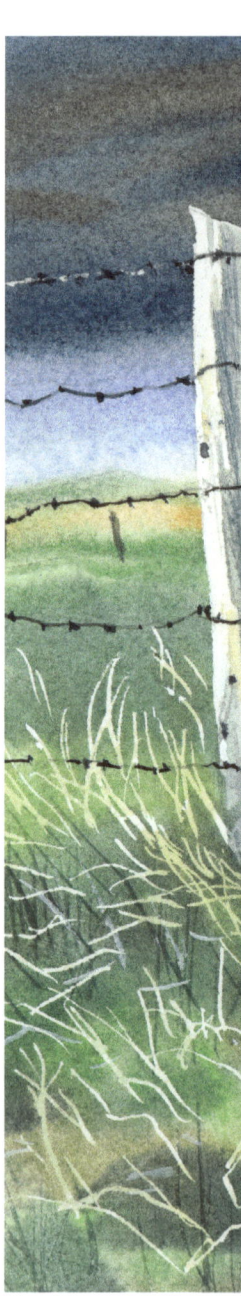

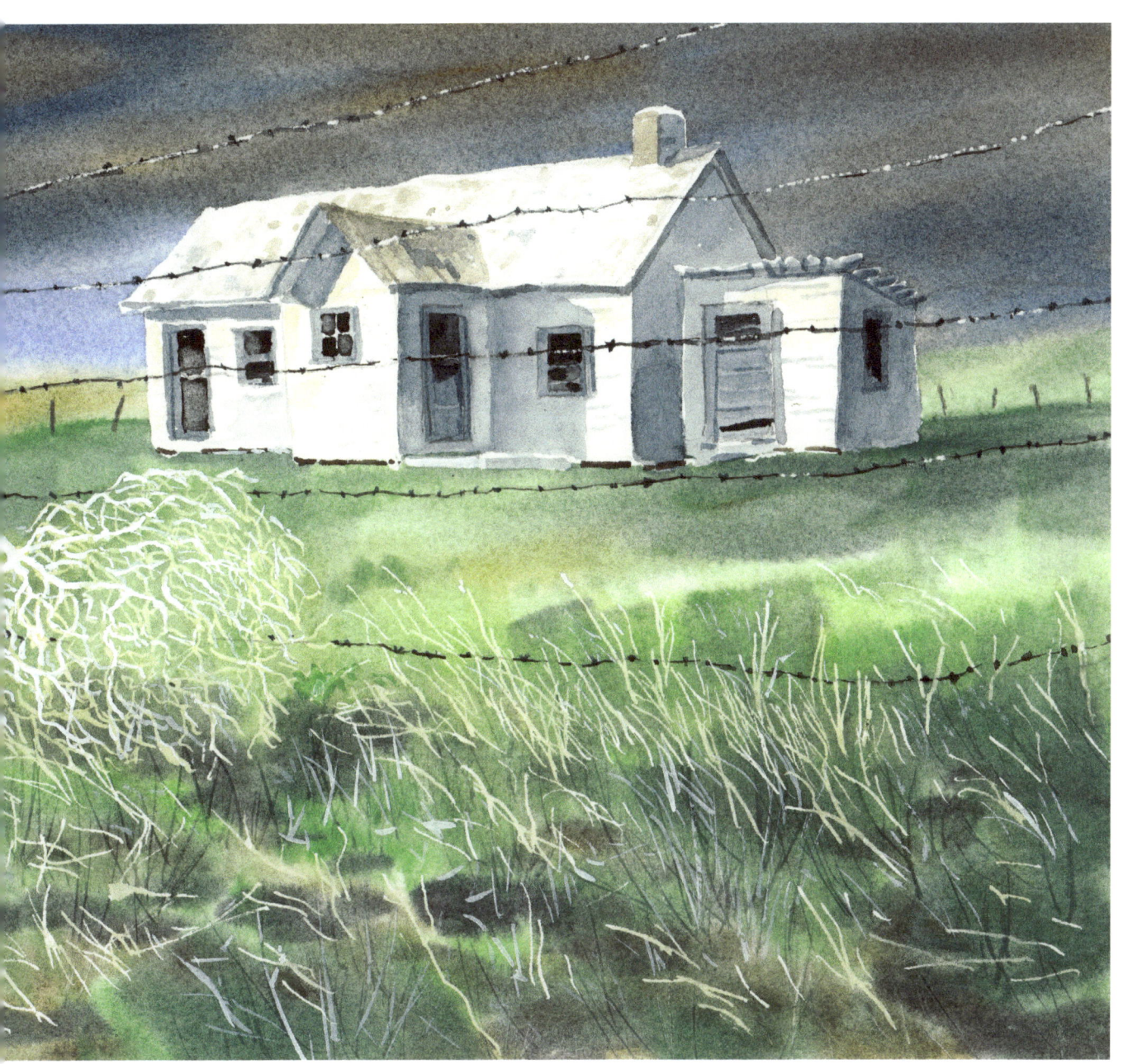

In to Town for Provisions

Because I lived in Valentine, and after obtaining an official driver's license at age sixteen, I was able to make a few trips in a ranch pickup to Valentine to purchase groceries, parts, visit my family, and give rides to other employees. One of my duties was to fulfill the shopping list of some of the other employees on the ranch. The list usually included resupply of the beer and whiskey inventory in the bunkhouse. Being under age, I could not make such purchases in regular liquor stores. However, Fred Nollett, the owner and proprietor of the only small general store and post office in Nenzel, Nebraska, knew that I might be stopping for last minute necessities (ice cream cone), possibly some mail before the regular three-day-a-week rural mail delivery to the ranch, and to fill my important shopping list for the bunkhouse. Fred would set the necessary liquor items on the counter and go to the back room. If they were gone when Fred came out and there was money in their place, that was okay with him, and most certainly okay with the thirsty gang in the bunkhouse.

A Man Named Pedro

One of the itinerant workers from Bill Jordan's Trading Post in Valentine was a Mexican national that we called Pedro, who was about eighteen or nineteen years old. I am not sure if Pedro was his real name. He came out to the ranch with a couple of other itinerants from Arkansas. Pedro had one good English word—"Wheaties"—which he used to refer to almost any food we had in the cook house. He was a good worker.

One Saturday night about two weeks later Pedro went to a dance in Cody with three other employees, including the two from Arkansas. On their way back to the ranch about 3 or 4 a.m. the next morning, the driver, having had too much to drink, took a sharp curve in the road too fast and rolled the car two or three times. The occupants were also plenty inebriated, except for Pedro. Most unfortunately, Pedro lost his life in the wreck. No one knew how to contact his family or what to do for him. To the best of my knowledge, he is buried in the Cody cemetery and none of his family could ever know what became of him. The curve in the road is now known as "Dead Man's Curve."

– MORRISON HETH, VALENTINE

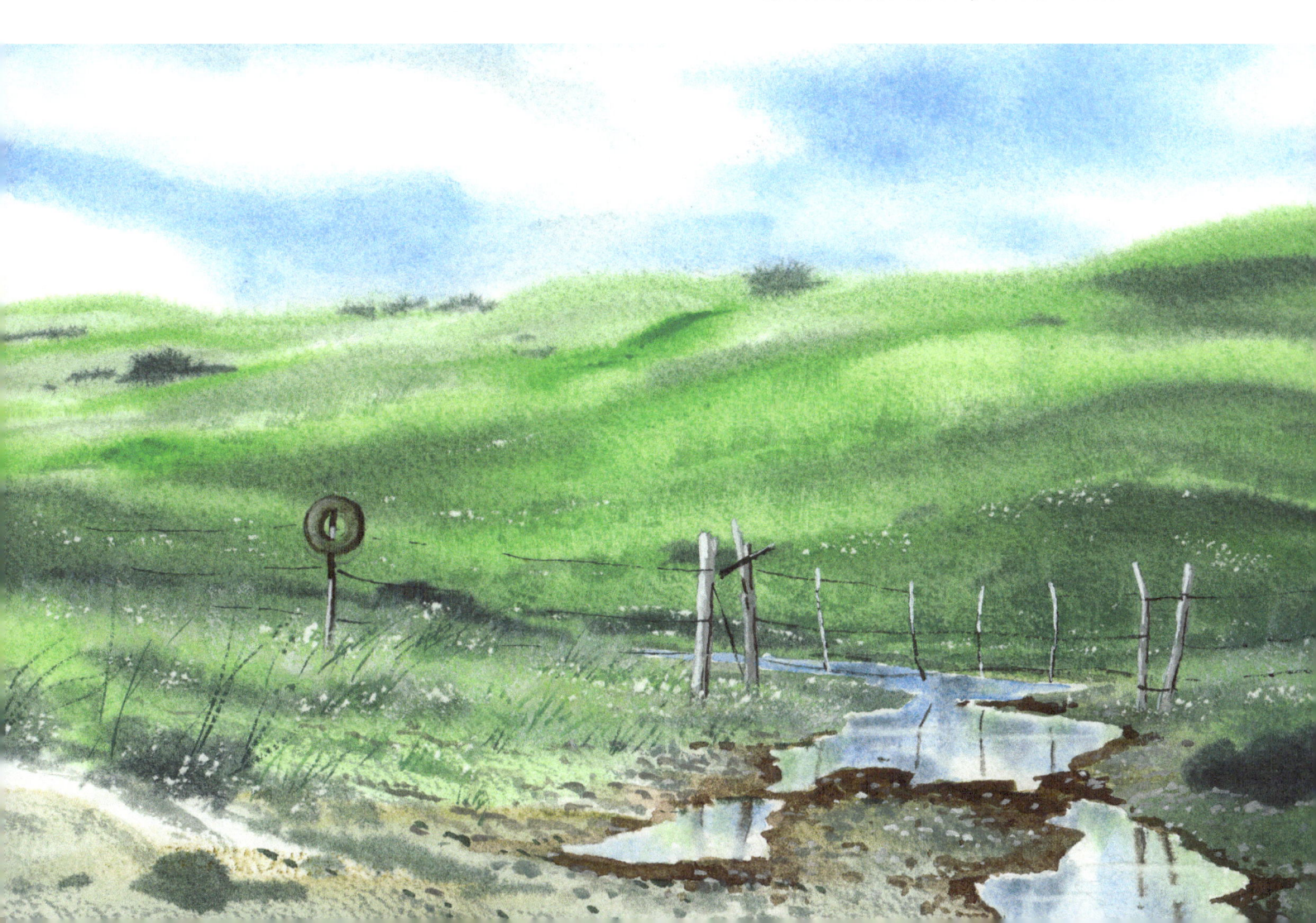

The Homestead Act

The Homestead Act was the hope of the poor man. Many who had wanted a piece of government land felt that preempting, which required an eventual cash payment of $1.25 or more an acre, was too risky for the penniless. If the preemptor failed to raise the money at the proper time, in addition to building a home in the wilderness and making a living for a family, he lost the land and with it all his improvements, his work, and his home. The Homestead Act offered any bona fide land seeker 160 acres from the public domain with no cash outlay beyond the $14 filing fee and the improvements he would have to make to live on the place the required five years. His house, barn, sheds and corrals, his well, the tilled acreage and the fencing—all counted toward the final patent to the land, and most of these improvements could be made by the homesteader's own hands—his and the family's.

—MARI SANDOZ,
OLD JULES COUNTRY

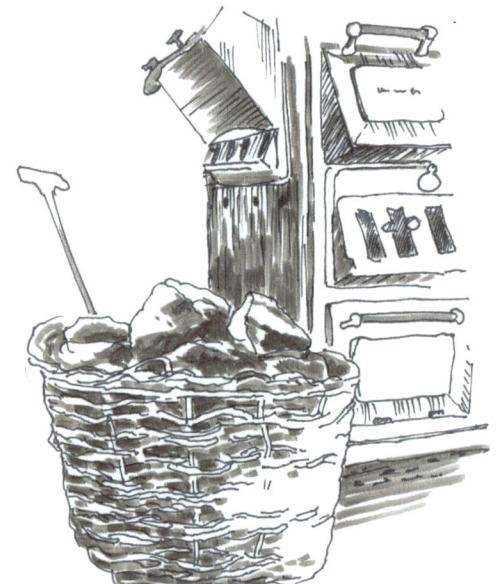

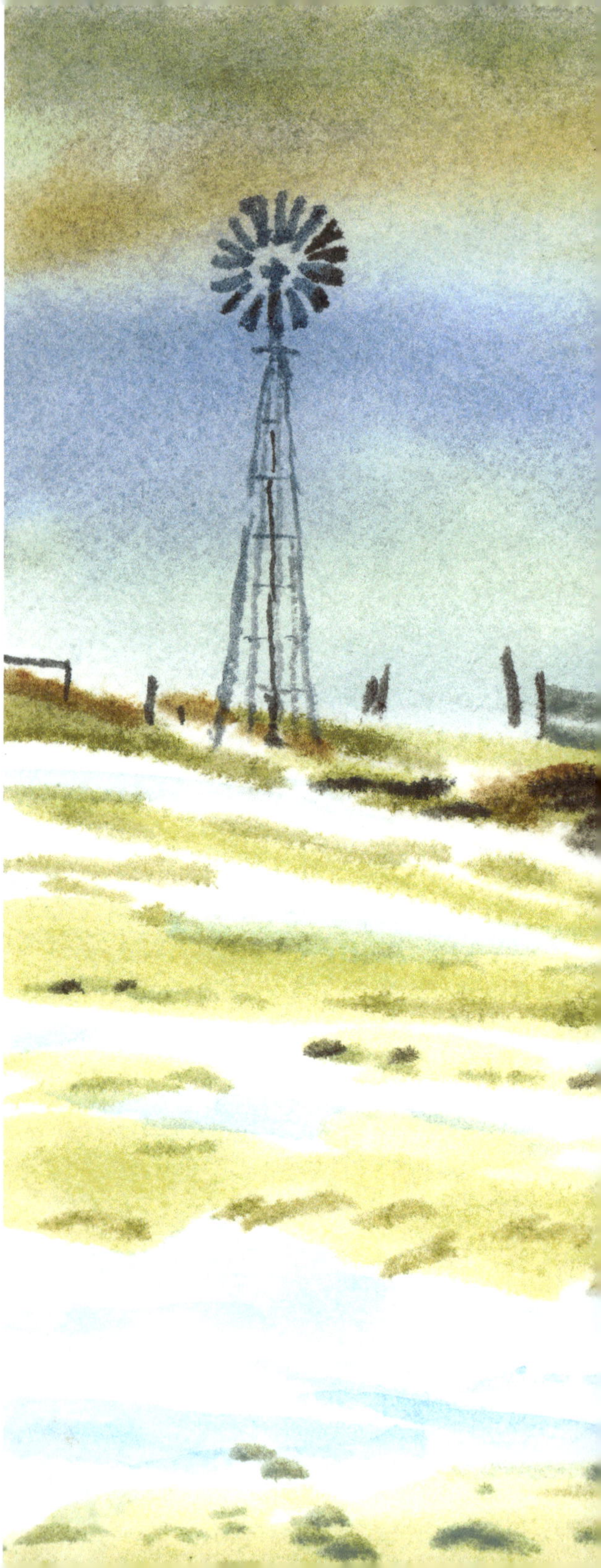

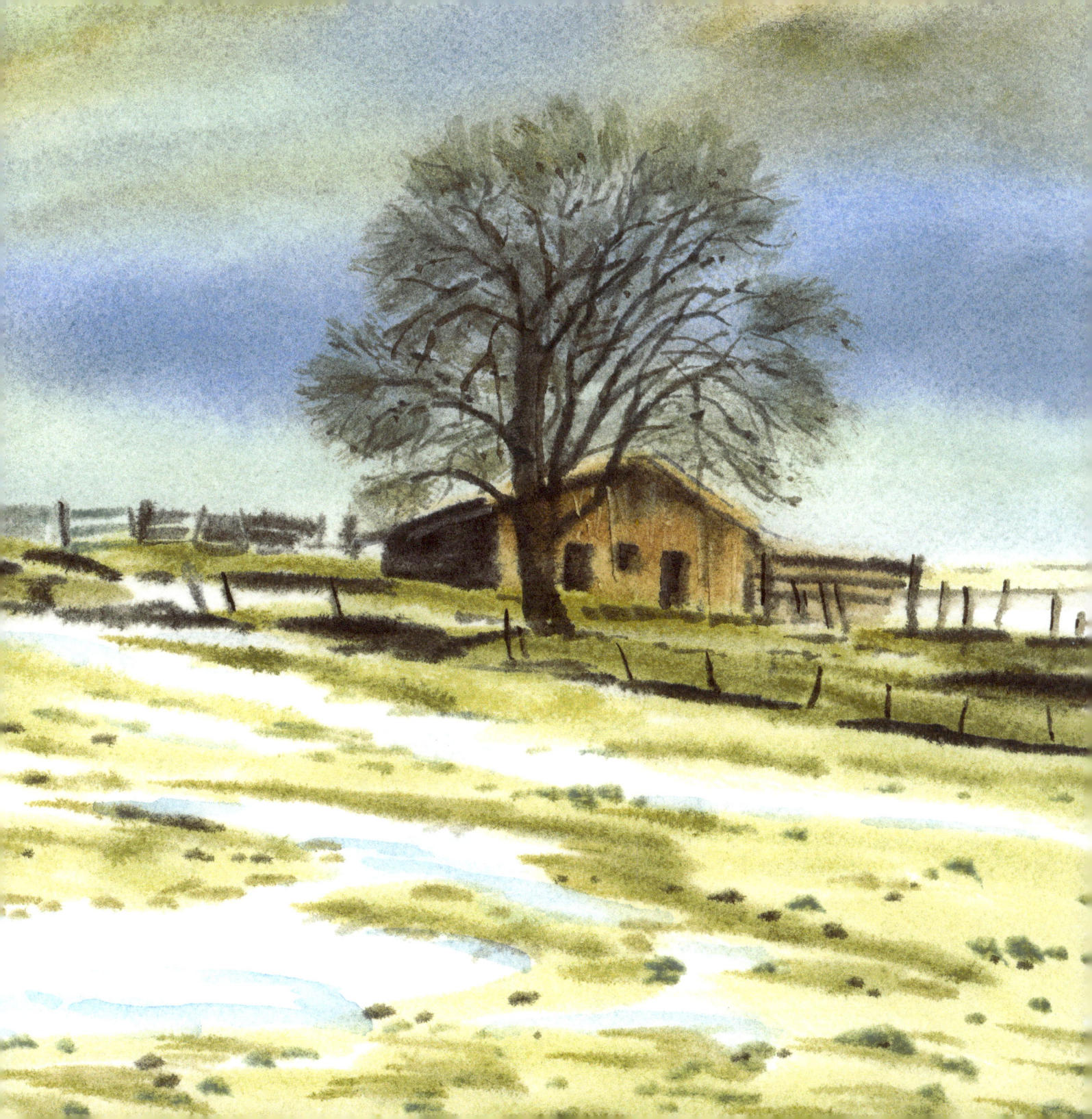

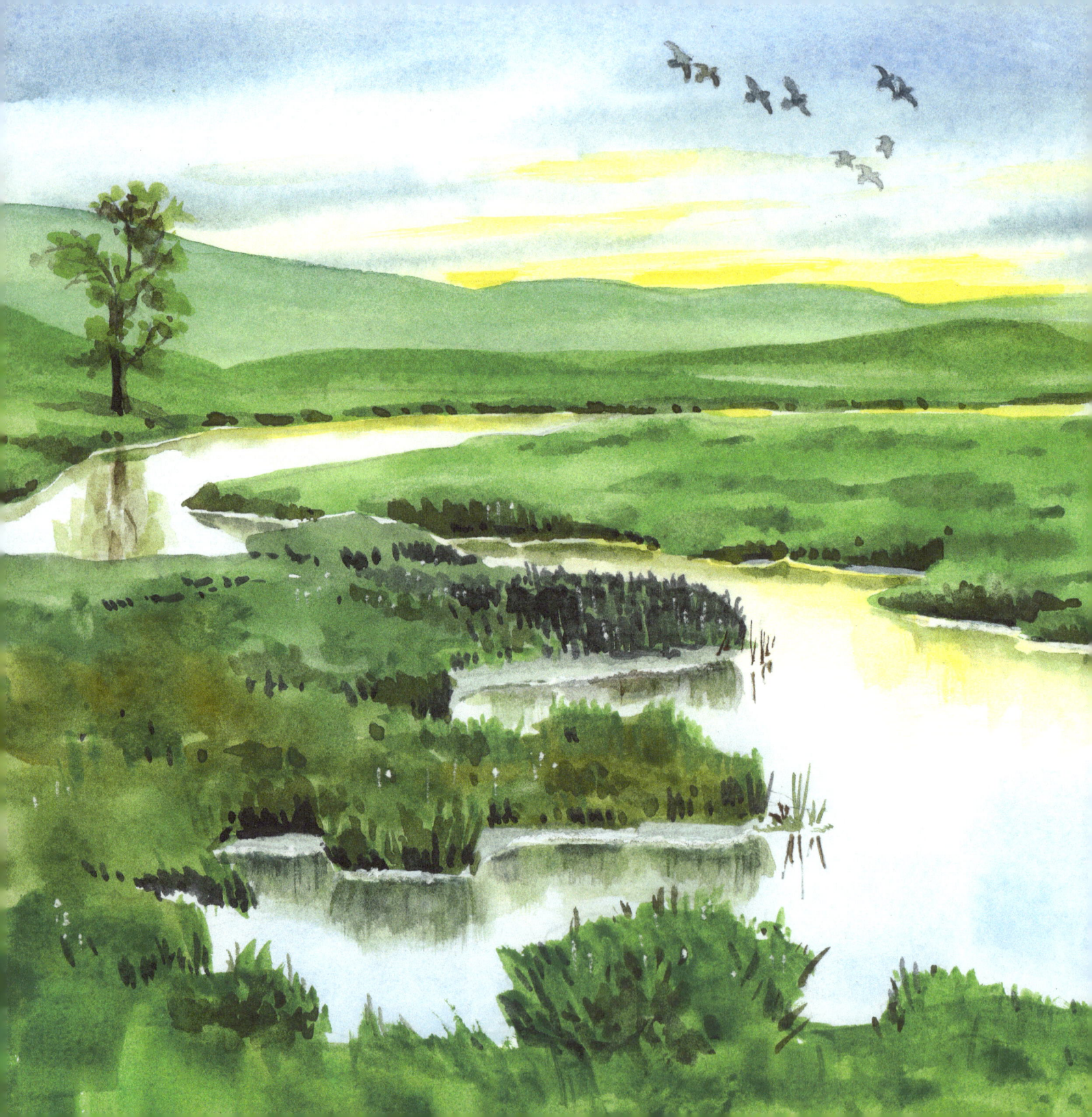

Homesteads

More and more came up the trails without any dream of gold or at least without the heart and the pocketbook to try for California or the more sedate Oregon. These and hundreds of others sought homes no farther west than necessary, looking for the first likely quarter section of the public domain, all practically free during the early years of residence. At first, land along the trails was open only to squatters' rights, to be defended against claim jumpers by gun or combination of guns in the claim clubs, but after the surveyors came and the land offices were set up, the entries were legalized.

–MARI SANDOZ, *LOVE SONG TO THE PLAINS*

Mail-Order Brides

The homesteader got most of his outside items through mail-order catalogues, including, sometimes, his wife, if one could call the matrimonial papers, the heart-and-hand publications, catalogues. They did describe the offerings rather fully but with, perhaps, a little less honesty than Montgomery Ward or Sears Roebuck. Unmarried women were always scarce in new regions. Many bachelor settlers had a sweetheart back east or in the Old Country, or someone who began to look a little like a sweetheart from the distance of a government claim that got more and more lonesome as the holes in the socks got bigger. Some of these girls never came.

"We married everything that got off the railroad," old homesteaders, including my father, used to say.

–MARI SANDOZ, *OLD JULES COUNTRY*

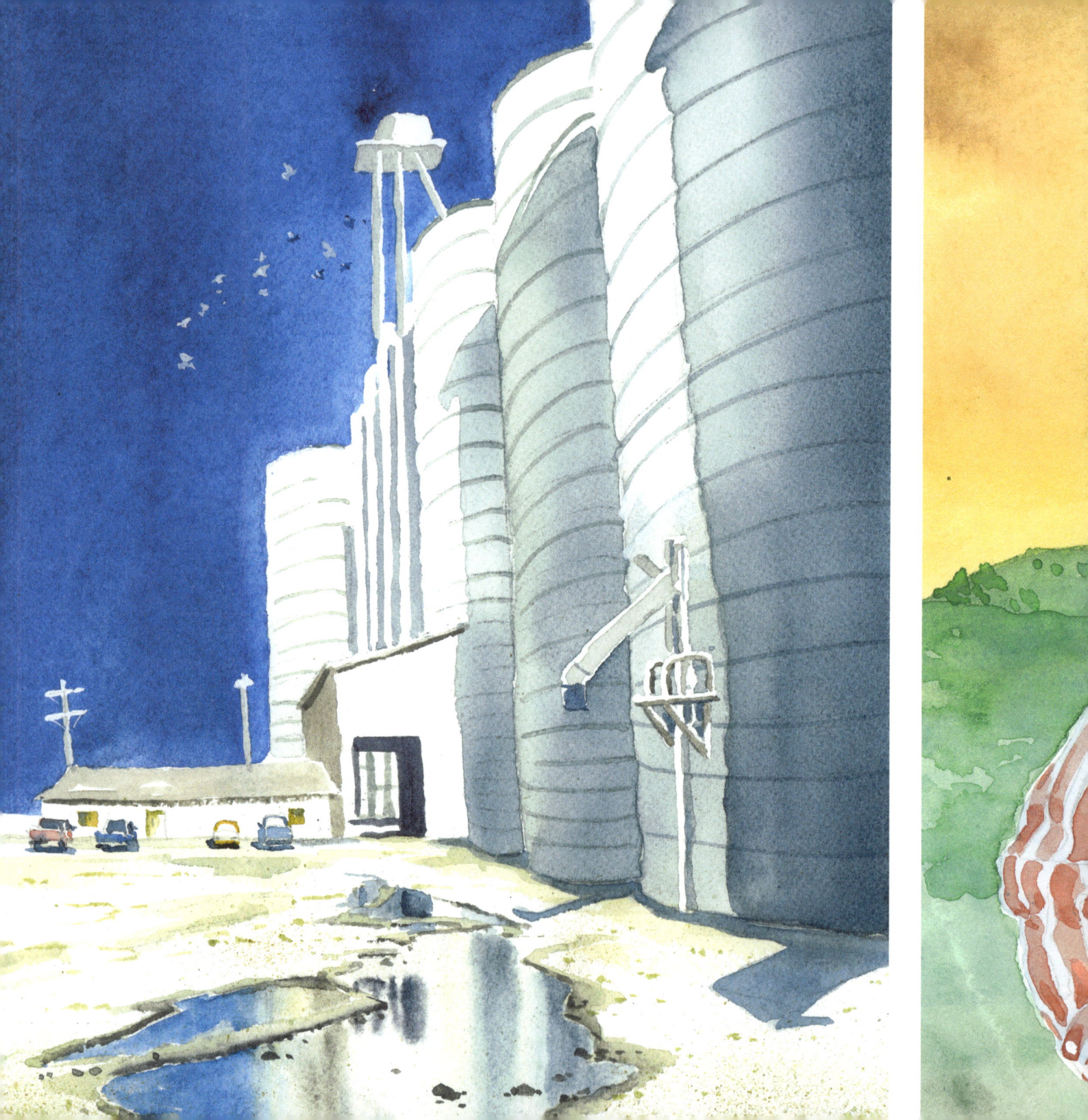

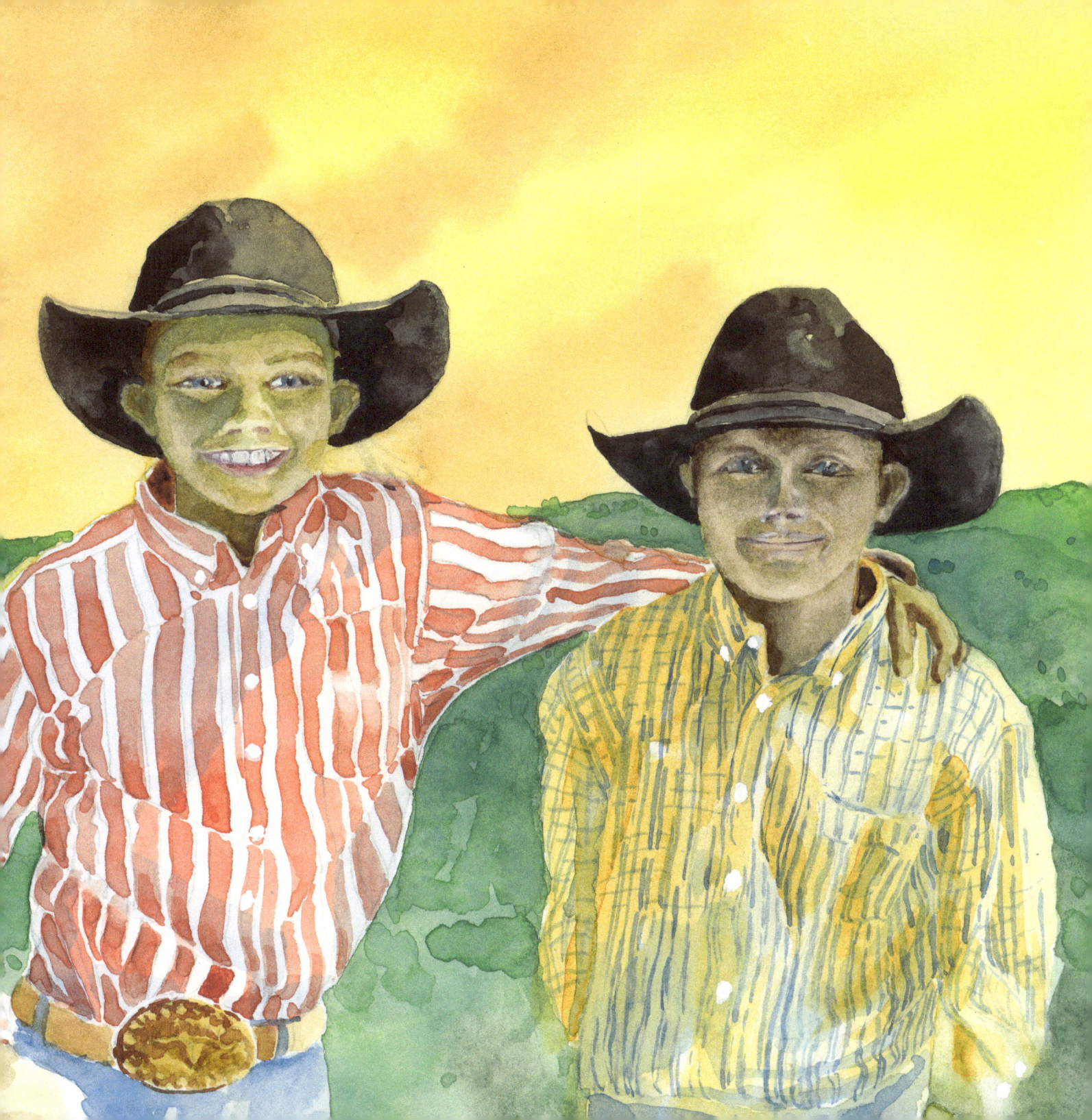

The Railroad: Steaming Into the Future

When the last rail was set and the golden ceremonial stake driven, a new era opened in the West. The Union Pacific and the Central Pacific met at Promontory Point, Utah, on May 10, 1869, linking one coast to the other. The UP was financed by private investors and was also sanctioned by the Federal Government. As an inducement to spur the construction of a national railway system, the UP was given title to land on both sides of the track.

Small hamlets grew to become boisterous cities along the Iron Route as laborers came for work; investors looked for get-quick-rich opportunities, while others were just hangers-on. Lawlessness, licentiousness, and liquor were rampant. In time, these communities settled down as some workers moved on to other fertile fields and a system of law and order prevailed.

It was a time of great excitement, especially for settlers in the Sandhills. No longer would they feel isolated and forgotten. They could occasionally visit friends and family back home, ship their cattle to markets, and receive ranch supplies and goods ordered from a Sears catalog. Even though ranchers and farmers might not travel, it was a good feeling just to know they could. Optimism and excitement reigned just as proud Americans celebrated a man landing on the moon a hundred years later. The railroad had opened a new world of opportunity.

Soon, the Burlington Road established a route across Nebraska transporting passengers and freight between Chicago and Denver. Eventually, the line extended to the Pacific Northwest as well as joining small towns together in Nebraska. The line underwent several acquisitions and is known today as the BNSF, Burlington Northern Santa Fe Railroad.

There were railroaders in my family. My Uncle Fred was a proud engineer for many years. I remember him dressed in a pinstripe suit, white shirt, diamond stick pin in this tie, and a large pocket watch on bob tucked into a pocket just made for such an important instrument. He left his house to begin his "run" dressed like a banker. Reaching his station locker he slid into body-length coveralls that protected his clothing from the ashes and soot of the coal burning steam engine. With goggles protecting his eyes, he protruded his head outside the cab to view the road ahead.

My Uncle Royd worked in the Burlington Shops in Havelock. In those days, railroaders had a system of communicating with moving trains. A station master would use a hoop to provide orders to a train that did not stop but passed through a small town. The hoop looked like a large wooden sling-shot. Tied to the free ends was a loop of string on which were attached the orders. Uncle Royd occasionally traveled to the sandhills on an employee pass. On a hot, sultry, moonless night Uncle Royd cooled his legs by hanging them out the window of the passenger car. The trainman on the platform mistook the extended leg for the outreached arm of the engineer and Royd awoke to find the orders dangling from his ankle.

Another proud trainman was Melvin (Shorty) Ingraham. He received the nickname in high school because of his small stature. However, in time he grew to be a handsome, strong young man, but the nickname stuck. A bright student, he graduated from high school at sixteen. He wanted to go to college but the money wasn't there. He worked jobs as a hired hand or delivered milk for several years before landing a job as a fireman on Burlington locomotives. He loved the job, although it was hard to imagine why anyone would like to shovel coal into a hot furnace. The mark of his trade was a pair of white gauntlet gloves. These were elbow length gloves that protected his hands and sleeves from burning. They were white when new but soon became blackened by coal dust. He carefully watched

"He loved the job, although it was hard to imagine why anyone would like to shovel coal into a hot furnace."

and learned the mechanics of railroading, eventually becoming an engineer in the Ravenna Division of the Chicago, Burlington and Quincy Railroad. Later he was transferred to the Alliance Division. By that time he had a wife, three children and a home in Edgemont, South Dakota.

Families of railroad employees were able to travel free on the line. Melvin Ingraham's daughter, Roberta, remembers traveling alone to visit her grandparents in Broken Bow when she was seven years old. Her parents placed her on the train in Edgemont, said "Good bye," and left her in the care of a friendly conductor. She remembers him as smartly attired in a starched white coat and a black cap with the polished brass emblem of the Burlington Railroad. Roberta sat alone on the bench with her tiny legs dangling from the seat; her little red velvet purse clutched against her tummy guarding the twenty five cent piece she would need to purchase a pillow. If any pennies were left, she would scramble into station at Alliance and buy a couple of Chicklets before boarding train #42 to Broken Bow. She memorized all the station stops so that she would always know the progress of her journey. Roberta's aunt ran a restaurant in Alliance. Between trains Roberta sometimes ran swiftly to her aunt's diner. She would climb up on the red vinyl-covered chrome stools while her aunt fixed her anything she wanted to eat. After a special meal, Roberta ran as fast as she could back to the train.

Melvin had a fine career that eventually carried over into the diesel-powered age. He commanded the respect of his peers and his community. He loved being a fireman. It was a profession. . .possibly what he might think of as a "calling." He never lost his love for power and steam and after retiring, he was chosen along with his best friend, another engineer, to be the crew of the 1880 steam-driven train running from Hill City to Keystone, South Dakota, and back carrying tourists in the Black Hills. Walt Disney decided the train and the older crew to be perfect for his movie "Scandalous John" with Brian Keith, and so ended a proud railroad career that is forever memorialized on a Disney celluloid film.

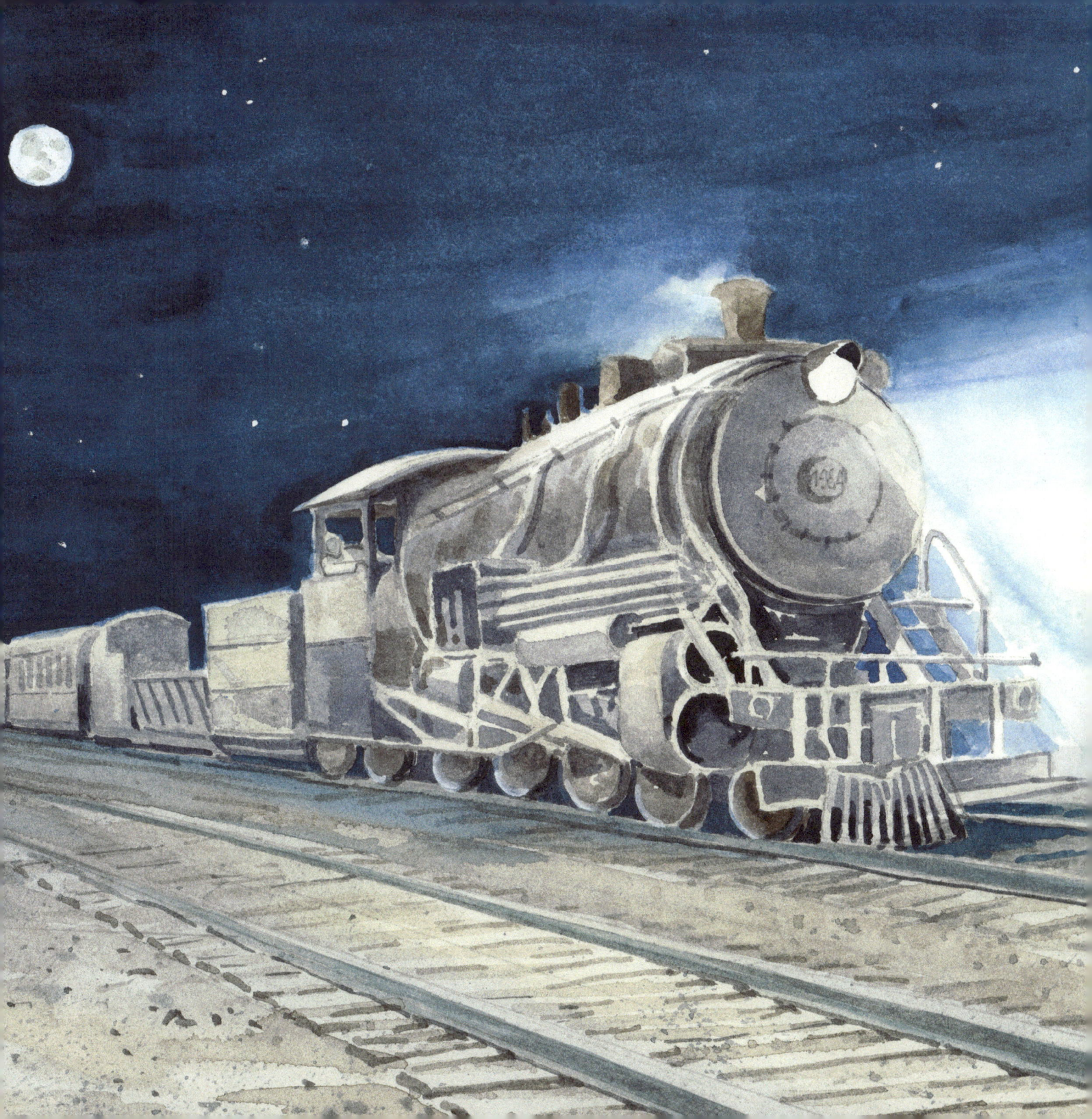

Kinkaiders Giving Up

The first week in May brought the sun and summer winds. Snow water filled the valleys and the cellars, drowning out the alfalfa. This was the buyer's opportune moment. The music teacher, weak from a severe cold, was one of the first to sell. The shrewder, the more courageous, sensed the promise of the latent hills and mortgaged their claims to buy out their neighbors. So walls gaped open to the sun, making good rubbing places for the cattle, lousy from lowered vitality. But we scarcely noticed the Kinkaiders go, so busy were we with the extra work of Father's new orchard.

–MARI SANDOZ, *SANDHILL SUNDAYS*

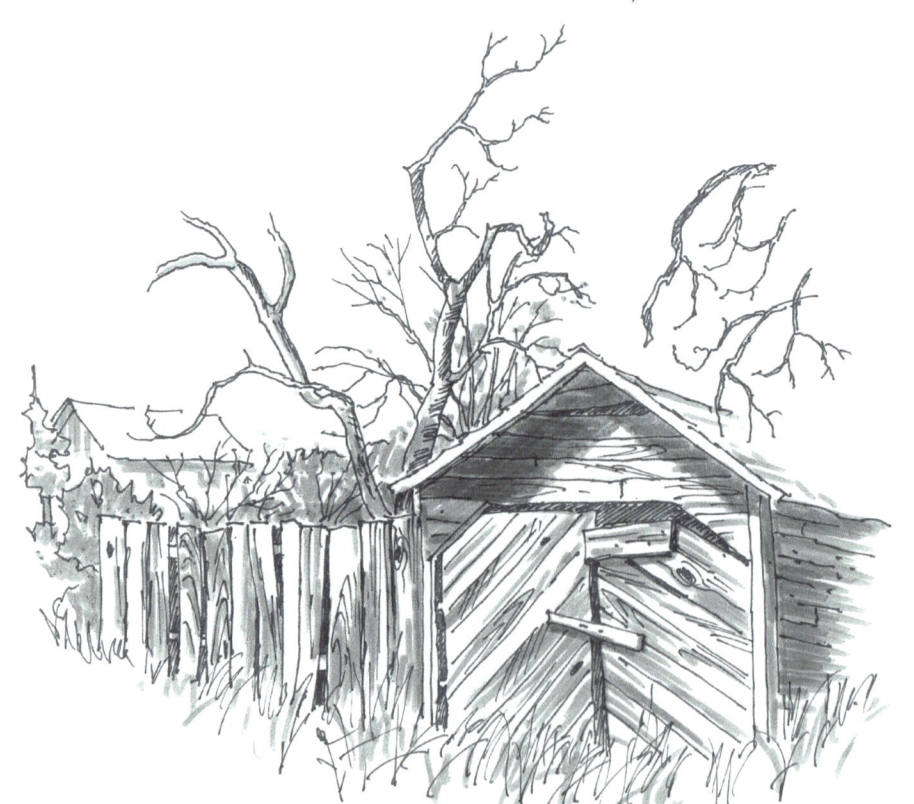

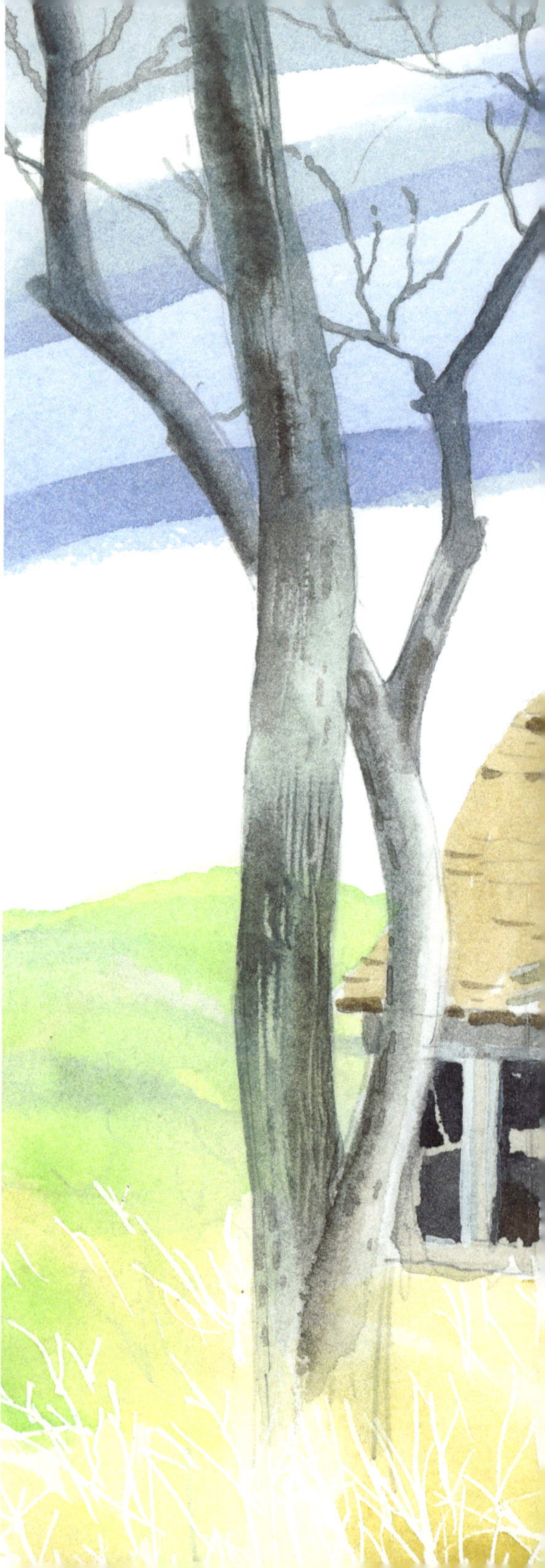

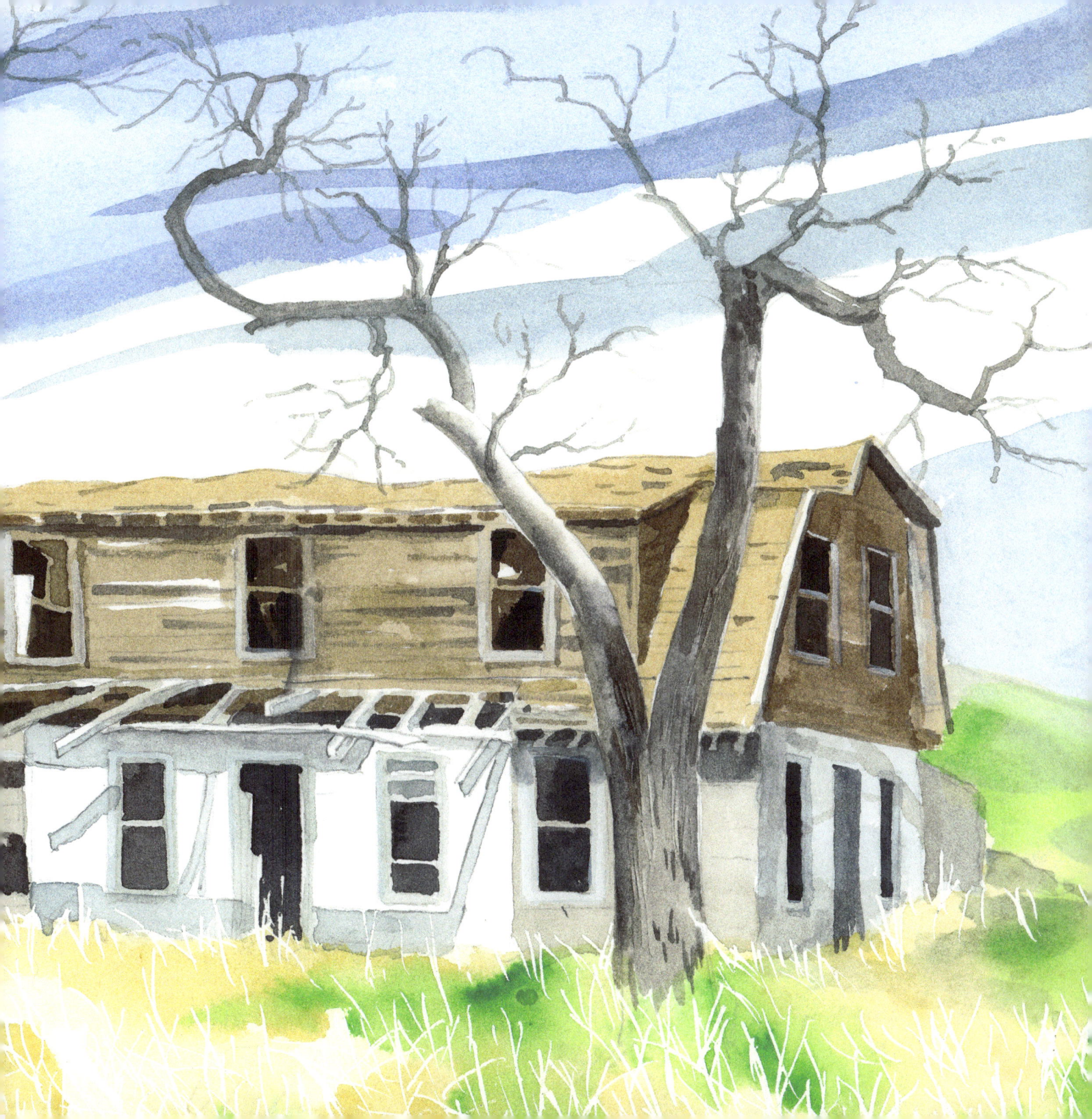

The Dismal River

I don't know why they called it the Dismal. It's just a lazy Sandhill river, set at the bottom of a cedar-lined canyon. The channel doubles back on itself repeatedly, as though it had all the time in the world to join up with the Loup and meander toward the Mighty Mo. Occasionally it runs swift and deep, and some stretches are notorious for quicksand. Just here, it drifts along slowly, around sandbars and willow islands, under the overhang of plum brush and wild roses.

–LYN MESSERSMITH, *MY SISTER MARIAH*

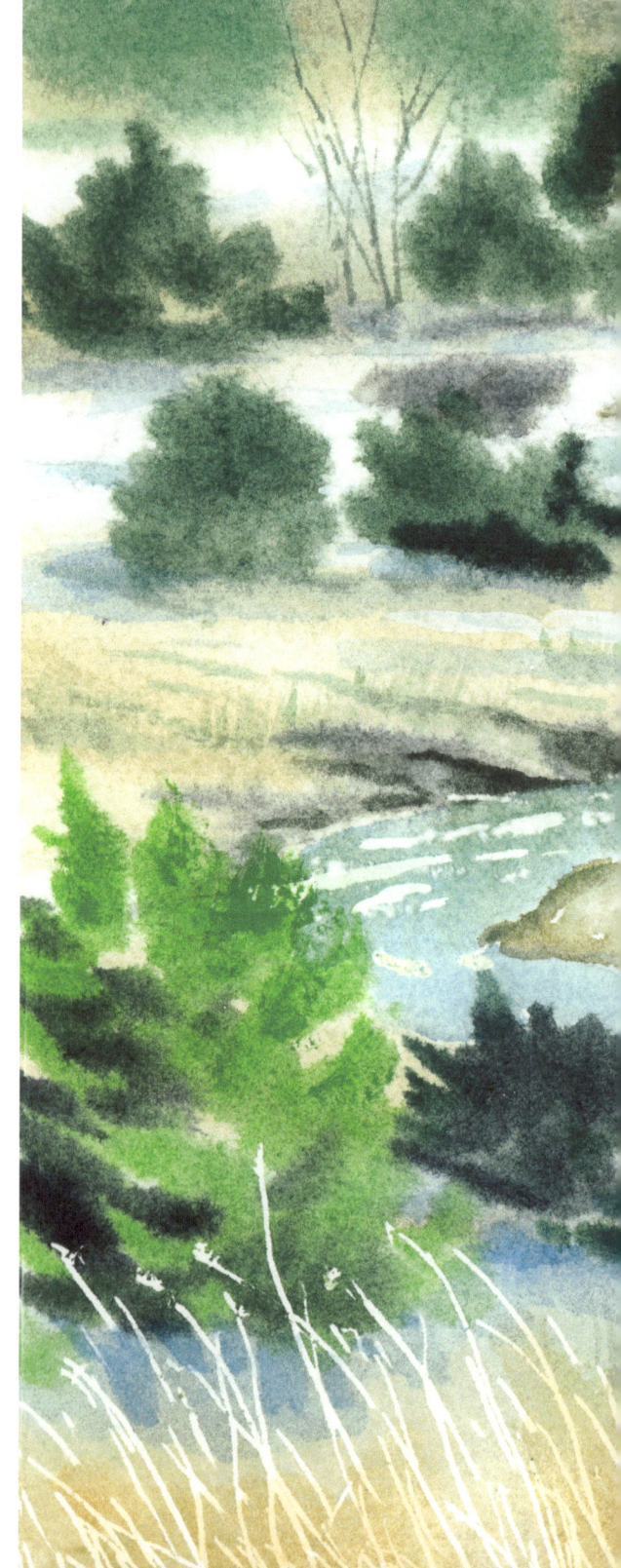

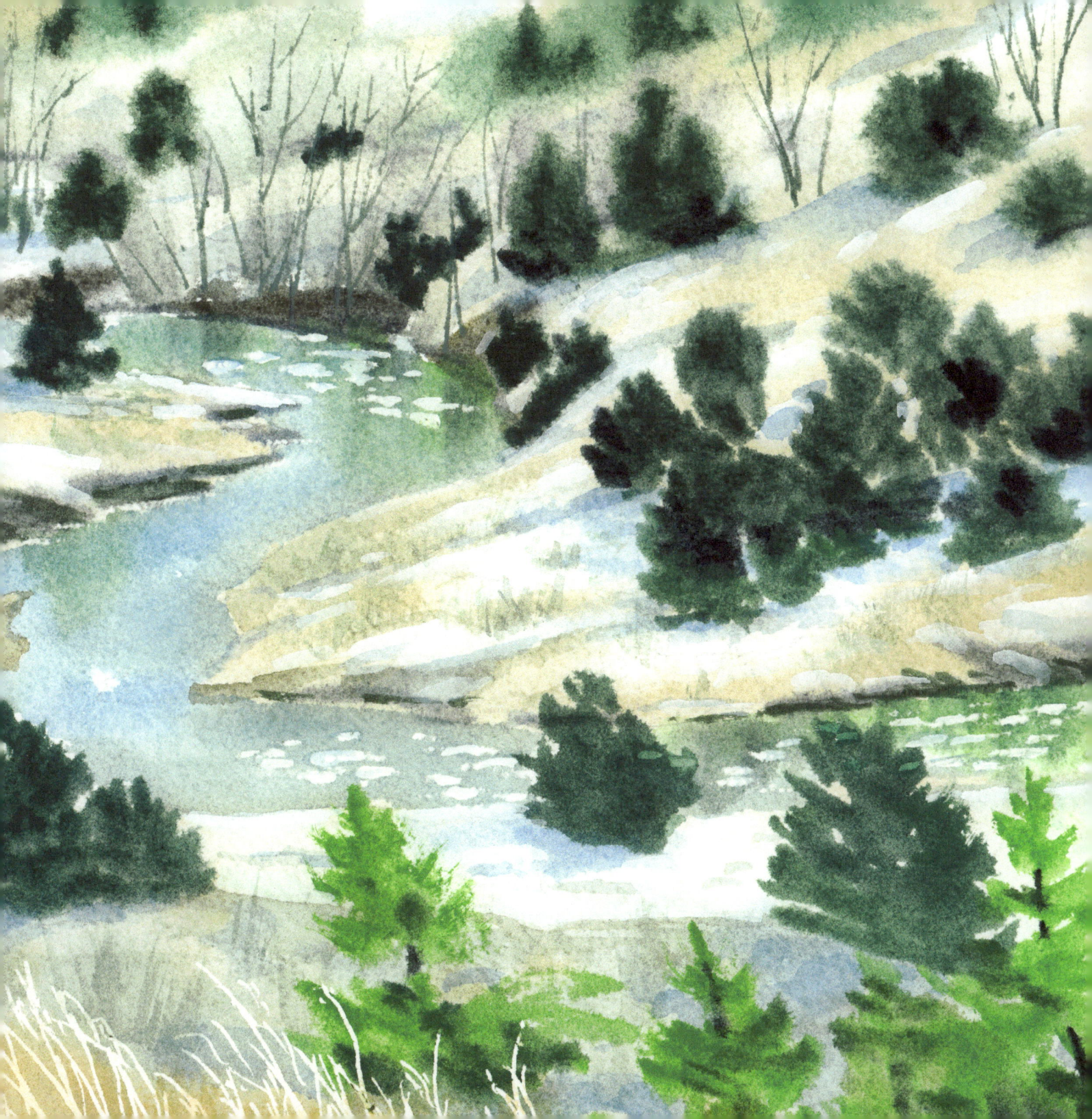

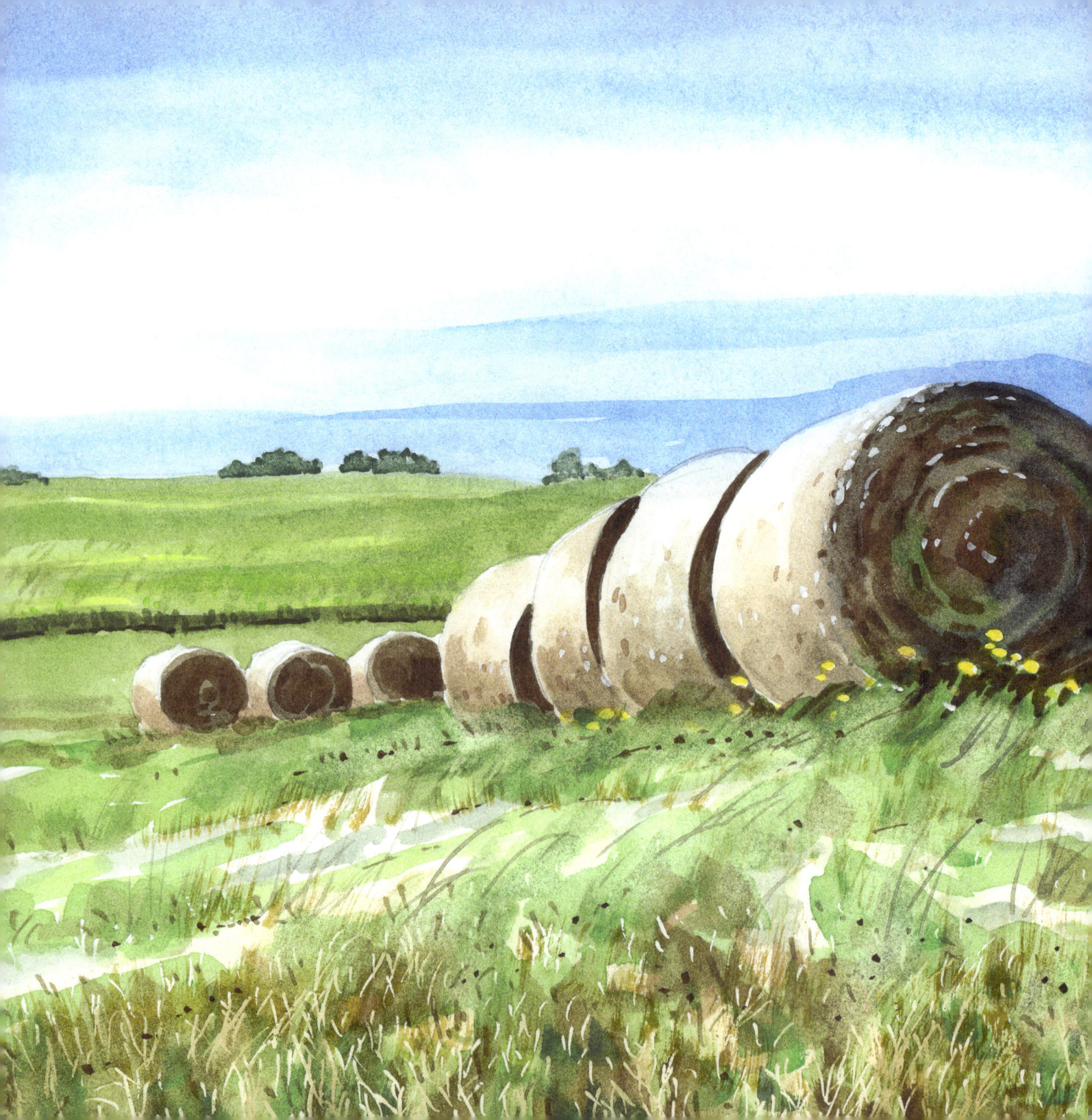

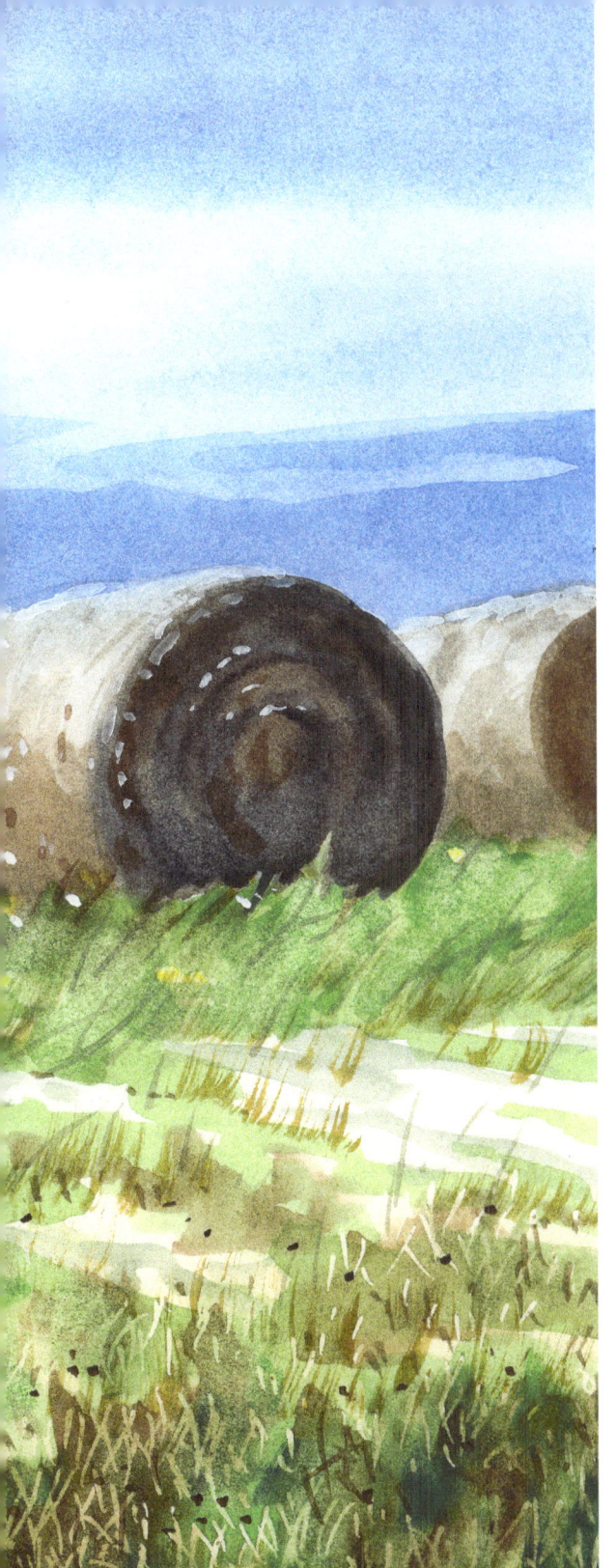

Hay Fields

. . .I love hay fields. Before they're cut, when Mariah tosses grasses like an endless green sea, later on the clatter of sickles, smell of mint, and graceful stems falling over the bar. Raking the fragrant windrows and watching the baler spit out neat bundles of promise for winter. Driving past them at night; the scent of fresh cut clover washing in the window, walking barefoot through noonday stubble, sliding my feet so as to smooth out prickly ends, keeping an eye peeled for cactus and bumblebee nests.

–LYN MESSERSMITH, *MY SISTER MARIAH*

Arthur, Nebraska

Dappled light from under a canape of Elm and Cottonwood trees decorates the park in Arthur, Nebraska, population 140. Nothing seems to be going on in this sleepy village. However, over at the Bunk House Café there is a string of twenty cars parked on the gravel main street. The café is the popular gathering place and watering hole for folks from miles around.

This spunky village boasts of two "must see" attractions in guide books: "The smallest county court house in America" and the oldest church built with bales of hay. That piqued my interest.

The while-washed, Pilgrim Holiness Church sparkled brightly in the morning light. I was told by a passer-by that Ruth Jagler at May's Place next door would be pleased to unlock the church and give me a tour. The church has a proud history having been built in 1928 of baled hay. The bales had been stacked on end with strips of wood driven through each one for support. The walls were stuccoed on the outside and plastered inside. The hay insulated the church against the hot summer sun and frigid winter Sundays.

Nineteen different preachers served the church. . .most for only a year or two. Behind the altar were four rooms that provided the families a home. Several babies were born in the church.

My next stop was The First Arthur County Courthouse and Jail. It measures twenty-six by twenty-eight feet and occupies the center of the town park. There is a simple latch on the door which opens a cell with only two small barred windows for light. The exterior is painted white but beginning to blister from the hot summer sun.

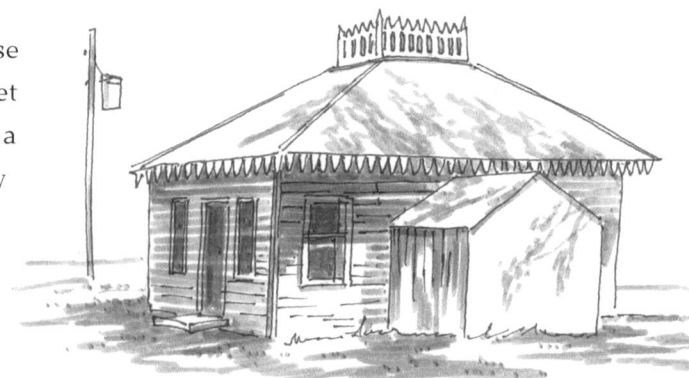

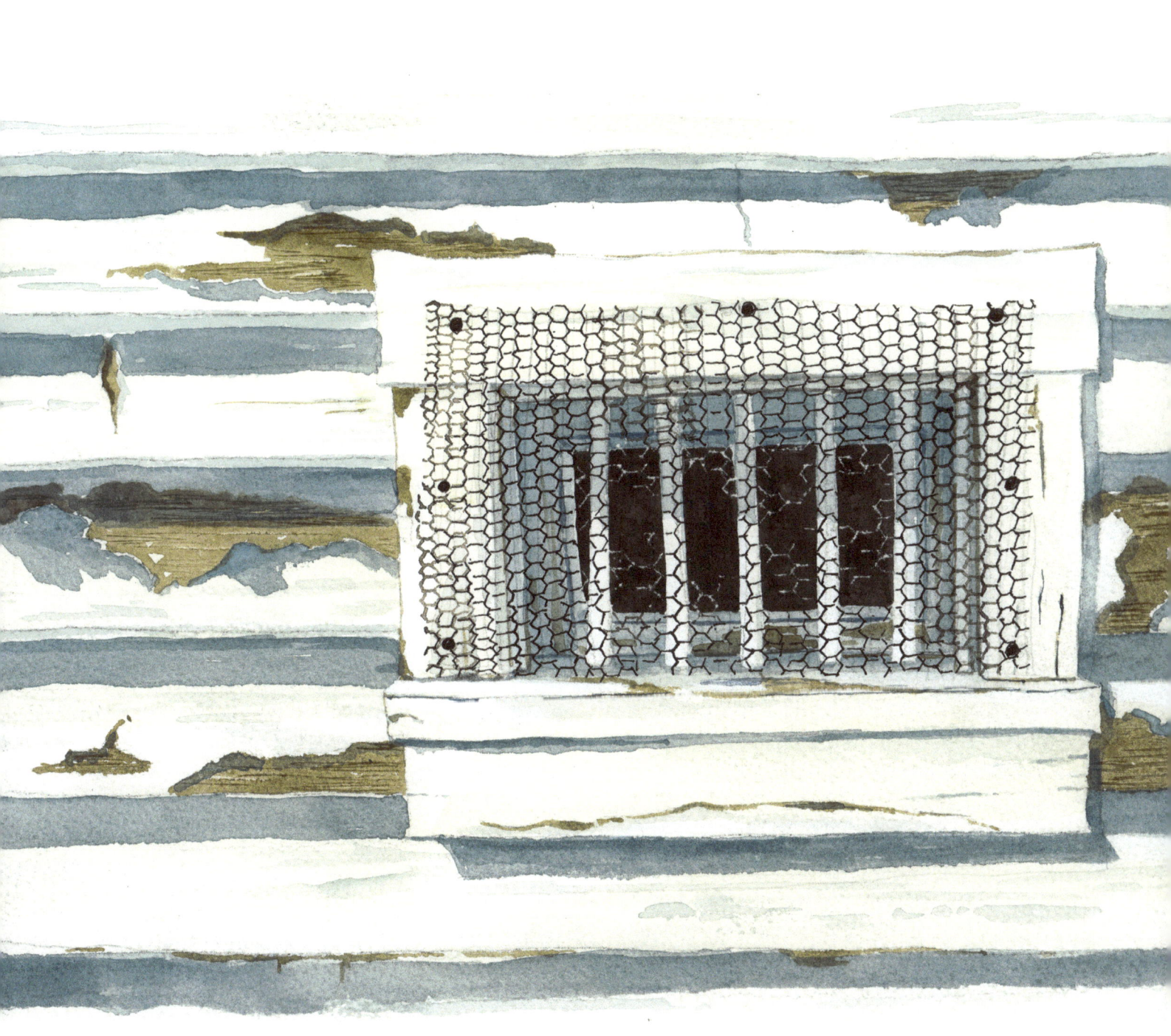

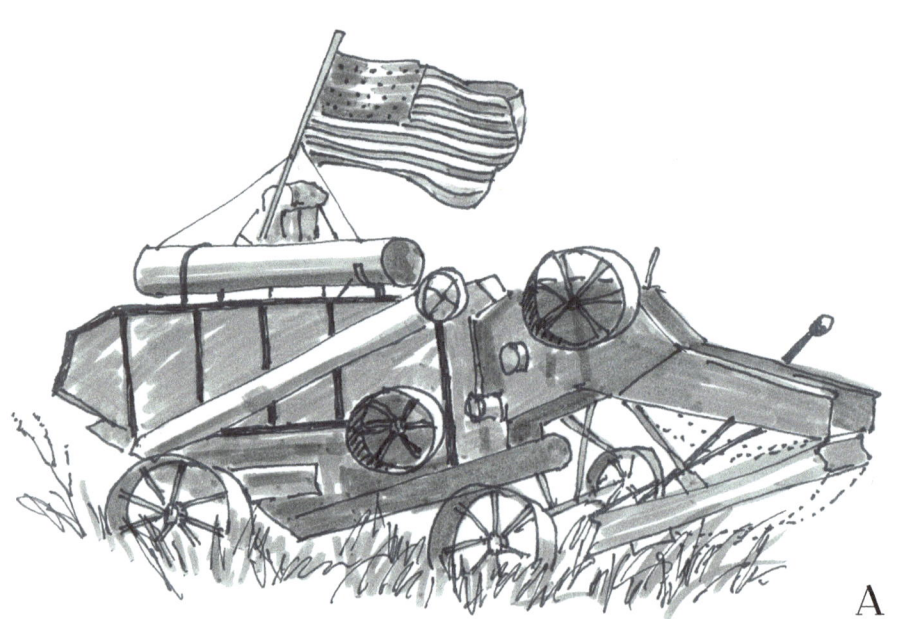

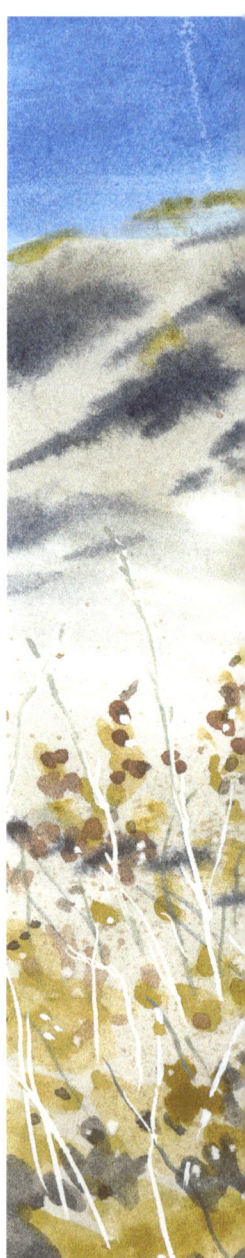

A Strange Sight

I saw one of these new homemakers in the south Sandhills of Nebraska not so long ago. Twenty miles from the nearest boxcar depot, an old Model T without a top, fender, or windshield drew out of the rutted trail to let us pass. In place of an engine the motive power was an old flea-bitten mare, the single-tree slack against her hoary fetlocks. The car body was rounded in a neatly tiered mound of cow chips, the native coal of the Sandhills. In front, his feet reaching down to brace against the dash, sat the driver, a young man in frayed-bottom trousers, In the back was a young woman in overalls and an orange felt hat that still carried a hint of the jauntiness of a good shop. Beside her was the battered old washtub used to gather the fuel.

–MARI SANDOZ, *SANDHILL SUNDAYS*

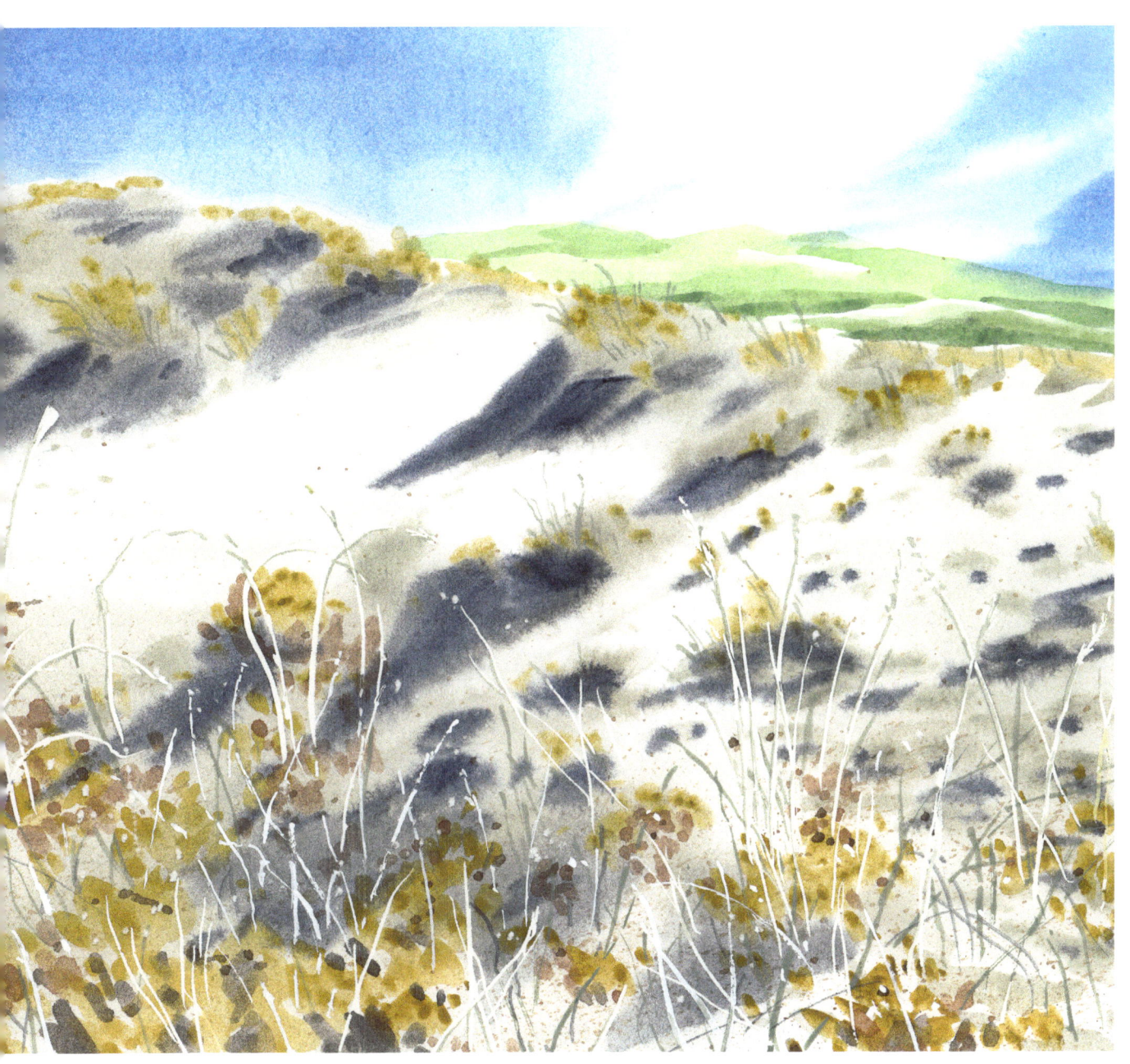

Niobrara River

The Niobrara has its inconspicuous headwaters at an elevation of about 1,500 meters within an area known as the Hartville Uplift, in Niobrara County, Wyoming. It remains a rather scenically unimpressive river in its leisurely passage over the Panhandle region of western Nebraska. The Niobrara Valley then cuts directly through the northernmost edge of the western Sandhills. There it splits off a segment of the Sandhills that crosses the Nebraska border and extends a short distance into South Dakota, mostly in southern Bennett County. Between these two Sandhills sections the Niobrara River runs freely, eventually cutting down to a bedrock channel near Valentine.

—PAUL A. JOHNSGARD, *THIS FRAGILE LAND*

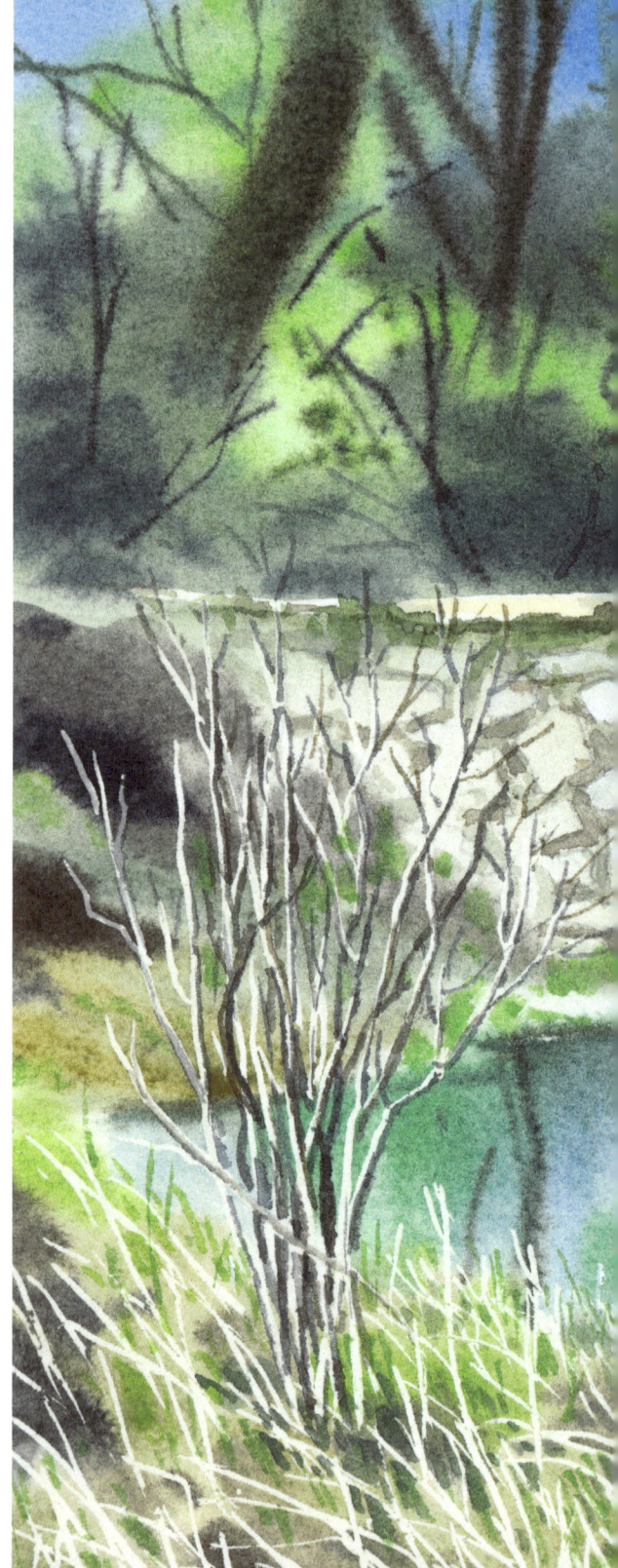

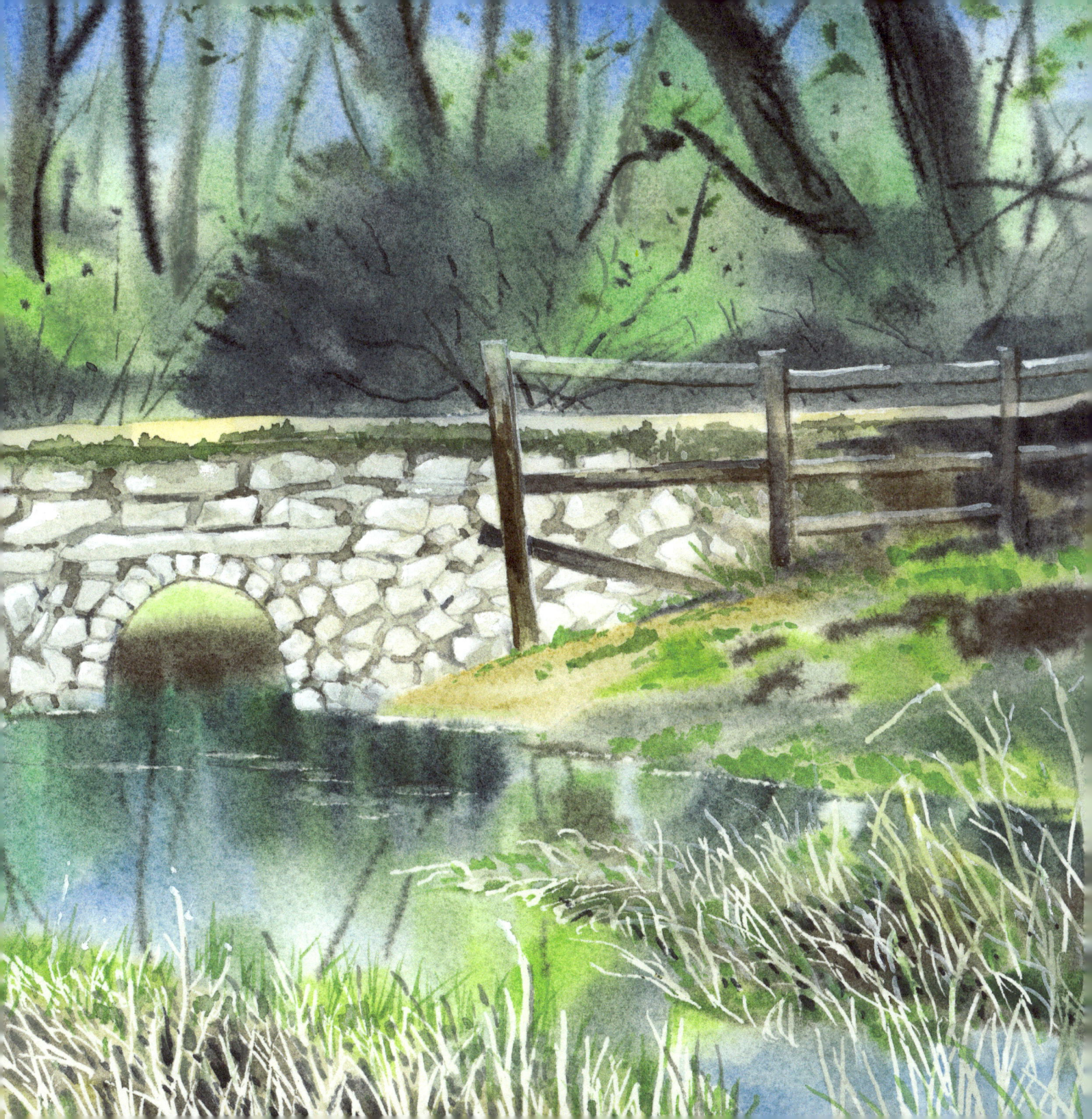

Windmills in the Sandhills

Dotted among the hills are wells that are giant straws that drink precious water from the underlying aquifer. When the land was first settled a big market sprung up for windmills. On the vanes were names like Everlasting, The Iron Screw, The Dandy, Favorite and Aeromotor. Although the energy was free, service and repairs were expensive. Ranchers had to know how to fix them and have a ready supply of replacement parts when things went wrong.

The mills vary in size, height, and depth; reaching ground water that is retained in water-bearing sands beneath the tangle of roots and sod of prairie grasses. The water is fresh and cool and is sucked to the surface using wind power and piped into stock tanks. Ranchers place them in strategic locations in order that their herds may be shifted to different pastures as the grasses become stressed. Even though "live water" may be accessible, Lyn Messersmith explains that well water is safer for her cattle to drink rather than stream water that can often be contaminated with bacteria from animal waste and agriculture chemicals.

Many of the mills today are decaying. The cost of repair or replacement is often prohibitive and some are being replaced by submersible pumps where electrical power is available.

> In the late 1870s windmills came into use on the plains, first the homemade ones that almost anyone could afford if pipe and pump rod for those deep wells could be managed somehow. Later the manufactured product was produced in several Nebraska communities. Soon many western cow towns looked like flower gardens with the daisy faces of the windmills turned busily into the wind. But there were still pretty girls pumping water.
>
> –MARI SANDOZ, *LOVE SONG TO THE PLAINS*

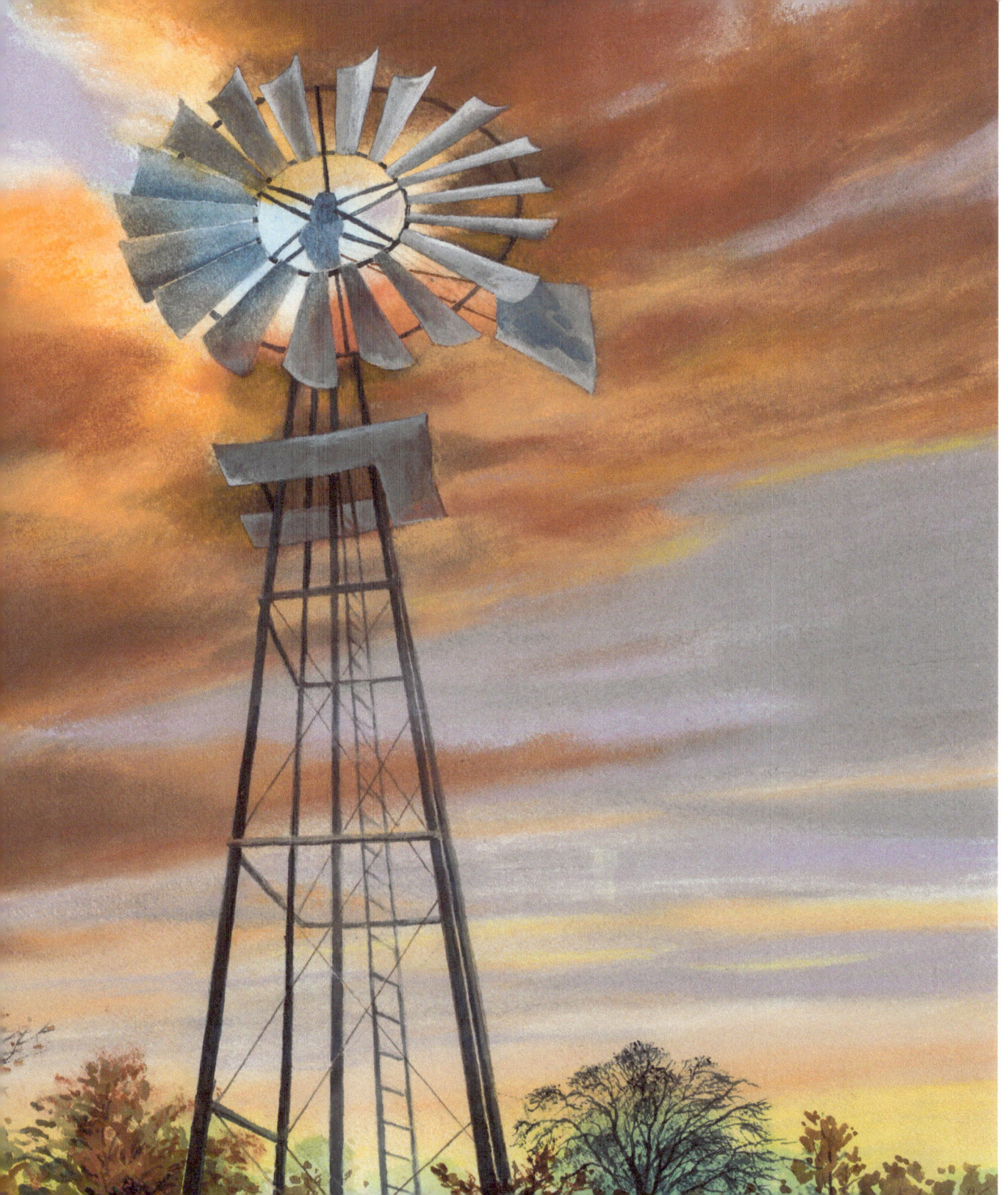

Willa Cather Writes About the Sandhills West of Moonstone

Willa Cather, the American novelist, based her best stories on memories of her Nebraska childhood. She modeled many of her characters from remembrances of people she knew growing up in Webster County. Cather must have loved the Sandhills since she provides lengthy descriptions of them in her tales. Cather moved and rearranged locations and people on her mental story board before weaving them into sensitive descriptions of immigrants and pioneers of the West.

In *The Song of the Lark,* Cather's principle character, Thea Kronborg, is a young aspiring artist in piano and voice. She is twelve years old when an older admirer, Ray Kennedy, takes her to see the Sandhills. Cather writes:

> She liked him, too, because he was the only one of her friends who ever took her to the Sandhills. The Sandhills were a constant tantalization; she loved them better than anything near Moonstone, and yet she could so seldom get to them.

Later…

> On her thirteenth birthday she wandered for a long while about the sand ridges, picking up crystals and looking into the yellow prickly-pear blossoms with their thousand stamens. She looked at the Sandhills until she wished she were a sand hill. And yet she knew that she was going to leave them all behind some day. They would be changing all day long, yellow and purple and lavender, and she would not be there.

Her friend, Ray Kennedy, dies and leaves an inheritance to Thea Kronborg to further her vocal studies in Chicago. In a tearful parting with family and friends, Thea departs with Dr. Archie on the train for Chicago.

> Dr. Archie had gone into the smoker. He thought she might be a little tearful, and that it would be kinder to leave her alone for a while. Her eyes did fill once, when she saw the last of the Sandhills and realized that she was going to leave them behind for a long time.

Her life in Chicago is consumed with study, rehearsals, and lessons. To broaden her experiences, Thea is given tickets to a performance of Dvorak's New World Symphony. When the first movement ends, she has a dramatic epiphany that she is destined to be a vocal performer. This is a life-changing, "Sandhills," experience.

> Here were the Sandhills, the grasshoppers and locusts, all the things that wakened and chirped in the early morning; the reaching and reaching of high plains, the immeasurable yearning of all flat lands. There was home in it, too; first memories, first mornings long ago; the amazement of a new soul in a new world; a soul new and yet old, that had dreamed something despairing, something glorious, in the dark before it was born; a soul obsessed by what it did not know, under the cloud of a past it could not recall.
>
> —WILLA CATHER, *SONG OF THE LARK*

Life in the Sandhills

My dad traveled to Nebraska from Missouri in a covered wagon with his parents and siblings to homestead a ranch of his own, at the crest of the hill overlooking the Dismal River off what is now Highway 83. He was sixteen, and had only an eighth grade education, which was not uncommon. Dad was a cowboy born in 1893. Before I was born, he rode the stagecoach, tamed wild horses, packed six-shooters, wore chaps, boots, and spurs. There were rattlesnakes and an occasional rustler on the prairie. Eventually dad also became the local well driller. Ranchers came from all over the county to hire him to drill or fix a windmill. By the time I left home, the ranch had grown to 3,000 plus acres.

My mom married my dad when she was twenty-one and moved onto his homestead. Shortly thereafter, a tornado came through and they watched as it sucked the house up and carried it away, leaving only the porch. My dad sold the property and purchased a ranch to the north with a sod house. Our home was a two story (two rooms up and two down) with windows on the lower level and wood floors. The walls had been constructed of stacked sod blocks six inches by ten inches by two feet. The outside was cemented over. Inside, the walls were plastered and then covered with wallpaper. Two lightning rods had been set on the shingled roof to guide lightning strikes from the rods along heavy braided wires attached one on each side of each rod to the ground for protecting the house. Earlier, my mom had been struck by lightning while in the yard. With God's grace and dad's help, she survived.

> *"Shortly thereafter, a tornado came through and they watched as it sucked the house up and carried it away, leaving only the porch."*

On March 18, 1941, at age forty-five, Mary Elizabeth Adkins Florea welcomed her eighth child into the world. No doctor or midwife was there to attend to the

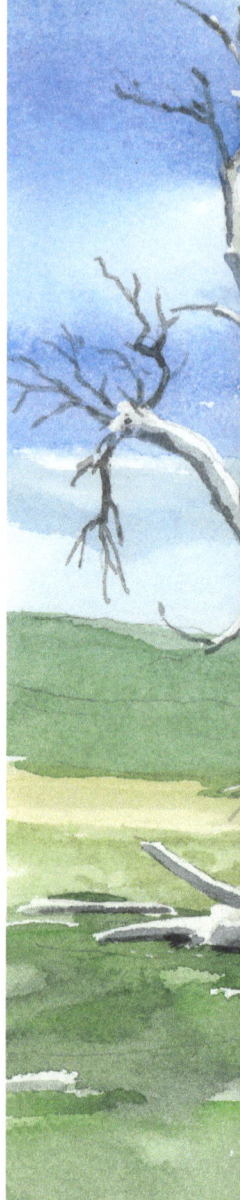

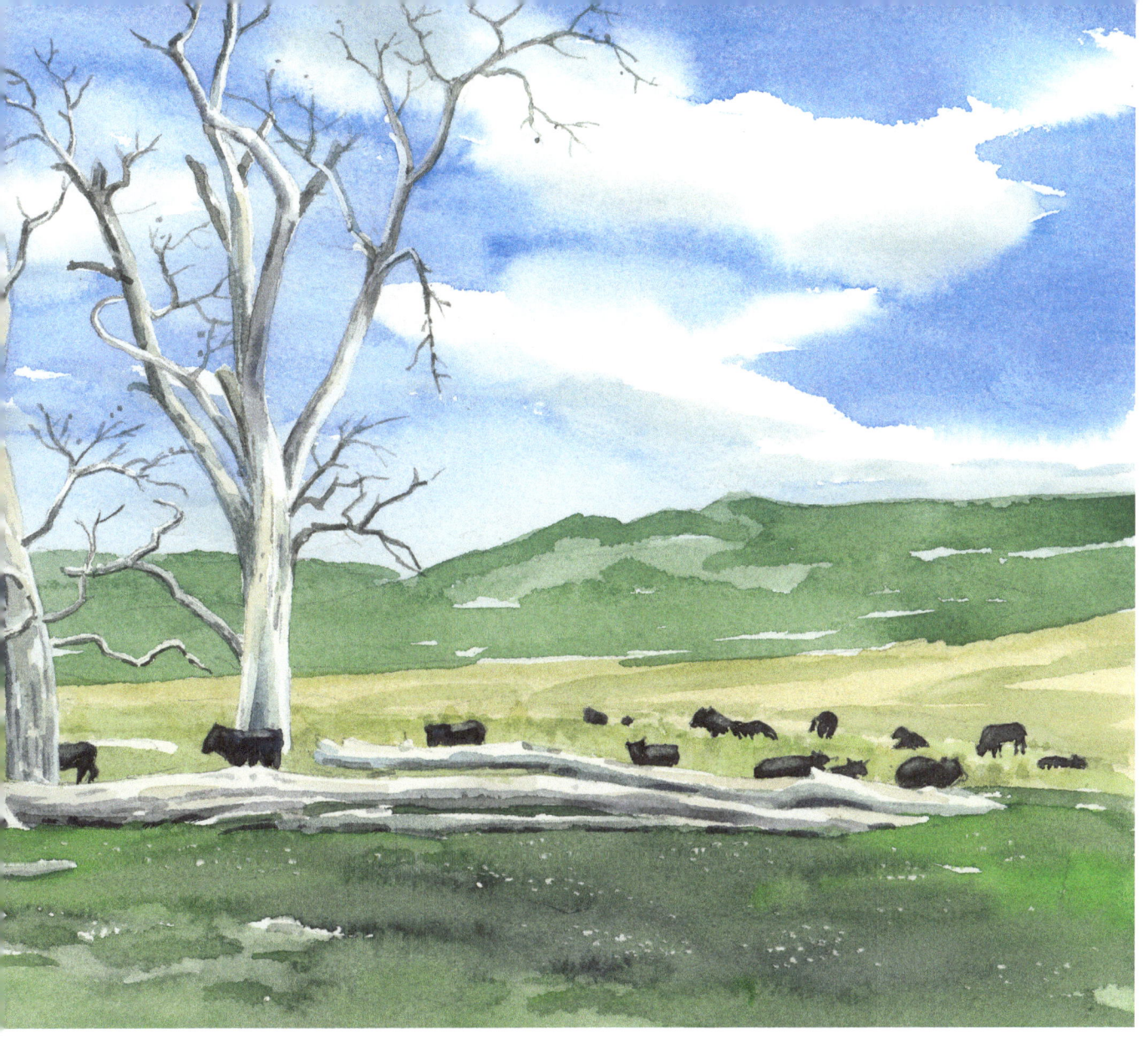

birthing as country doctors came and went. Instead, two of her sisters came to help. One babysat the other small siblings while her maiden sister, Belle Adkins, delivered the baby. Mary named her new baby Laura Belle Florea and my life began.

–LAURA FLOREA RAMIREZ

The Demise of a Town

Trains still thunder by in the night, singing wheel songs that were my childhood lullabies, but no cattle bawl in stockyards, and the depot and roundhouse are gone. Been no school there on the hill for many a year, and grandpa's bank now houses the post office. There's a cafe and bar in the old light plant building, but general stores and other businesses have gone the way of the school and Catholic Church. Grandma's house is in sad disrepair, and the only reminder of her lovely yard is the big old cottonwood I used to try to stretch my arms around.

–LYN MESSERSMITH, *MY SISTER MARIAH*

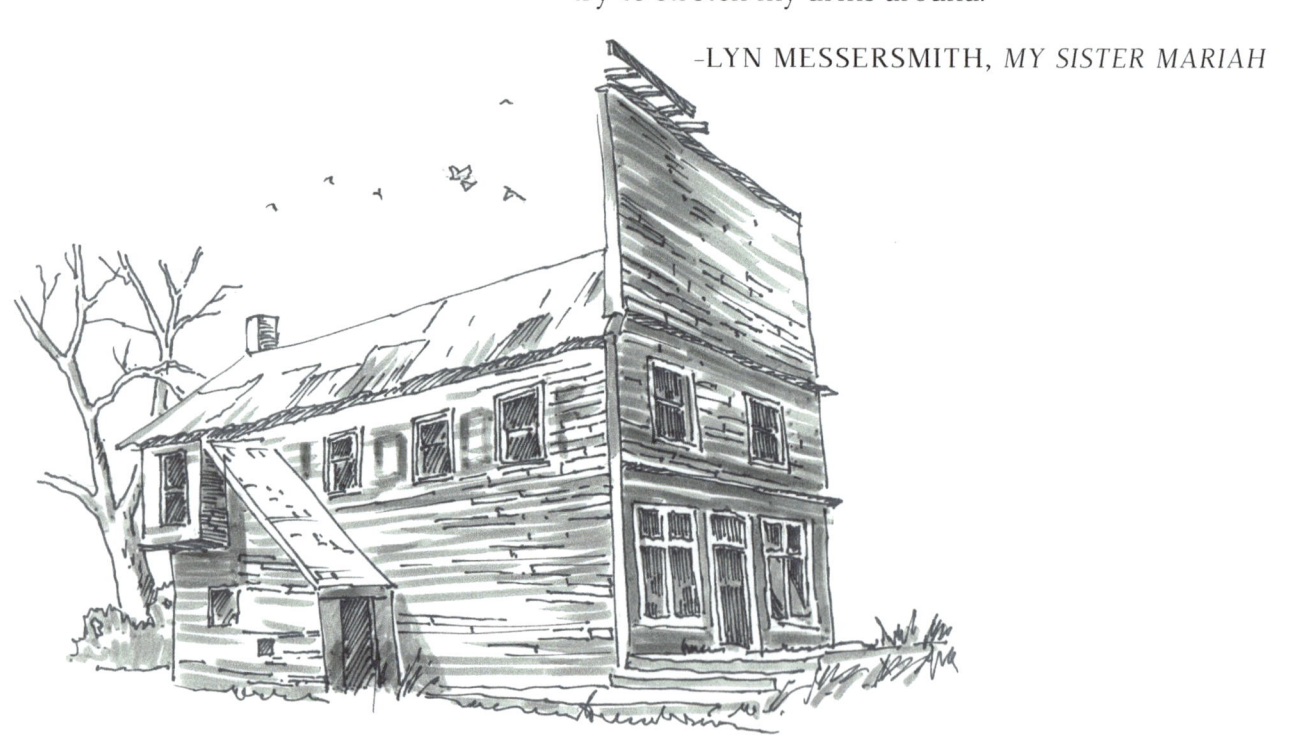

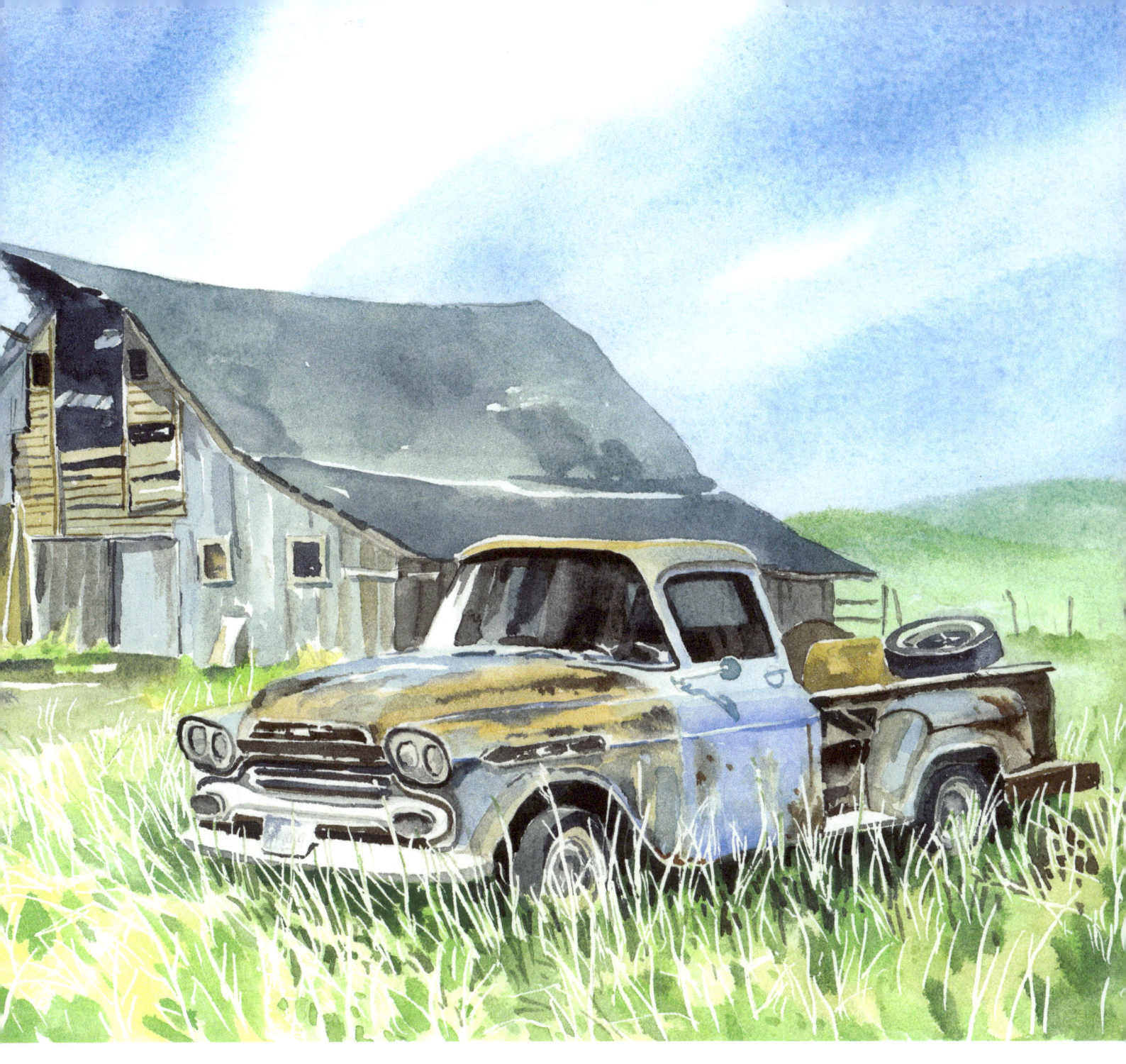

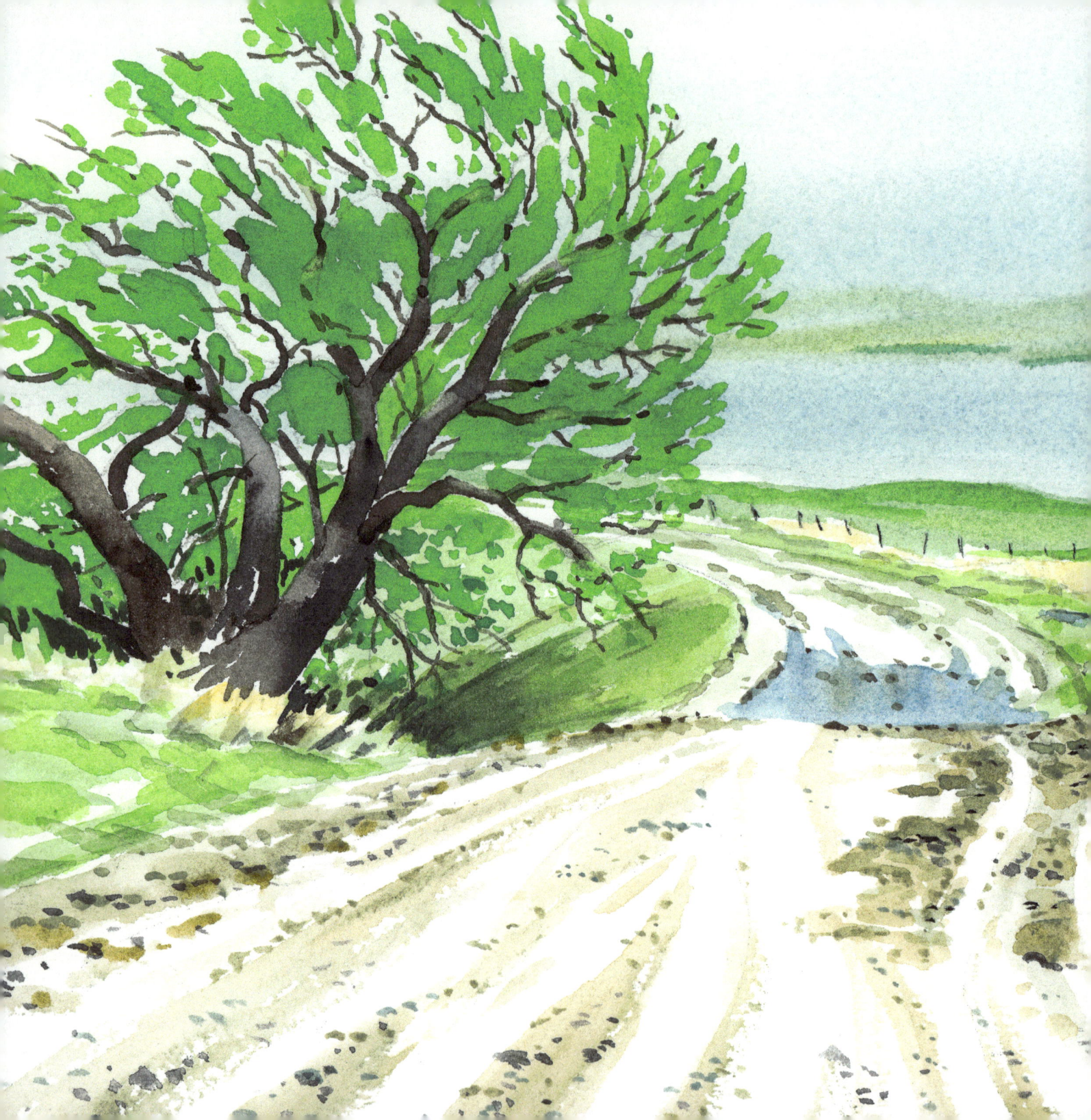

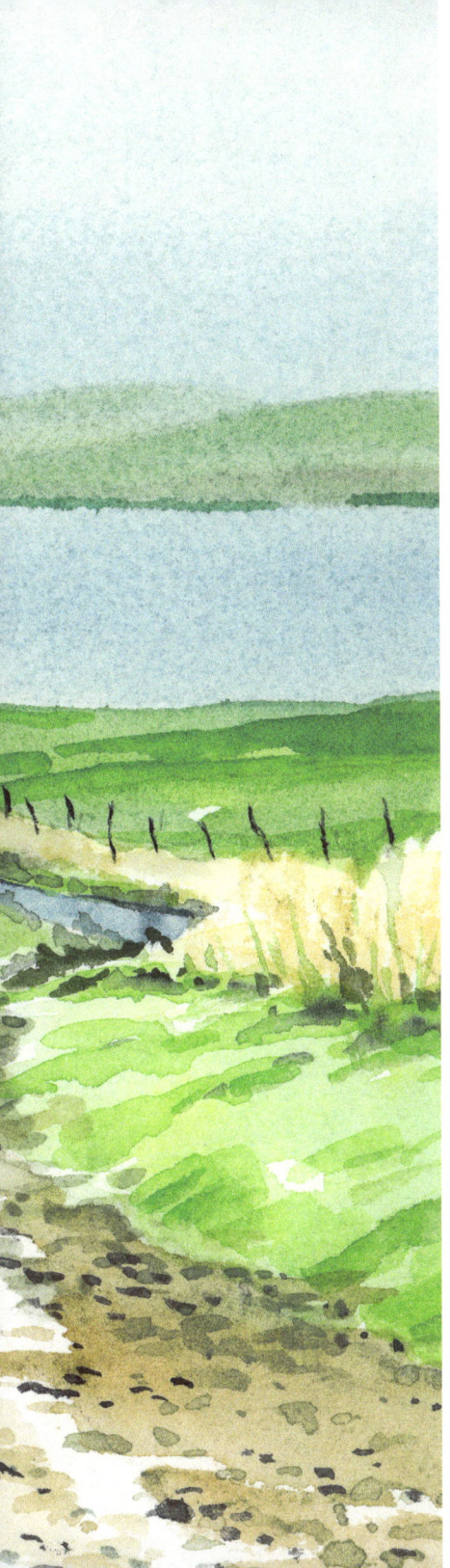

Memories of Growing Up

I was raised seventeen miles south of Long Pine and Ainsworth, Nebraska, in the middle of the Sandhills. Our ranch was ten miles by 10 miles about. Had lakes on it. I started trapping beaver, mink and muskrat in third grade. Drove to school picking up neighbor in third grade also. Before that, rode horse four miles or dad took us and we walked home. UP HILL BOTH WAYS! Had a sister killed by a cow when she was six. She went to call Dad for supper one Sunday afternoon. She walked in a pen where a cow had a new calf and the cow put her up against the manger and Dad came and fought the cow off with a pitch fork. They took her to the hospital but she died in Long Pine and they had another 10 miles to go to Ainsworth to the hospital. Was a tough life at times, but God was good all the time.

Best time to drive anywhere was when wet otherwise could get stuck in sand! Could dig post holes and about three or four feet hit water in places. Had creeks running year around but could drive through them anytime. Even if five foot wide and three inches deep! Those were the days. My dad back in the 1950s made $17,000 on Blue grass one year as a gift from God. The whole ranch was covered with Blue grass. That was a lot of money back then. It was the talk of the town how he made out so good for years. He did good at everything he did. Got in and out of things at the right times. Shetland ponies, Appaloosa horses, livestock markets, buying and selling ranches after he had polio and two-thirds of his stomach removed. Went from $100 in pocket to millionaire and loved by all, dying at seventy-four years old. As you can tell I admired the man.

–DON ATEN

House on a Hill

On a gatepost twenty-five miles over the wind-swept hills from the nearest railroad hangs a tipsy sign. Many winter snows, many summer suns have weathered it, mellowed it to a velvety gray. Precariously creaking on one nail, the first storm will cast it down, unlamented, into the jointed sandgrass. While the boiling engine of the mail truck cooled from the long pull through the sandy gap, I shook the wrinkles from my skirt and idly inspected the blurred legend: "Pleasant Home."

But in a clump of ragged sunflowers stood an old cook stove, the corroded oven door sagging to reveal hay and straw of a mouse nest where spicy cookies once baked. And suddenly it all came back; the little white beehive of a house with a green blind at the one window—the home of a spinster music teacher from Chicago. . .

–MARI SANDOZ, *SANDHILL SUNDAYS*

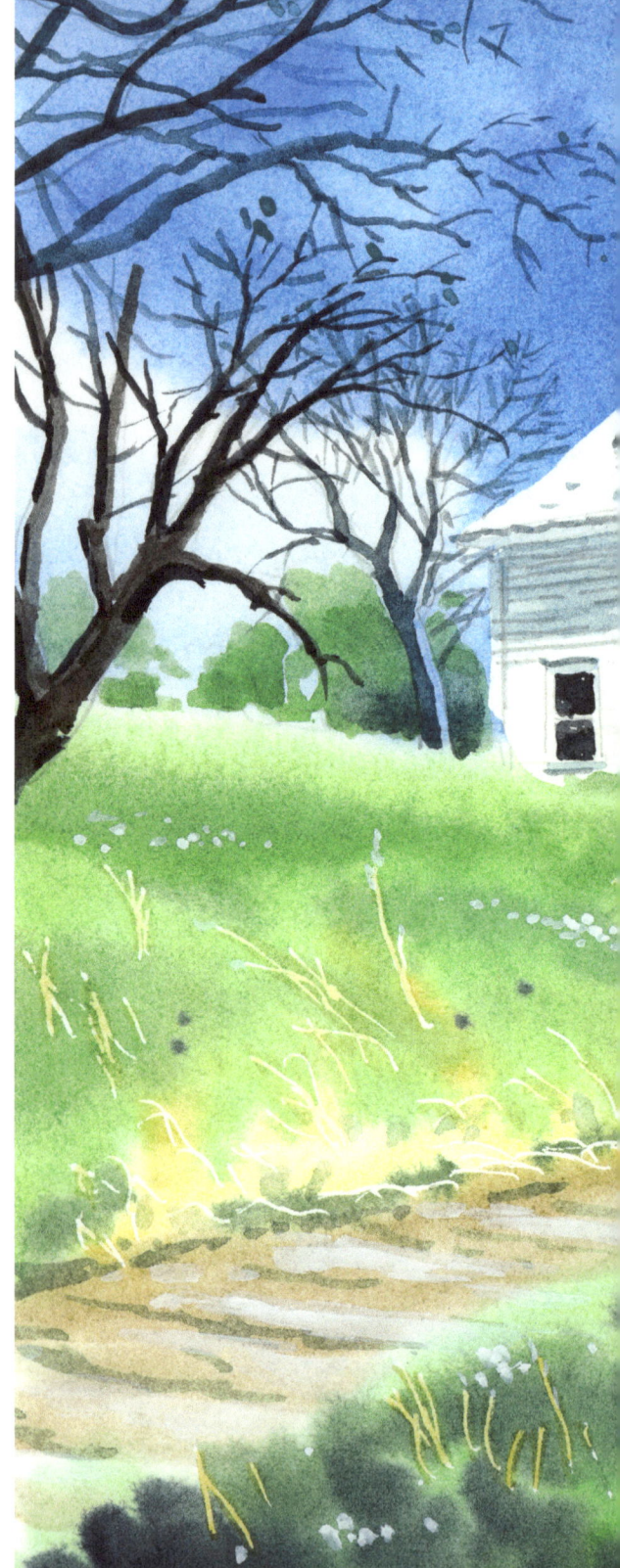

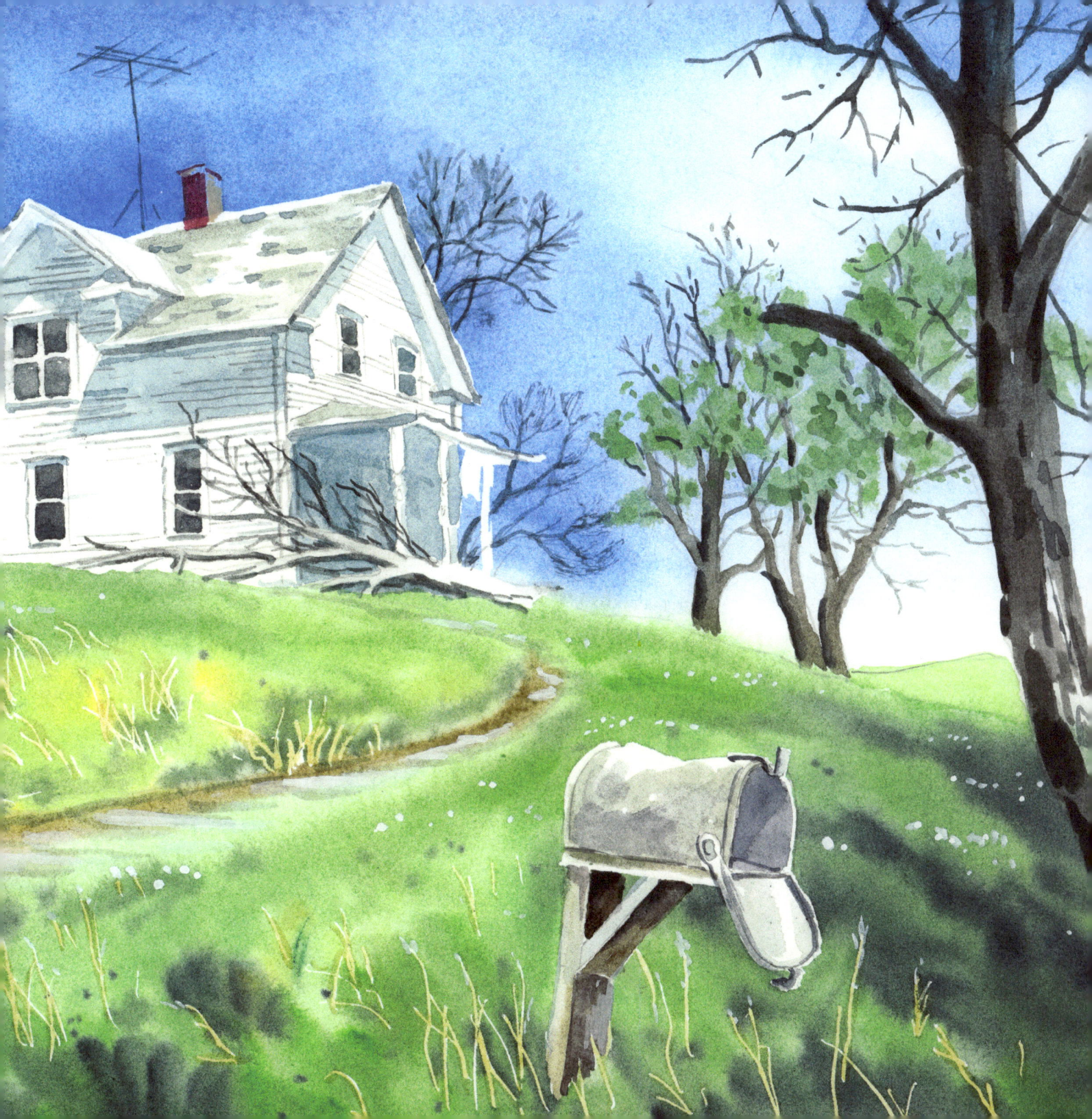

Dust Storms and the "Dirty Thirties"

Those were extremely difficult times. In the decade of the 1930's the land was drought—stricken. The Dust Bowl covered a large area from Texas to southern Nebraska. Many new farmers were inexperienced and broke prairie sod to plant crops without thought of water or irrigation requirements. The prevailing thought was that if the land were plowed, rain would follow. This practice along with winds and lack of moisture only created a disaster.

Skies darkened when billowing clouds of dust and sand thousands of feet high raced over the land at speeds of twenty-five miles per hour or more. They swallowed up hills and settlements with little warning. Crops failed. Livestock died from lack of nutrition and lungs full of particulate matter. Both man and beast suffered from "dust pneumonia."

> "Ranchers, who depended on good pastures for their cattle, picked up and deserted their land..."

Ranchers, who depended on good pastures for their cattle, picked up and deserted their land leaving others to deal with foreclosures. The economic impact was oppressive to farmer's investments as well as their daily survival. There were some who took their own lives, unable to deal with the psychological darkness that overwhelmed them. The hardy ones, strong in resolve, somehow managed to survive. Those who had financial reserves bought up foreclosures, increasing their holdings, and in time, became successful farmers and cattle breeders.

Times began to improve in 1940 with better land management and government programs designed to prevent degradation of the land. The national economy slowly improved, relieving some of the pressure on the rural population. The war effort of the early forties increased a demand for food, defense products, and services.

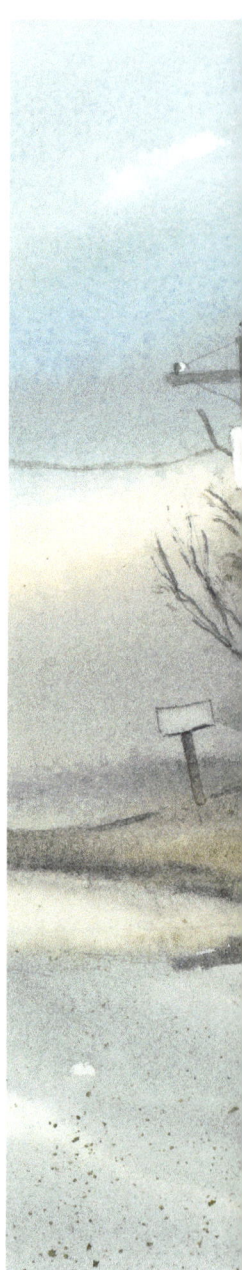

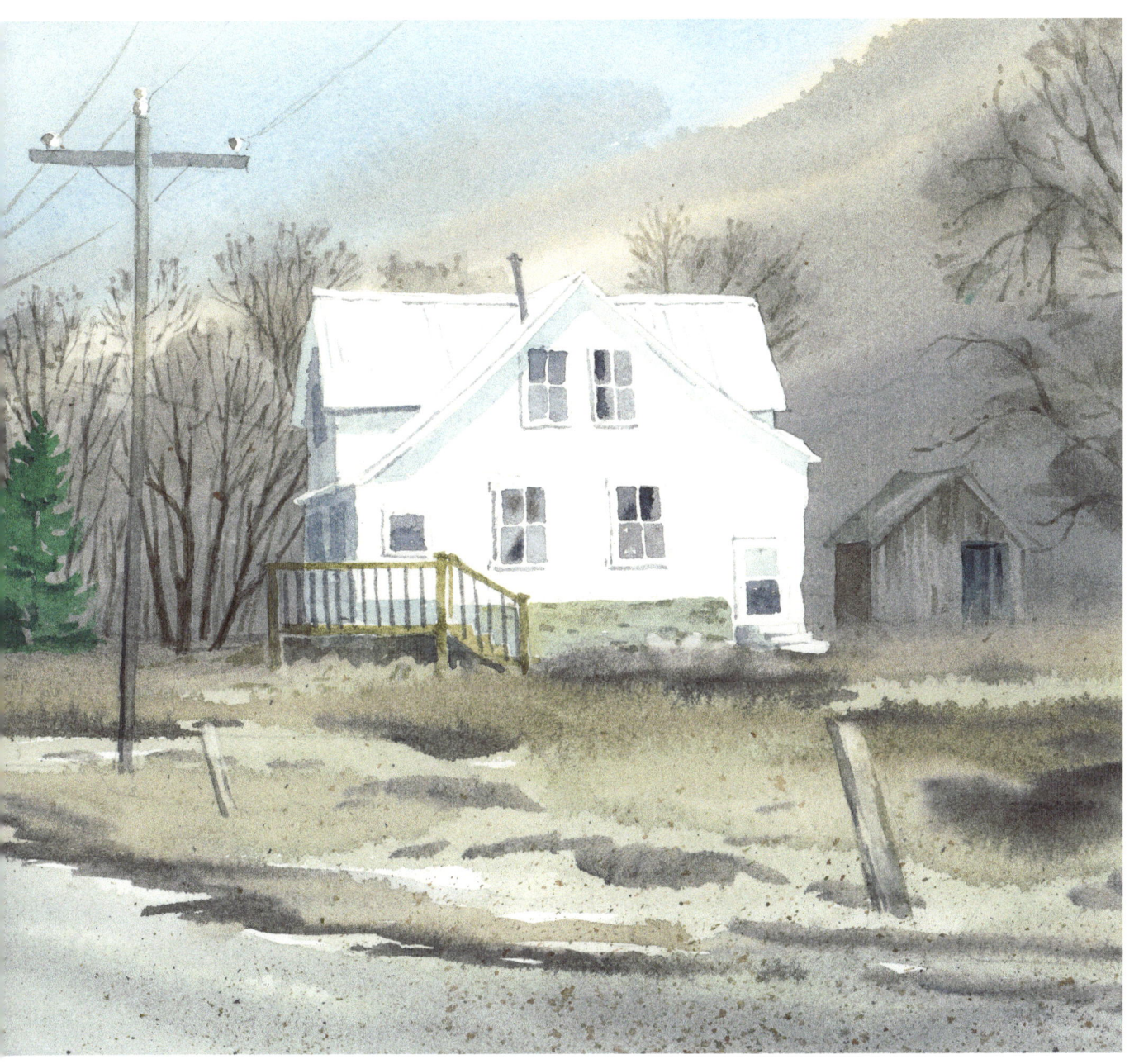

Saddle-up in Burwell

Dale and Peggy Prickett own and operate the County Line Saddle Shop. Folks from miles around know it only as "Dale's Shop" in Burwell. A stranger would have difficulty finding it, but locals know they can find Dale in the rear of The Western Shop near the town square. No sign marks his place of business since his reputation as a fine saddle maker is widely known. A back door opens to the street behind the building and is often used by customers coming and going.

When I visited Dale, he was patiently repairing a dog collar for friends. Although Dale is known for his fine saddlery, it is the repairs and small jobs that support his business. A large work table dominates the center of the one-room shop, while nearby a saddle-stand holds a saddle whose horn is being reattached. Dale and his father fashioned the stand from an old barber chair base. Dale can raise or lower the device using the hand pump. His roll-about stool allows him to work

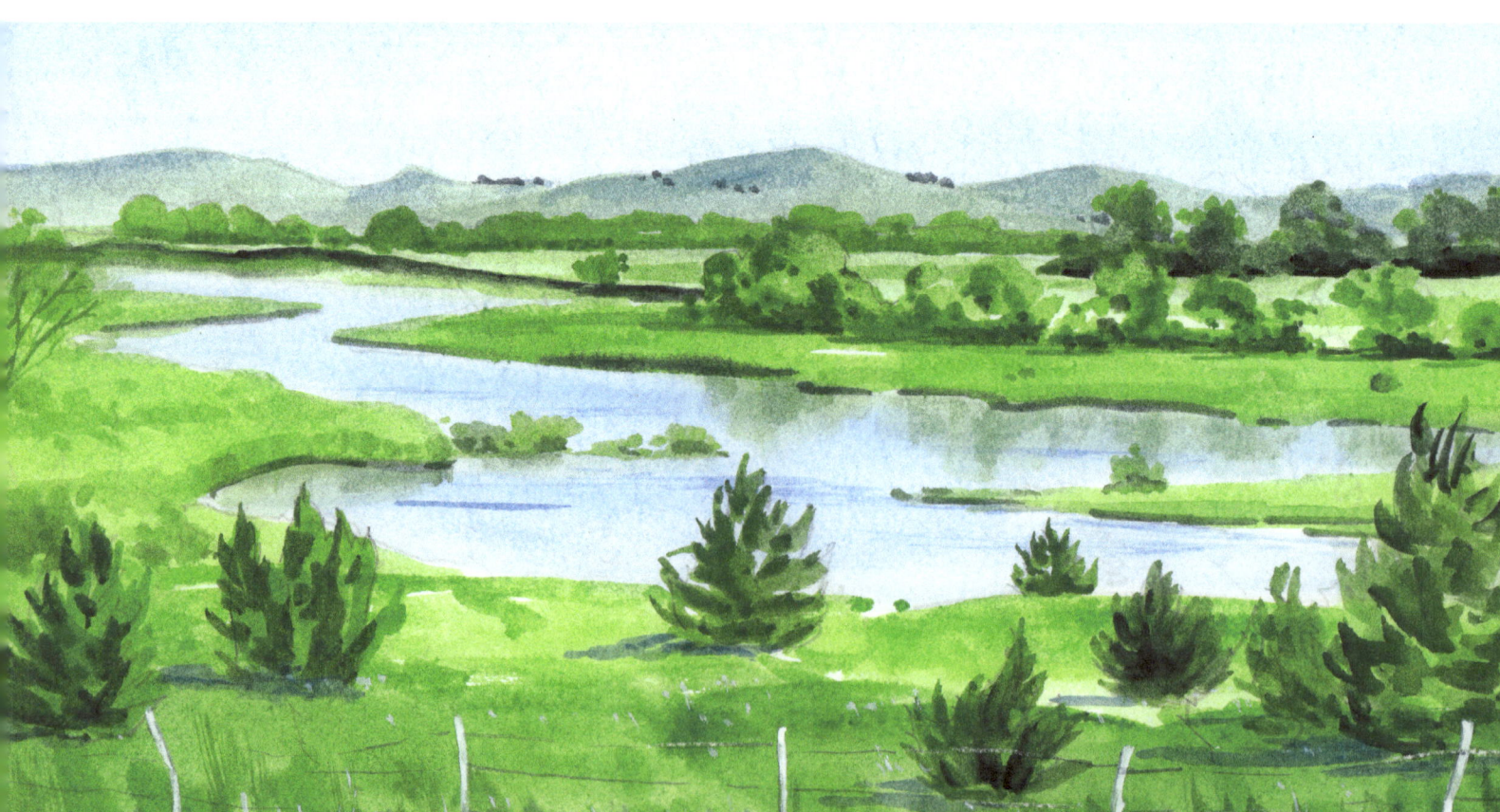

comfortably within reach of a workbench that is piled with tools, clamps, vices and other paraphernalia. Other tools—scissors, scrapers, and gouges, not needed for the immediate project—are more neatly mounted on the wall above. On another wall, a hundred photos of saddles Dale has made tell a story of his successful career.

I pointed to the ceiling where wooden forms hang that are used to begin the saddle construction. Dale explained, "They are called 'trees' and come in different sizes, from fourteen to seventeen inches in length. We build the tree to fit the horse and then build the saddle to fit the rider. Today, horses tend to have a different shape than they used to. They are bigger now and have straighter shoulders."

His Utah supplier provides the tree that has been wrapped with rawhide and varnished. Dale then begins to shape the saddle into a comfortable fit by adding layers of leather attached with glue and nails. He finds it takes longer to build a saddle in the winter than in summer because the time taken for the damp leather to dry between steps is dependent upon temperature and humidity.

Peggy does the artistic design tooling. She uses a priceless array of precision stamping tools provided by an Elko, Nevada, tool maker. The leather is slightly dampened before stamping. "There's a fine line between too wet and too dry that only experience can tell you."

Together the Pricketts create many leather products and awards that are commissioned by western organizations. They have crafted unique designs for the National Rodeo Association and the annual presentation given the World's Champion Livestock Auctioneer.

The Pricketts are at the height of their careers, having earned the respect and the appreciation of ranchers and community. It does not appear they will be saddling up soon to ride into the sunset.

A Sandhills Veterinarian: A Life Dedicated to Profession and Community

A gravel lane circles to the top of a hill where a red bungalow and two barns are cloistered among shady trees. This is the home of retired veterinarian, Dr. Dale Karre. Although his home looks over the town of Ord and the prairie beyond, much of his professional life was spent serving ranchers in the Sandhills to the north. His dedication and love of community is a testimony to the strength of the people who helped each other during hard times. Dr. Karre wrote his rememberances of one of those events.

My experiences started on November 17, 1948. I had only been in my veterinary practice since June of that year. Several mornings a week, I tested cows for tuberculosis for the government in their quest to eradicate T.B.

Dr. Frank Christ was a federal veterinarian who lived in Arcadia and was in charge of quite a large area, so he welcomed all the help he could get. He would ride with me occasionally to see how things were going and helped me all he could.

When we T.B. tested cattle, we injected about a tenth of a cc of tuberculin in the hairless fold of skin along the tail head of the cow. Then in seventy-two hours, we went back and observed the injection site. If there was swelling at that site, it meant that the cow was sensitive to the tuberculin and probably had been exposed or was actually infected with tuberculosis. Then it was up to me to make a judgment as to how to dispose of the cow: either call her a suspect or send her to slaughter.

The morning of November 17, a Thursday, the sky was cloudy when I left the house at six a.m. The previous Monday I had injected several herds of cattle about fifteen miles north of Burwell, just off Highway 11. Dr. Christ was going to ride with me that day. He was going to stay in the Burwell Hotel and I was to pick him up there.

When I picked him up and as we started north through the canyon road, it started snowing. The flakes were those big ones that splattered on the windshield almost like rain. The car radio said "clearing by night".

When we turned off Highway 11, and went west to our first ranch, it was snowing pretty heavily. The road from there on would be a sandhill trail. That is where the road just starts off across the country, requiring one to seek the valleys or low hills, and go until you come to a gate that leads through to another pasture.

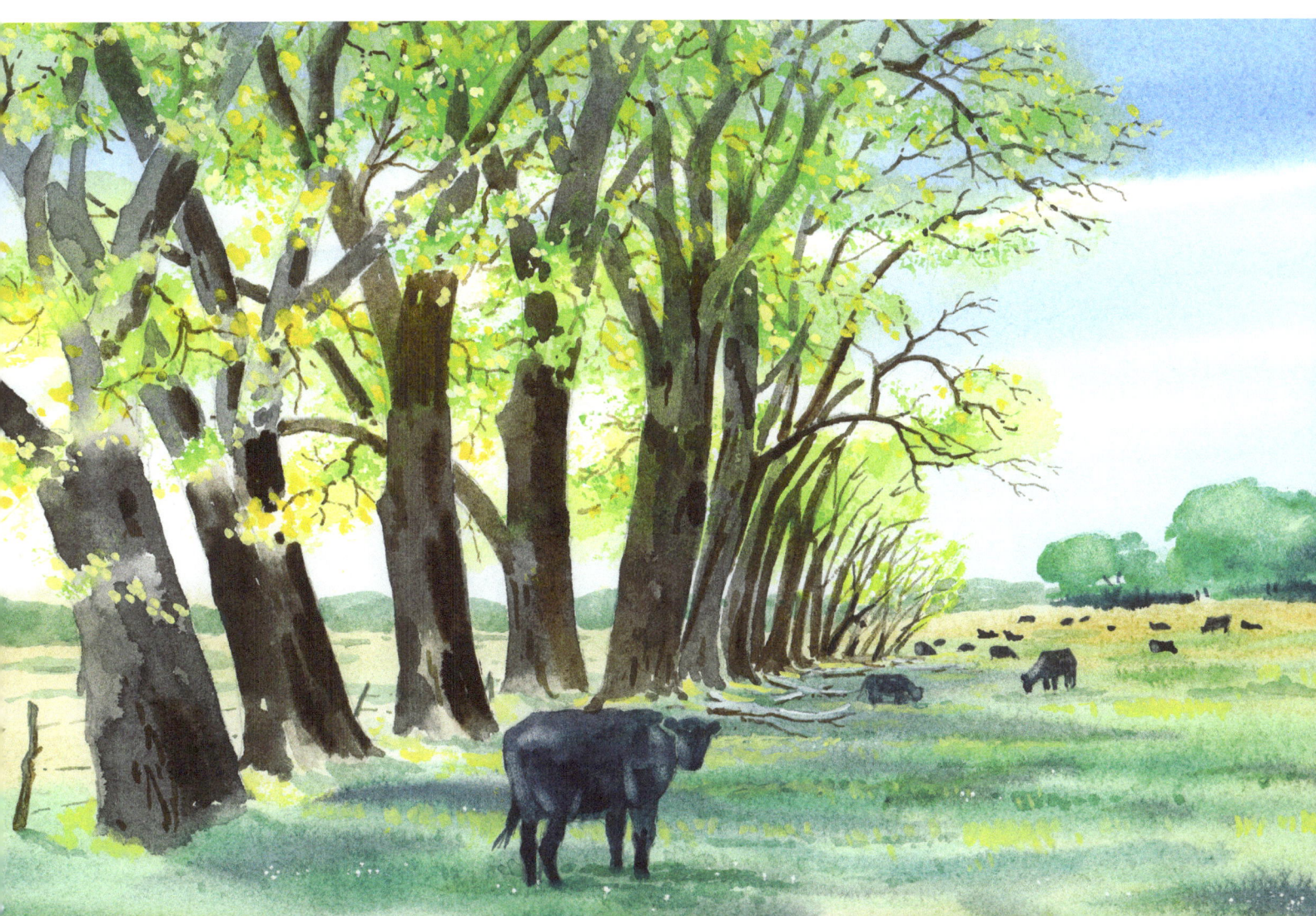

The first place happened to belong to my Uncle Howard Karre. He had the cattle in the barn, so we examined all of them and headed on up the trail about a mile to Leonard and Fay Butts's place. They weren't home, and I knew they wouldn't be, because they were over helping Bill Crandall get his cattle in, which was our next stop, about ne and a half miles on west. By that time the visability was getting terrible. Sometimes, I had to roll down the window and try to determine the edge of the trail by looking for tufts of grass that were not covered by the blowing snow. We finally reached the Crandall's and that is where we spent the rest of the day and all day Friday. We checked the cows that were in the barn, then went to the house to weather out the blizzard, which by that time was blowing and snowing and drifting.

The Crandalls were very nice people and treated us very well. Of course, the Butts were there also, so we visited and ate and slept and looked out the windows at the storm, wondering if it would ever end. The outside toilet was on the other side of a snow drift, but we all managed to make it. I helped Bill do some chores but there wasn't much we could do. The cattle didn't come out to eat what little hay we could find for them.

Sometime after noon on that first day, the phone rang. The Crandalls and Butts about fell off their chairs because the phone line only ran between their two places, which meant there was someone at the Butts's house. It was my Uncle Howard. He had worried and walked up to the Butts's place. He had really risked his life and did, in fact, get lost a couple of times during that trip.

Any cows that were out in that storm were almost blinded by the wet snow freezing on their faces and over their eyes. Man had the same trouble so we worried the rest of the time over if Uncle Howard had gotten back home.

The storm raged on Thursday night and all day Friday, snowing, howling, and drifting. We all got real acquainted and almost became like family. I felt that we couldn't have been stranded at a better place.

Saturday morning was beautiful. The sky was perfectly clear. The sun was shining bright, and everything was white. The wind had blown so hard most of the snow was in large drifts with bare spots in between. We dug out my car and finally got it started, then we headed for home. We drove on the bare ground until we came to a drift, then I drove through as far as I could and we scooped the rest of the way through. We finally got to Highway 11 and down the highway about five miles by dark. When we went by my Uncle Howard's place, he joined us.

When we got as far as we could, we went back to his place to spend the night. We knew the canyon road just north of Burwell would probably be worse than what we had been traveling on, so my uncle offered to take us in with a team and wagon. I left my car in a man's yard along the highway and we took off.

We got to Burwell Sunday evening and had to dig Dr. Christ's car out. When we lifted the hood, all one could see was snow. We finally got it started and headed for Ord. I walked into my house in Ord about dark on Sunday evening to greet my wife of two months who hadn't known where I was for four days!

That was the start of one of the worst winters in the history of Nebraska—the winter of '48-'49. I had several team and wagon rides that winter and a few on the tractors. People didn't have the snow removal equipment that they have today.

The Army Corp. of Engineers sent soldiers with bulldozers into the area to help open the roads and to make trails to haystacks so farmers could feed their cattle. The farmer's wives were so glad to see them and so grateful to be dug out after a month to six weeks of total isolation, they invited the soldiers in to feed them no matter what time of the day or night they came through.

Then when the snow thawed in the spring, we had another problem—MUD! Roads were impassable and bridges washed out. Sometimes when I think back on it, I can't believe that I stayed here in this county another forty-five years!

—DALE L. KARRE, DVM, ORD, NEBRASKA

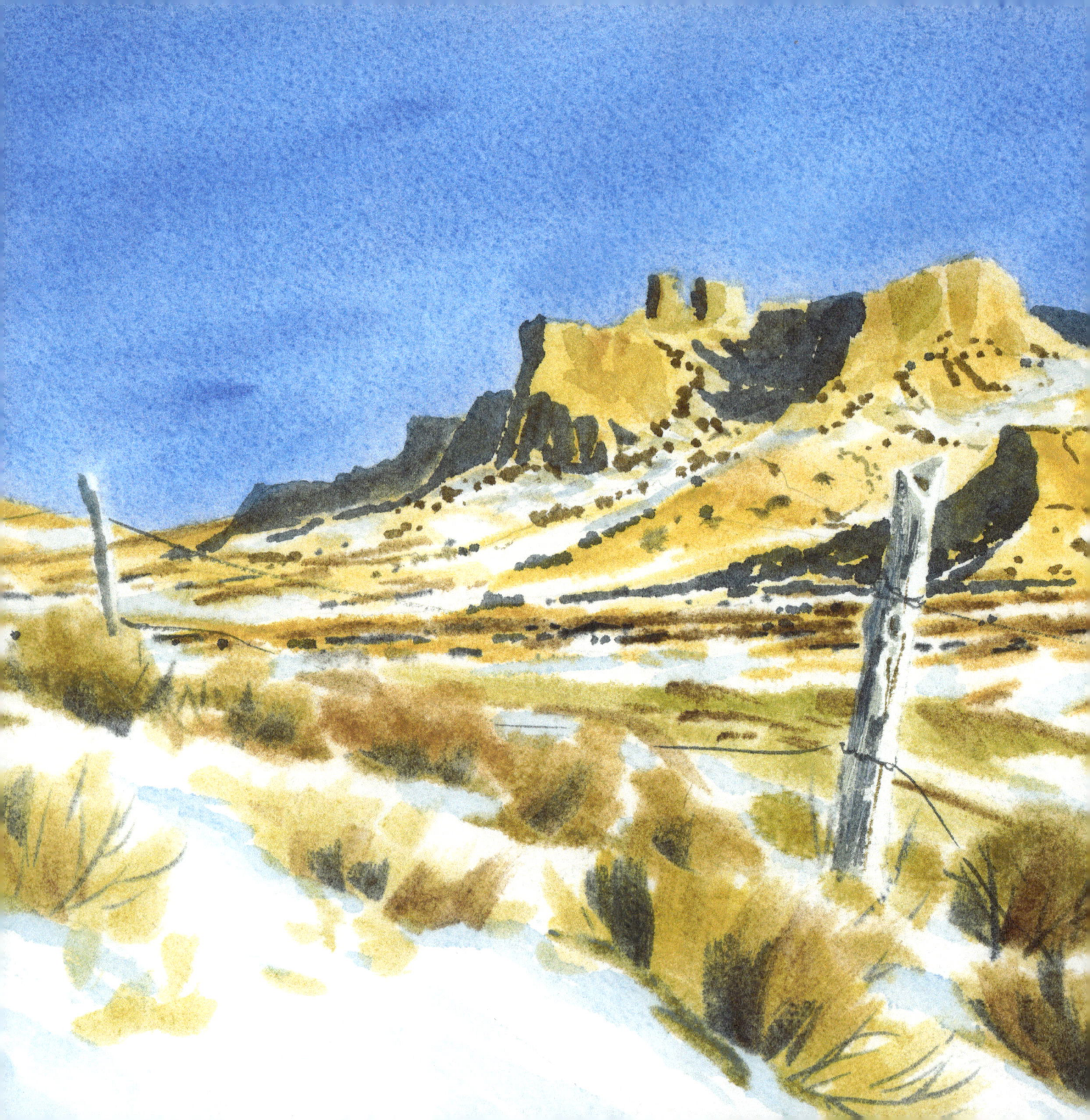

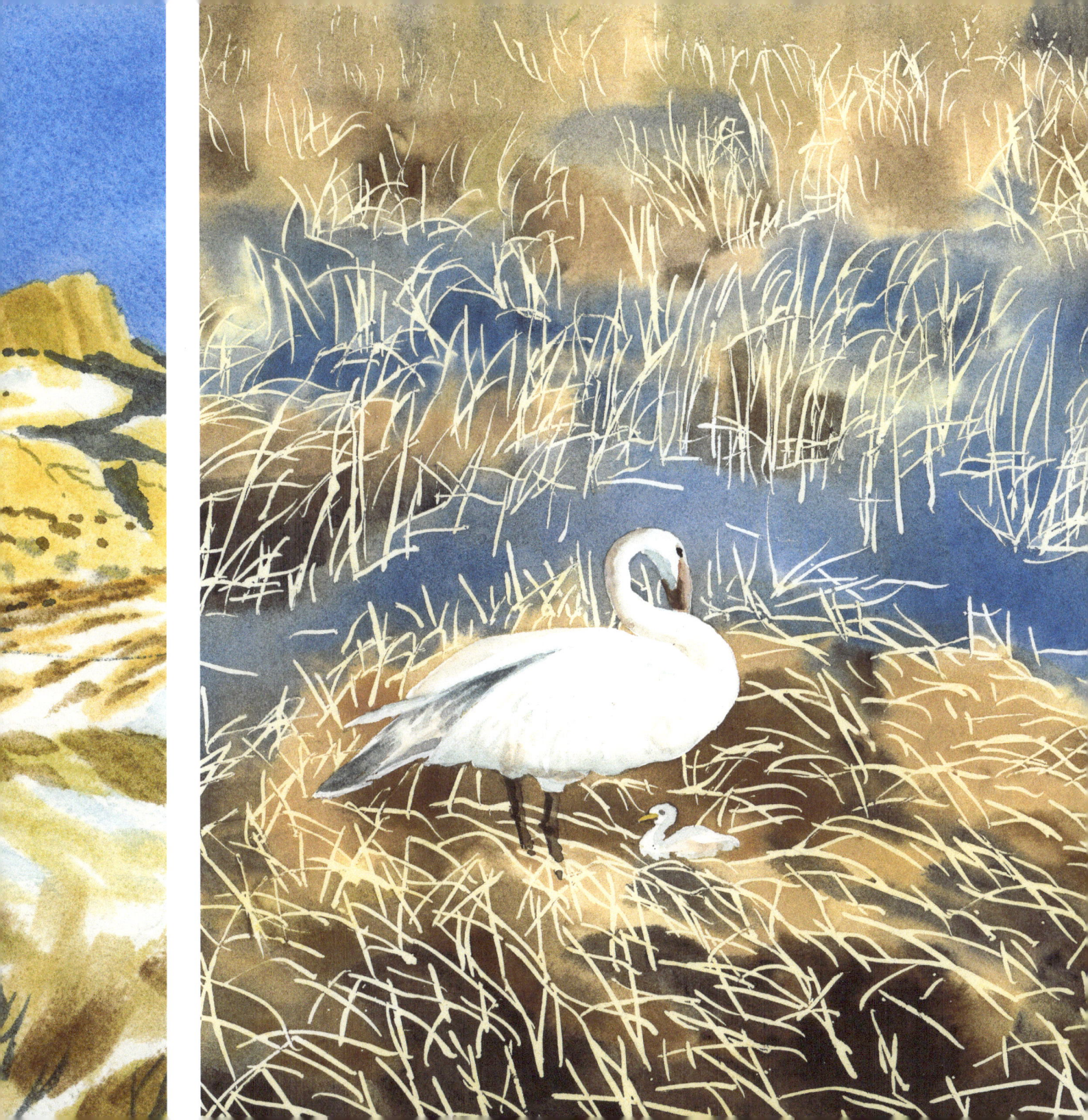

Building Character: Prayer and Pranks

Ron Hamilton, age eighty-seven, was born in his grandparents' sod home between Ellsworth and Gordon. There were no hospitals nearby; however a doctor came from Alliance in his Model T Ford to help in the delivery. When mother and child were ready, they returned to their own sod home twenty miles east in Survey Valley. No established roads existed in those days, only sandy trails across the prairie. Travel was slow and painstaking. It would take a half day if the family wanted to travel just 32 miles to Gordon from their home.

When young Hamilton started school, he rode his horse four miles over the ridge to join four other children in a small class. When his pony broke his lead and returned home riderless one night, his mother was horrified. The anxiety ended when he was found safely back at school.

Hamilton remembers the "Thursday Night Prayer Meetings" in the home. A circle of chairs were set in the kitchen with the faithful kneeling in front of each chair in prayer. As a six-year-old, he recalls the fear in his heart of praying out loud when it became his turn.

At fourteen, Hamilton left his family's home to stay with his grandparents and began working as a ranch hand on the "Young Jules's Place." Young Jules was the son of "Old Jules," who was the subject of Mari Sandoz's biography. Hamilton did odd jobs on several area ranches, stacking hay, and breaking horses during the summer months. Sandoz told him, "I will give you $5 for any of those wild horses you can ride." He could not refuse the offer. In those days, $5 was a lot of money.

When Hamilton was about fifteen, he was building hog houses with two buddies. When smoke was observed coming from the houses, the jig was up. He was found smoking cigarettes. In high school, he and others "took a cow up two flights to the assembly hall and tied her there. The teachers found a terrible mess there the next morning," he confessed.

Hamilton had a '33 Ford with no brakes. He could slow it by down-shifting gears and allowing it to roll to a stop. The County Sheriff slept most of the time in his parked DeSoto on Main

Street. When young Hamilton and his buddies sped up and down the street with tires squealing; the sheriff was awakened into action. "He chased us twelve miles to the South Dakota border where he had to drop off the chase."

Still, there was more mischief left in him. He attempted to steal watermelons at the Sandoz place. However, the Sandoz boys were on the lookout for thieves and hid beneath blankets used to protect melons from frost. When Hamilton was discovered in the act, the two sons of Young Jules sprang a counterattack, pushing a cultivator onto the road to block his escape route. Hamilton gunned his '33 Ford and detoured around it, taking out part of the fence in his successful getaway.

Apparently God honored the Thursday night prayers. Ron Hamilton became an upstanding citizen. He served honorably in the United States Air Force in Korea. He held several responsible positions and finally retired from Braniff International Airways after twenty-eight years as Manager of the Ticket Counter.

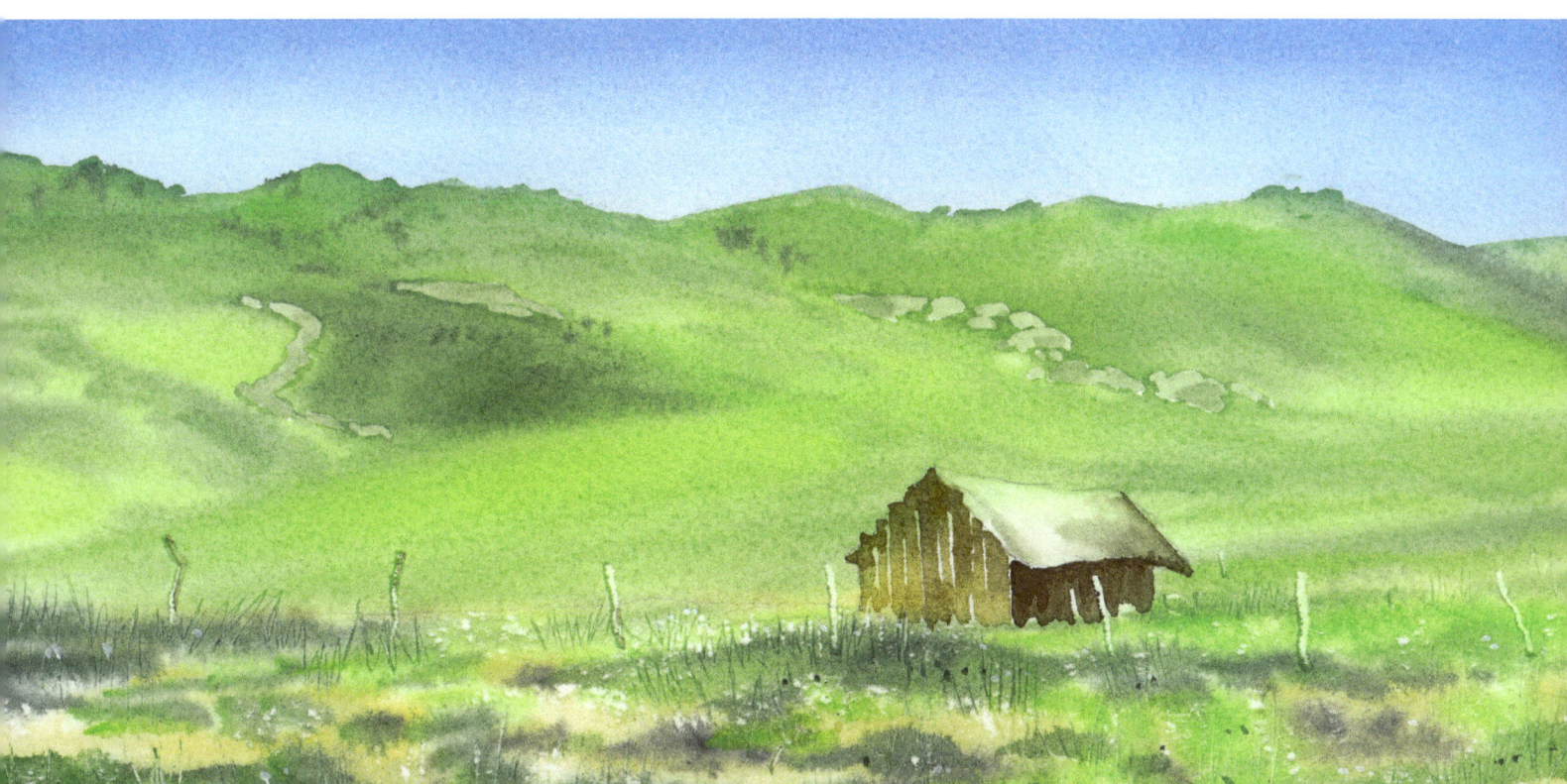

Fences

Wire fences might mark the end of a man's pasture, but they could not shut in his thoughts as mountains and forests can. It was over flat lands like this, stretching out to drink the sun, that the larks sang—and ones's heart sang there, too. It was, somehow, an honest country, and there was a new song in that blue air which had never been sung in the world before.

–WILLA CATHER,
SONG OF THE LARK

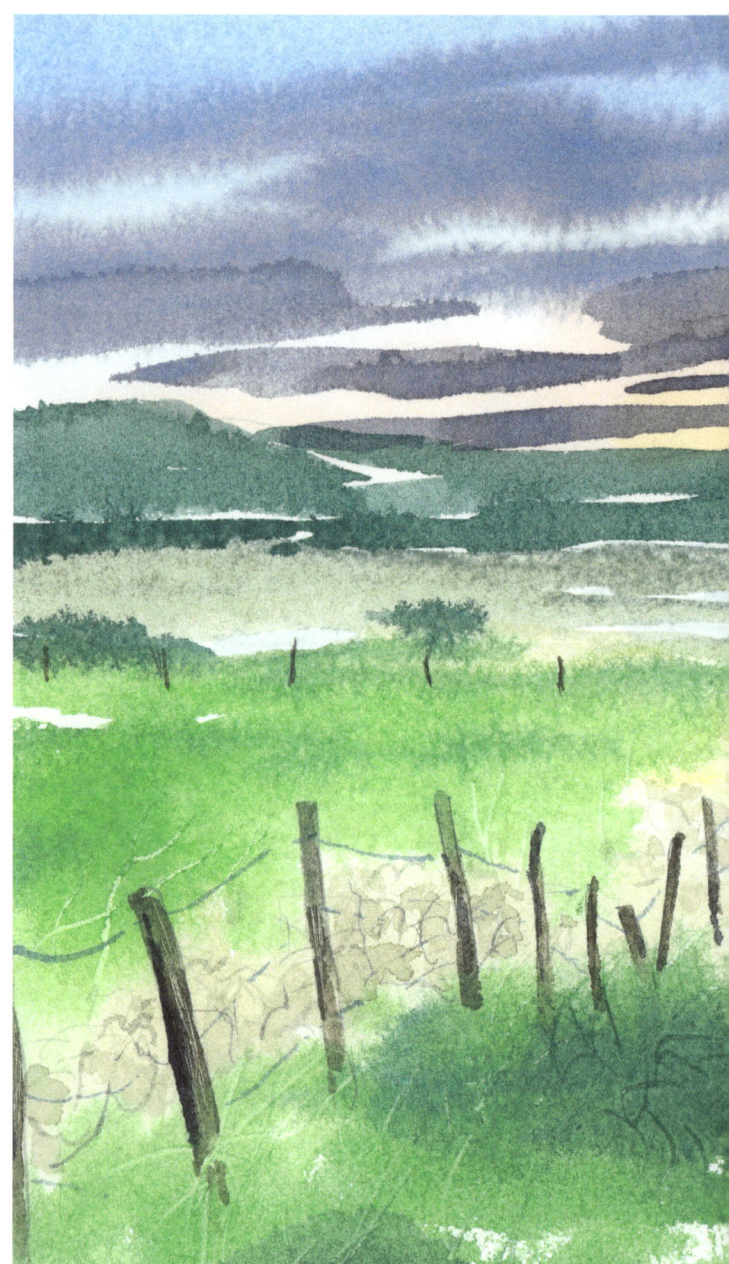

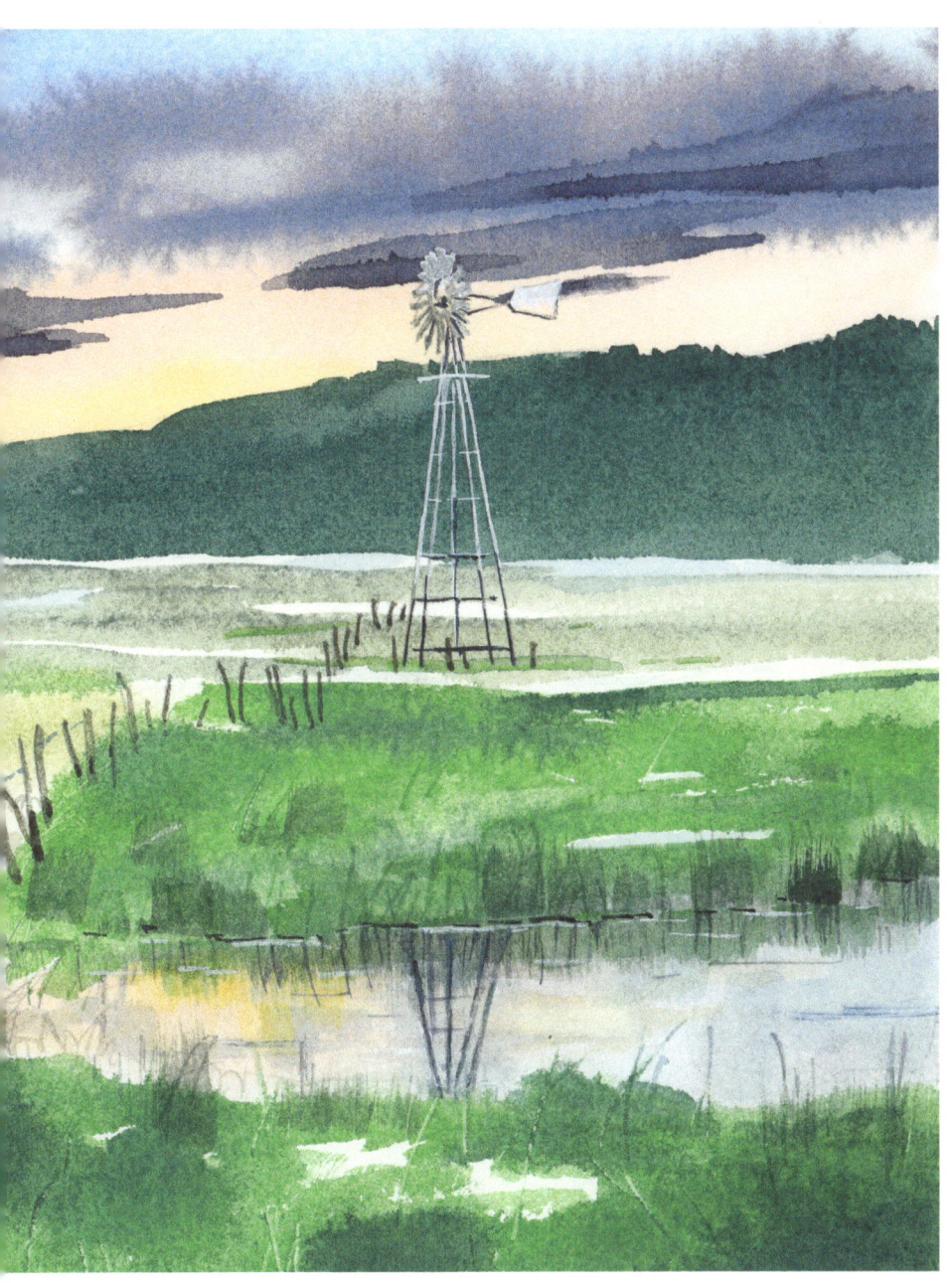

Fence Mending

Fence mending happens in spring. Before pairs (a cow and a calf) go to grass, we'll walk every mile of boundary fence on the place, checking for broken posts, places where wire has been cut by intruders, or downed by heavy snow, and areas where sand has covered the bottom wire, or blown out enough soil to allow calves to crawl under.

Internal fences can wait a bit. It's not such a calamity if our own cattle mix, although we prefer they don't and will get to those before turnout if possible.

–LYN MESSERSMITH,
MY SISTER MARIAH

Dances at the Bohemian Hall

At first sight, it might be considered an abandoned school house. However, it is the old Bohemian Hall in Sioux County. It was also known as the ZCBJ Hall by the Bohemian community. The acronym decoded is Zapadni Ceska Bratrska Jednota which when translated to English is Western Bohemian Fraternal Organization. There are a number of halls in Nebraska and in other parts of the nation, most larger and more substantial in construction. The halls were centers of Bohemian culture—for gatherings and fellowships, and especially for dances.

On a windy day in March, I lingered a while, bracing myself against the gusts that swept across the prairie. Window shades flapped in the old building to zephyrs that whistled through broken windows and slat-wood siding. Softly at first, then increasing in magnitude, the jaunty notes of a fiddle and a button-box accordion floated from the building. I could hear staccato clicking and clacking of shoes on the wood-plank floor. Laughter and gaiety spilled from inside. Then, as the wind abated on its journey across the prairie, music and voices began to quiet, and I was again alone with my thoughts.

For amusement, the young woman in the orange hat will go to the Sandhill dances with others of her kind, perhaps in an outmoded party dress, but most likely in a mail-order print, perhaps made by hand or on the sewing machine of Marlizzie. Their men will be in overalls, turned up jauntily at the cuffs, with open shirt necks and loose ties.

The women will sit on planks over boxes along the wall as their grandmothers did. Now and then the older women, like Marlizzie, will dance to the same fiddle and accordion of forty, fifty years ago. And at midnight there will be cake and sandwiches and coffee.

And toward morning the crowd will scatter, on horseback, in wagons, and in a few old cars that cough and sputter in the sand. The women go to their homes, the straw ticks and cottonwood-leaf mattresses, and to refreshing sleep.

–MARI SANDOZ, *SANDHILL SUNDAYS*

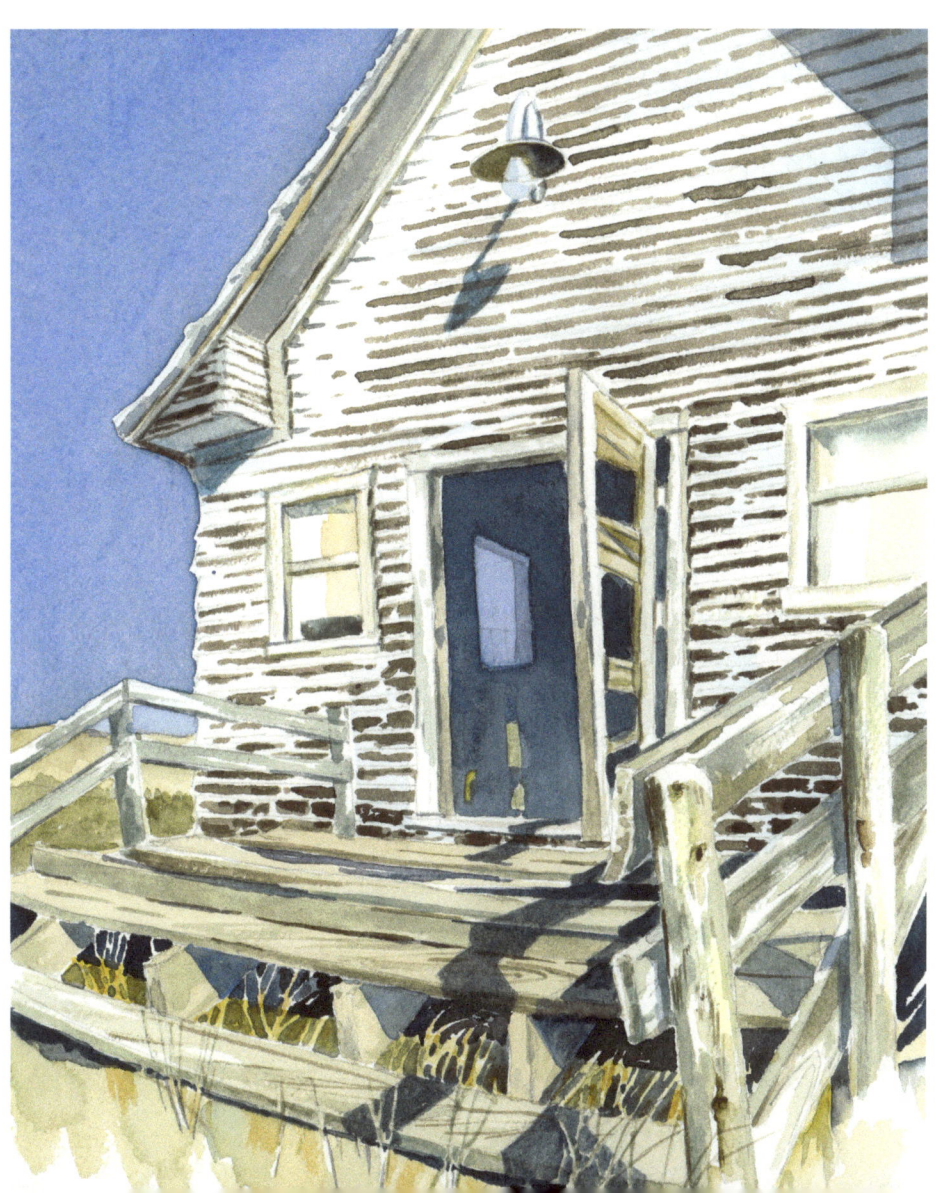

Early Life on the 6H Ranch, Long Tree

Our barn had milking stalls and we milked seven cows. I milked one while my uncle milked six. It had a pulley system where one work horse would pull a big fork-full of hay up to the haymow at a time and release it. One of the kids would lead the horse back and forth. It had stalls for two horses each with mangers. The saddle room had a real old ice box where we kept medicine for the cattle. We had a shed at the back for cattle, but it would be used only for sick cattle or a cow nearing calving in bad weather.

We used to saddle up our horses in this barn to ride to school four miles and sometimes drive a team of Belgian work horses. When I was in the third grade my father let me drive our pickup and asked the patrolman if it was okay. He said, "Can he see over the steering wheel?" Dad said, "No, but he looks between the steering wheel and the dash." The patrolman said, "All but one fourth of a mile is on your ranch, so if he has an accident, pull it over to your land and call us!"

–DON ATEN, BROWN COUNTY

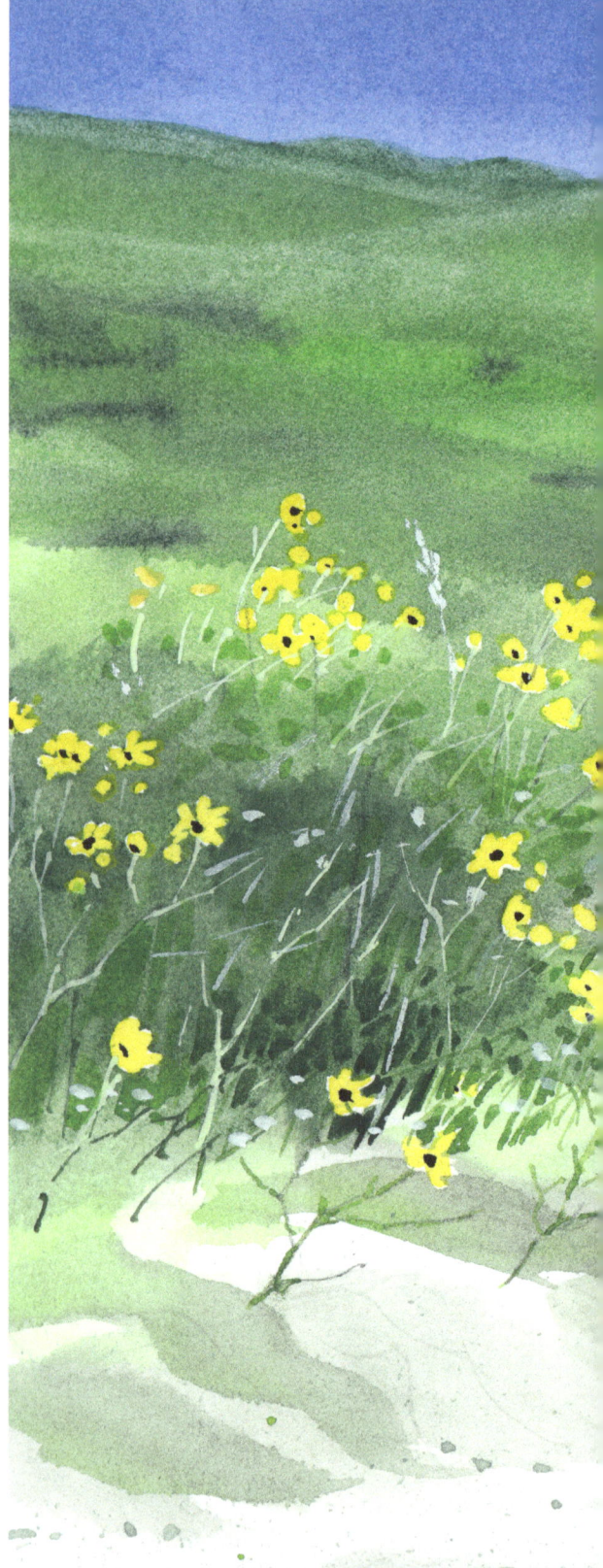

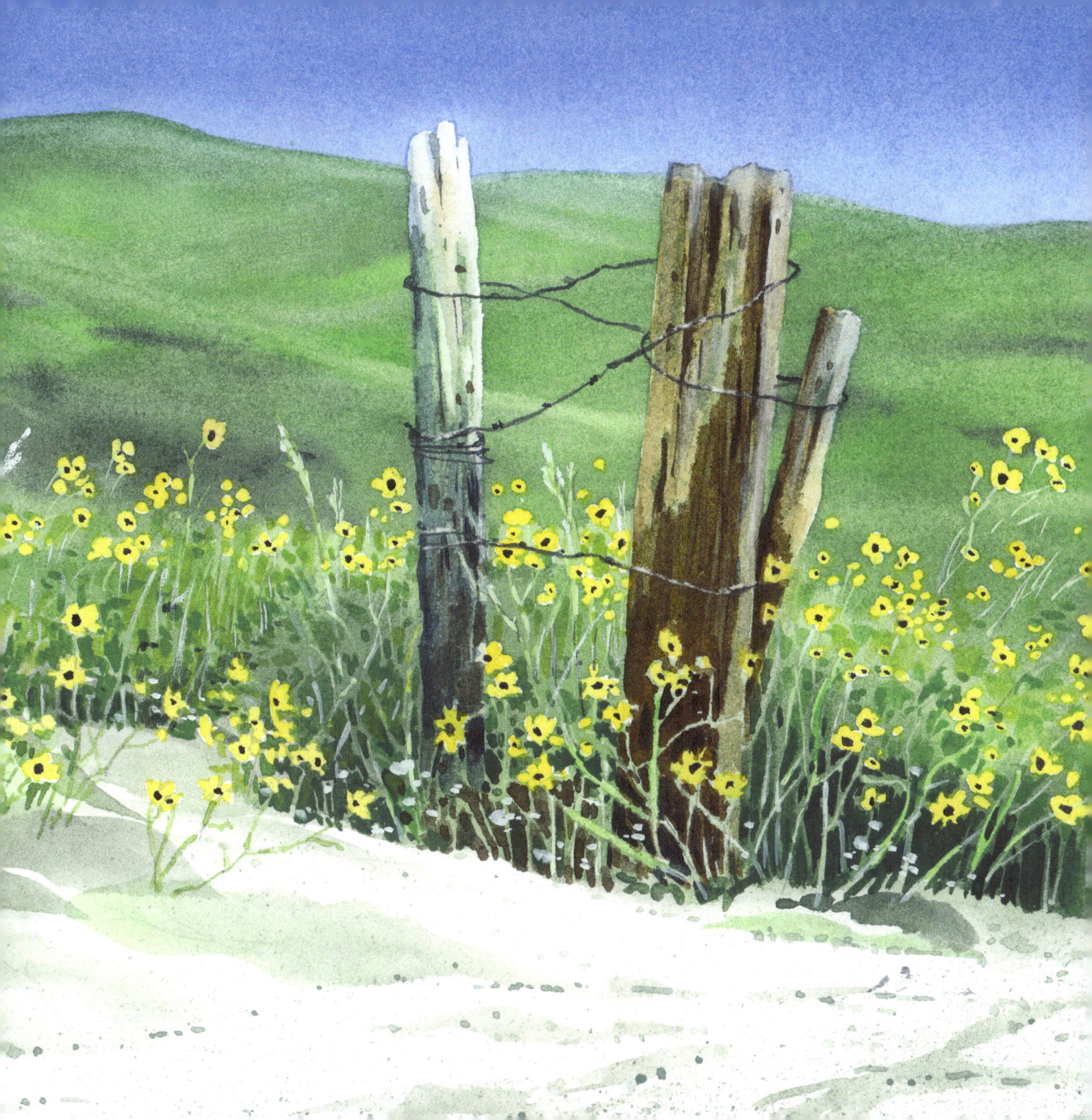

When Work Was Done, There Was Time for Fun

Through growing-up years, there were events that were so exciting and fun. A neighbor rancher, Guy Parsons, had a large barn with a hay loft for our monthly square dances with local ranchers playing fiddles. Uncle Ray was the highlight of the night, dancing a jig. As men would throw coins, he would dance faster and faster in a low crouching position. Dad was the square dance caller.

I attended a little one room country school from first through eighth grade with one teacher and a total enrollment of five or six. We produced a yearly Christmas program. Following the evening program we had a "box social." We girl students and all the mothers would create beautifully decorated covered boxes, placing a supper inside. These boxes were auctioned off. Dad was the delegated auctioneer. Depending on the creativeness, the beauty of the box, and possible knowledge of whose box it was, there would be a great competition between the men bidding to determine which lady they would get to share supper with. It was so exciting for us kids.

Another social event that was great fun was a charivari (shivaree). It held suspense and secrecy. When a young rancher married in our part of the Sandhills, we gave the newlyweds a brief chance to settle into their country home, and then we "welcomed them" with a shivaree. Each neighborhood ranch family would figure out the loudest noise makers possible: cowbells, metal pots and turkey roasters with lids. Word spread on the "party line" with a planned time and place for gathering, usually around nine p.m. Each family would prepare wonderful homemade sandwiches, cakes and cookies, along with coffee. At the designated time, we drove to the newlyweds' home with no car lights on, and on signal, car lights would come on with the honking of horns. We jumped from the vehicles with all the noise makers creating a thunderous commotion as we surrounded their home. Eventually, the sleepy husband opened the front door with the wife, crouched behind him wondering what was going on. We were all welcomed into their home. We covered the kitchen table with a cloth and set out a bounty of delicious food and drink. We would have a wonderful evening eating and visiting. What a special evening it was. . .never to be forgotten by the bride and groom or participants.

–FRANCES GOTSCHALL LEIGHTON

Essie Buchanan Davis—Pioneer Wonder Woman of the Sandhills

This is a story about a remarkable pioneer woman. Her story is not especially unique in the beginning; many immigrant women dreamt of a bountiful land and happy families. Most found only hard work, loneliness, and discouragement. Many gave up and returned to their earlier homes. Essie Davis shared some of those feelings, but what set her apart was a courageous determination not to be a quitter.

Essie was born in Illinois. The Buchanan family traveled to Nebraska and settled in Ogallala, where her father could pursue his dream of buying and selling imported stallions. Essie grew up and became a milliner in this small town. She created special hats for pioneer women who needed a no-nonsense hat that could be pulled down to the ears to brace against prairie winds.

Her future husband would be A. T. Davis. She met him on one of her frequent trips with her father to stock shows in Denver. He was born in Southern Illinois to Robert and Elizabeth Davis, where the family scratched out a living on a hardscrabble farm. The Davis family, with the hopes of a better life and the enticement of free land, moved to Red Willow County, Nebraska. Soon after filing for their homestead, Robert died, leaving Elizabeth and her children to save the homestead. The oldest child, fifteen-year old Al (known as A. T.), would grow in wisdom and stature, forsaking marriage for later to manage the family ranch.

At the age of fifty-seven, A.T. married Essie, in whom he saw a companion and a very smart lady. Sadly, after eighteen months of marriage, A.T. died, leaving Essie with a four-month-old son, a 3,000-acre ranch, and mountains of debt. In her book, *Sandhills Essie*, Martha McKelvie tells a story of a young woman who grew from not knowing anything of ranching and cows, to a predominant position in the cattle business. In the beginning, Essie was untrained and unprepared for a business dominated by cow-men. However, she was tough, determined, and had no fear of speaking up to men when negotiating deals. In time, she studied and built her herd into a thoroughbred line earning the respect of cattlemen, and the ire of possibly a few.

Essie was progressive in her respect for the land, receiving several important awards for soil conservation. She considered the Master Farmer Award in 1939 to be her greatest honor and the pinnacle of her career. She was the first woman recipient of the prestigious Nebraska Builders Award. A staunch Democrat, Essie generously dispensed her advice and opinions. Her work in breeding and soil conservation brought the attention of national leaders and she became the friend of both Republican and Democratic presidents.

This stubborn, cantankerous, but open-minded woman experienced difficulties and failures along with successes.

I thought it over through many weary nights, and then someone said to me that the worst that could happen would be failure, and that would be no worse than being a quitter. I decided right then to deal as a man would. No crybaby stuff was ever to enter in. I would take my losses as a matter of course (or maybe, ignorance). Best of all, as I have found out over the years, I decided to live my life each day and live it so that I could look any man in the face and tell him to go to hell!

–ESSIE BUCHANAN DAVIS

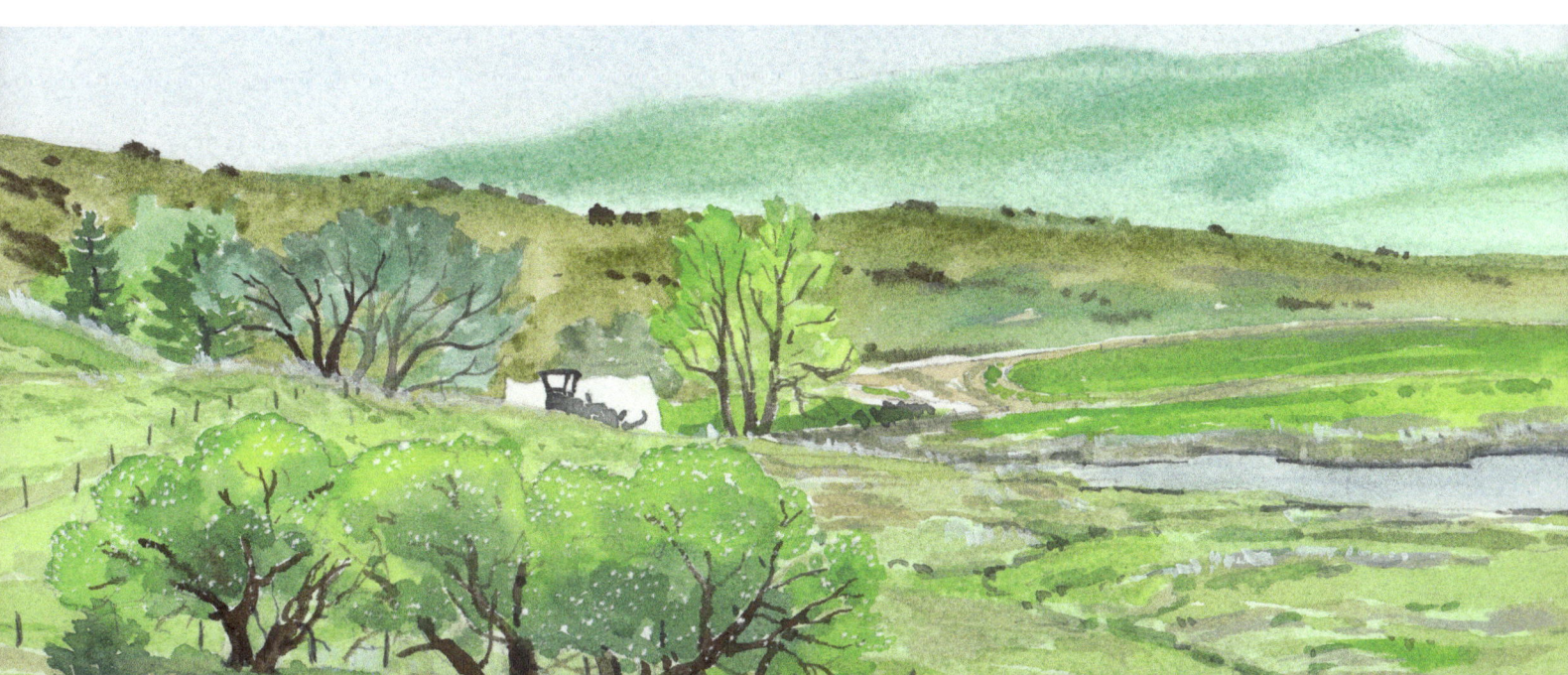

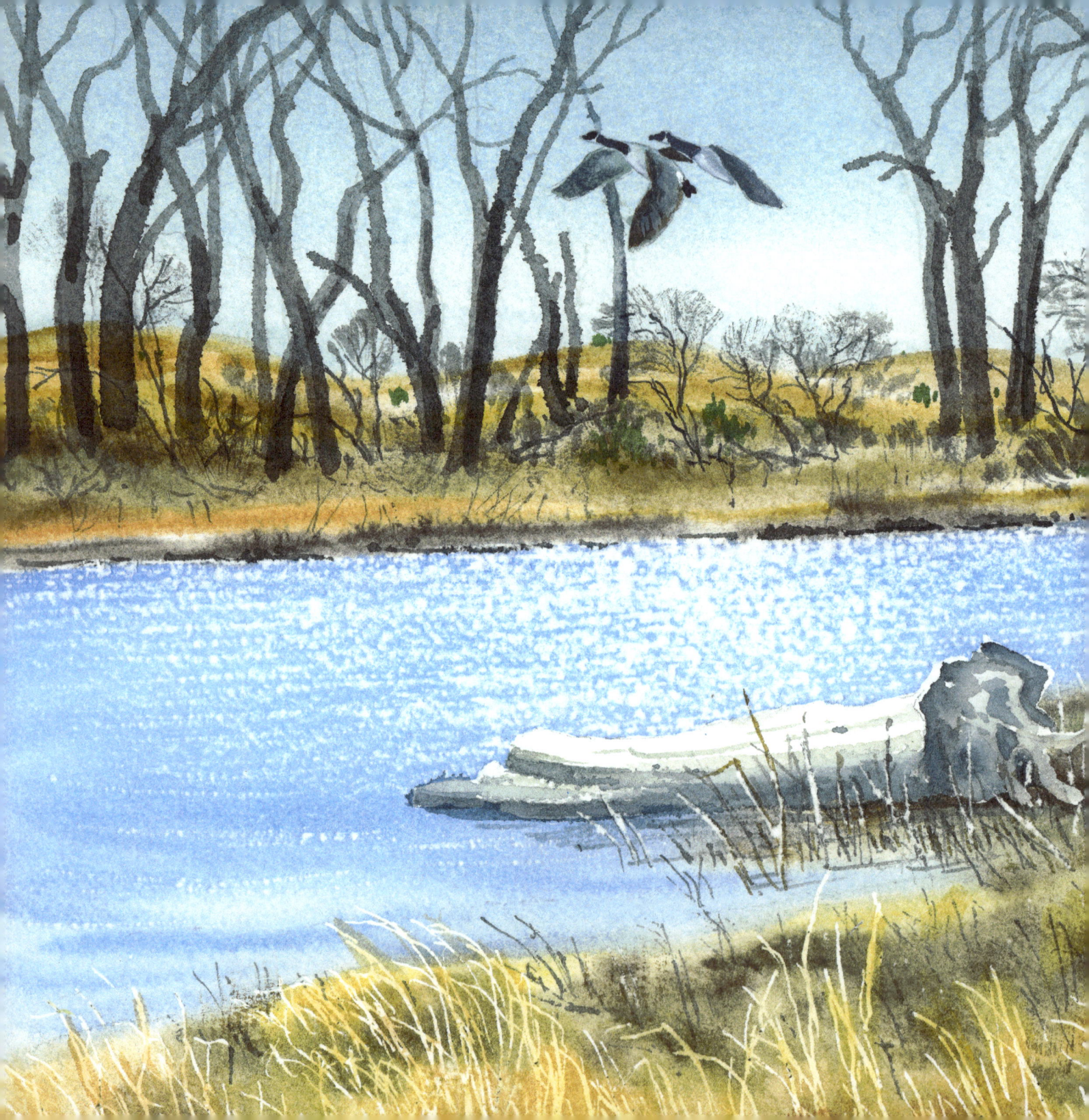

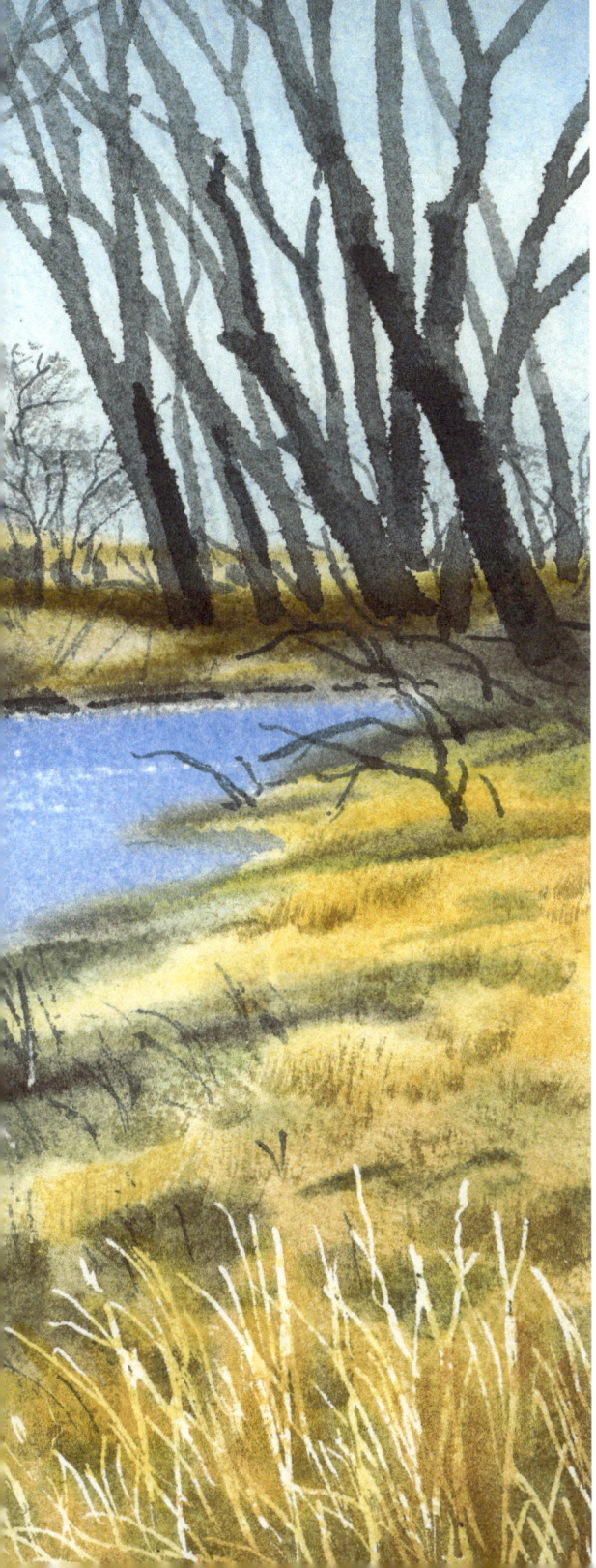

Streams

The streams of the Sandhills are sedge-lined. This life-giving circulatory system begins as innumerable tiny aquatic capillaries, which occasionally burst out unexpectedly from the bases of dunes as artesian springs, then sometimes flow into a Sandhills lake or wander aimlessly as clear, cool brooks through little valleys and wet meadows. These brooks gradually make their way in graceful arcs through nameless Sandhills valleys, usually headed toward the east and southeast, where they eventually reach and merge with the Cedar, Calamus, Dismal, and Loup Rivers, all of which are part of the greater Loup drainage and constitute about half of the Sandhills drainage system.

–PAUL A. JOHNSGARD,
THIS FRAGILE LAND

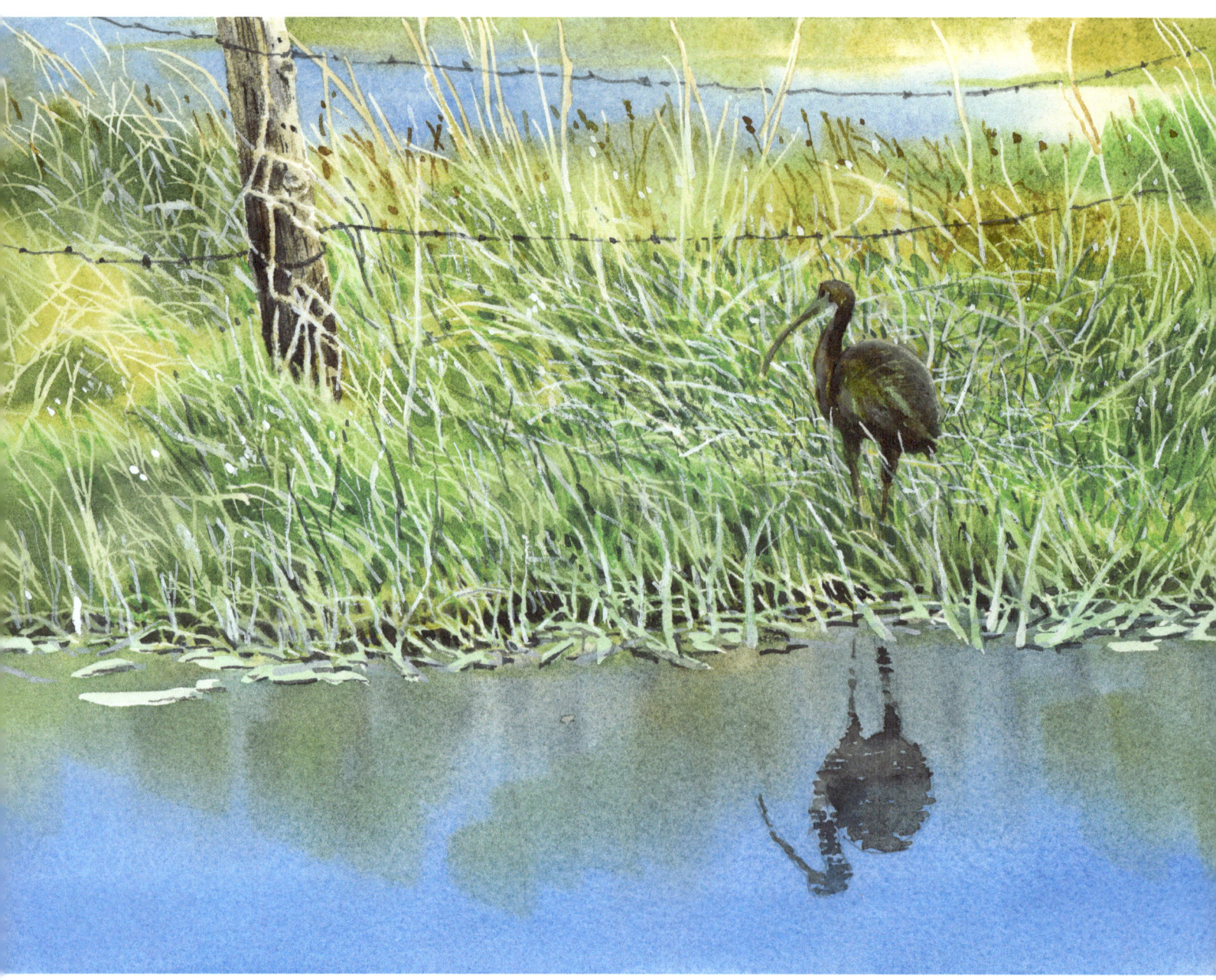

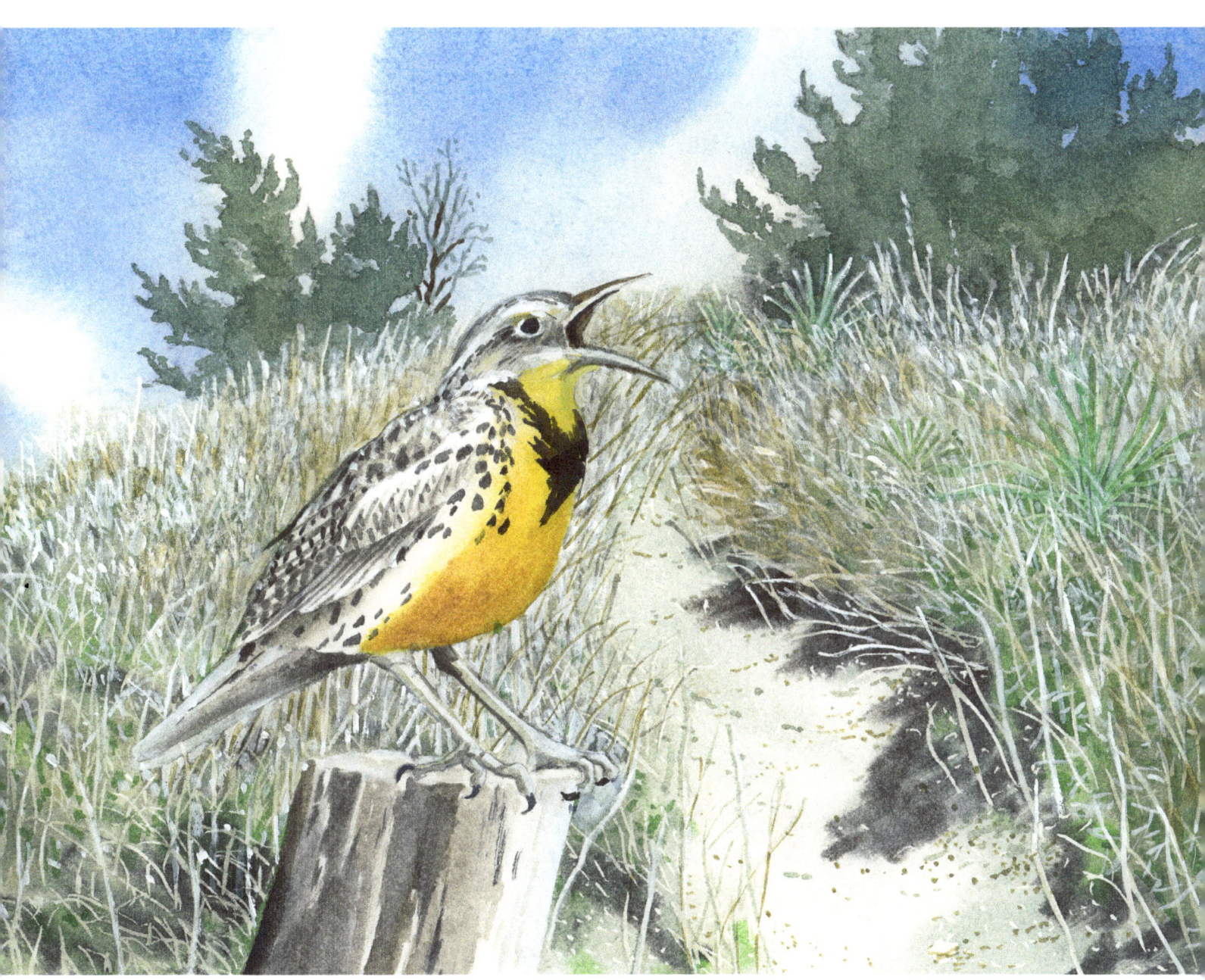

The Making of a Man and a World-Class Sculptor

Herb Mignery grew up on a ranch near Bartlett, Nebraska, on the eastern edge of the Sandhills. He studied four years at Wayne State College. But it was on the ranch that he received an advanced degree in human nature and animal behavior. He did not formally study equine anatomy, but on the ranch his strong powers of observation taught him what he would need to know to be a sculptor of cowboys, horses, and cattle.

After spending three years in the U.S. Army as an illustrator, Mignery returned to Nebraska. Sherry Shavlik was a young lady he had eyes on before leaving for the service. Although younger, Sherry grew up on a ranch near the Mignery's. They began a courtship, married, and soon moved to Hastings. Mignery knew at that time he would never again return to ranching. He had paid his dues there, but for him it was a lonely life. A social person, he felt a need for associations that the lonely prairie did not provide.

Mignery began his commercial art career at Dutton-Lainson. He illustrated products, designed catalogs, and drew cartoons of cowboys with Mignery-esque "tongue-in-cheek" characterizations. They brought smiles to those who had had similar predicaments or could appreciate some of life's tangled messes. In 1973, he cast his first bronze at Art Castings of Colorado. Sculpture would become his medium. He was determined to make art a life-long career and the couple moved to Colorado to be close to the mountains and nearby foundry.

Today, Mignery is recognized for his masterful representation of Western Americana. In 1984, he was elected to the prestigious Cowboy Artists of America, one of many awards and honors received. A man of generous spirit, he has never forgotten his roots or his gratefulness to his community. Beginning in 2002, Herb and Sherry began donating majestic bronzes to beautify the front lawn of the Wheeler County Courthouse. The installation has grown to twenty-five dazzling pieces in the midst of a lovely landscaped garden. Today it is known as The Bronze Garden of Bartlett.

"One of my goals in life as a chronicler is to tell the story of people like those I grew up with. I see myself as a vehicle to let their stories be known." Herb Mignery, Artist.

Mignery, In His Own Words:

I had no formal education that prepared me for art. My study was by osmosis—a preoccupation with movements of horses. I studied the sequence of how they moved their feet. Being a roper, athletically you have to feel the rhythm of the horse, think like the horse. I watched the other cowhands on our ranch. The idea of how a horse moves with grace, and the smoothness with which a cowboy rides in total unity with the animal was fascinating. To me, the horse has always been a work of art—their shape and muscularity— as is the human body.

I believe that you can tell in a Western painting or sculpture if the artist has spent much time on a horse. They might have a visual idea of the movement, but if they have not felt it, their picture may not be physically correct. There are certain movements that a cow or horse makes, and certain movements they don't make. If not artistically correct, it will not look right, and it probably won't make good art either. Sometimes, however, I must take artistic license to show emotion and energy. Every artist may need to stretch to emphasize a subject. You can't always apply formulas, tape measures or calipers to a design, for the subject will then appear too mechanical.

Cowboy humor was part of growing up. I remember one incident that still bothers me today. It was rather nasty mischief. When it rained, my cousin and I would add a ½ inch or inch of water to dad's rain gauge. Ranchers always gathered in town after a rain for coffee and reported their own gauge readings. Dad always had more rain than anyone else. I am sure everyone in town thought he was the biggest liar. As kids, we sometimes made fake arrowheads and planted them in the fields.

The Sandhills were obviously a big, big influence on my life. They provided me with technical experiences and anatomical knowledge that were to become valuable in my career. But more importantly, life there had a psychological influence. There is something about the loneliness of the ranch that affected me. You're out there all alone with only the meadowlarks, and that produces a certain melancholy. The positive effect was that it made me search for beauty and I began creating things in my mind.

–HERB MIGNERY, ARTIST
BARTLETT, NEBRASKA

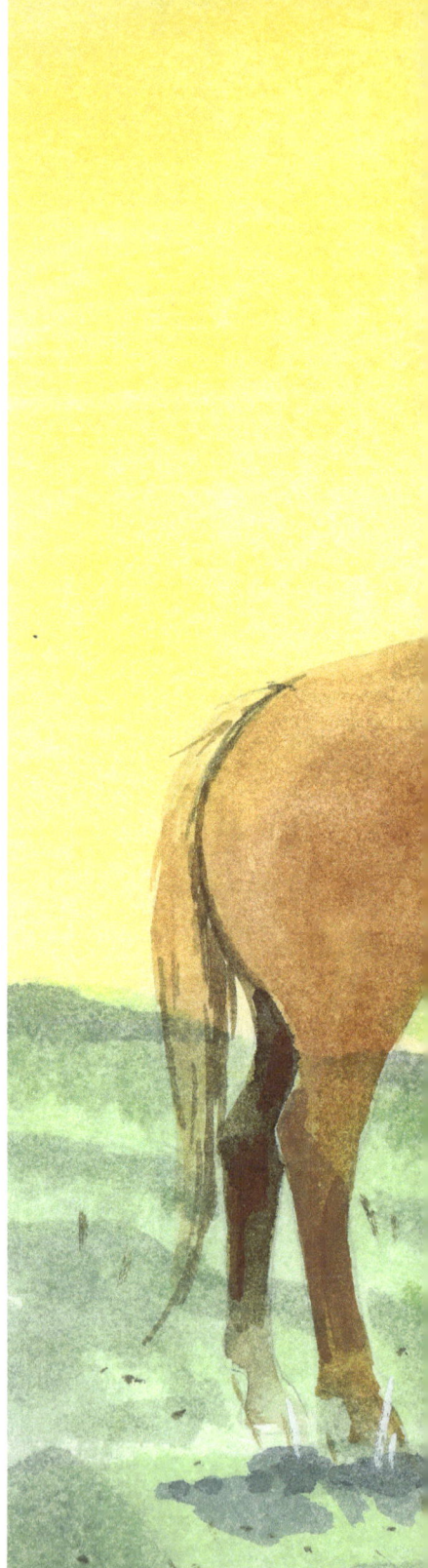

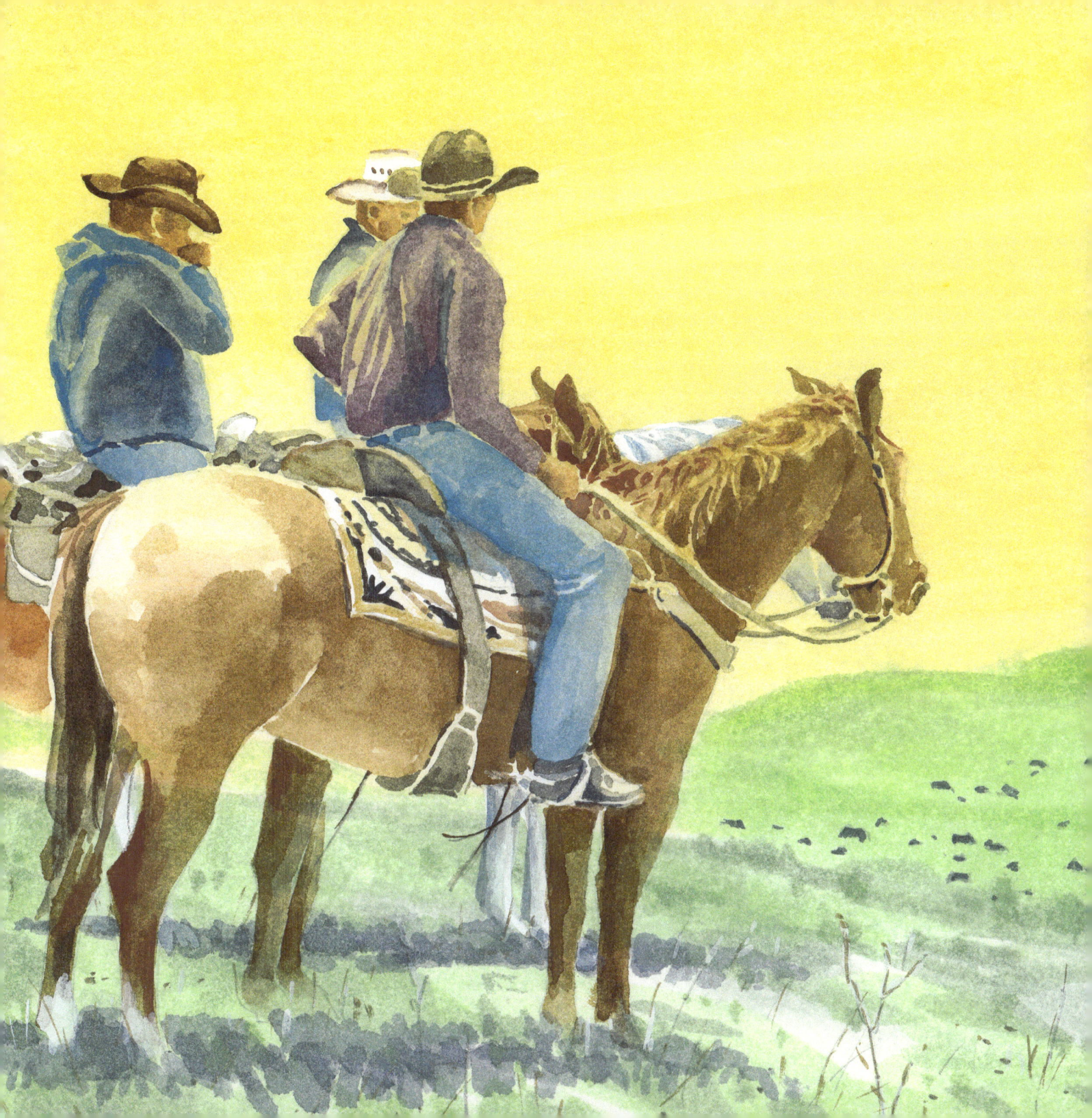

A Pilgrimage to Mari Sandoz's Grave Site

The April morning was beginning to brighten following an overnight rain. My plan was to visit the grave site of the respected Nebraska author, Mari Sandoz. I followed a good black-top highway south from Gordon. Twenty minutes later, a sign at the intersection of the highway and a ranch road announced, "Mari's Grave and Sandoz Fruit Farm—3 miles." So far, so good—I was following directions given to me. The damp, sandy ranch road wound through low rolling hills of springtime green. I was distracted by a panorama of hills dotted with black cows and newborn calves, and traveled five or six miles before I was aware I was off the track. Turning west again, I came upon a road grader. The operator instructed me to take a turn to the north on a less-traveled, one-lane road. After several minutes, I crested a hill that opened to a verdant valley below. I parked my vehicle among blooming sunflowers and walked the last 150 yards to the grave site on the side of the hill that appeared to guard the valley below.

It was a quiet, serene place for one's remains to spend eternity. Below, the fruit trees of Jules Sandoz's orchard are now sparse or broken with age. A wire fence circles the half-acre grave site; not to restrict visitors, but to prevent trampling by livestock. Near the entrance gate is an old mail box on a post. Inside is a piece of cardboard with a simple map drawn of the plot and a spiral notebook in which visitors can record their names. The grave marker is polished brown granite stone that rests on a plinth of similar stone. The modestly simple inscription understates the life accomplishments of one of the West's foremost chroniclers of pioneer life.

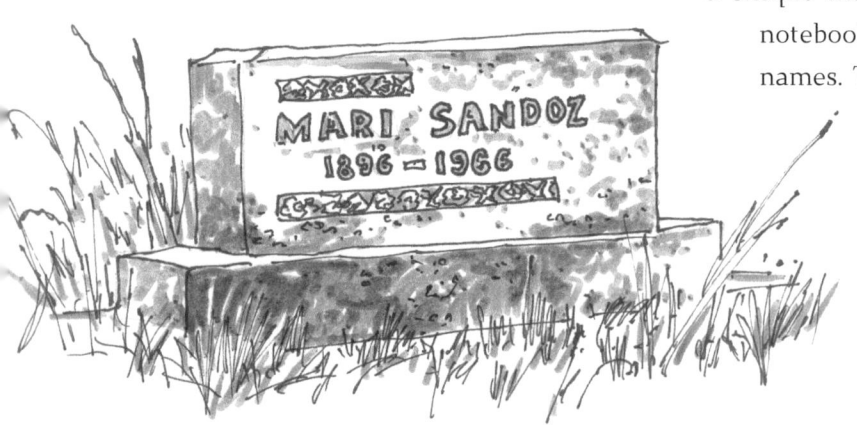

Homage to Mari Sandoz—A Visit to the Grave Site

The one-lane gravel road to Mari Sandoz's grave passes through a forest of sunflowers. They brush against the windows and tickle the undercarriage, making a crunching sound as the car rattles along. The sunflowers crowd up the desiccated hillsides, adding a welcome splash of yellow to the browns and russets of late summer.

–STEPHEN R. JONES
THE LAST PRAIRIE

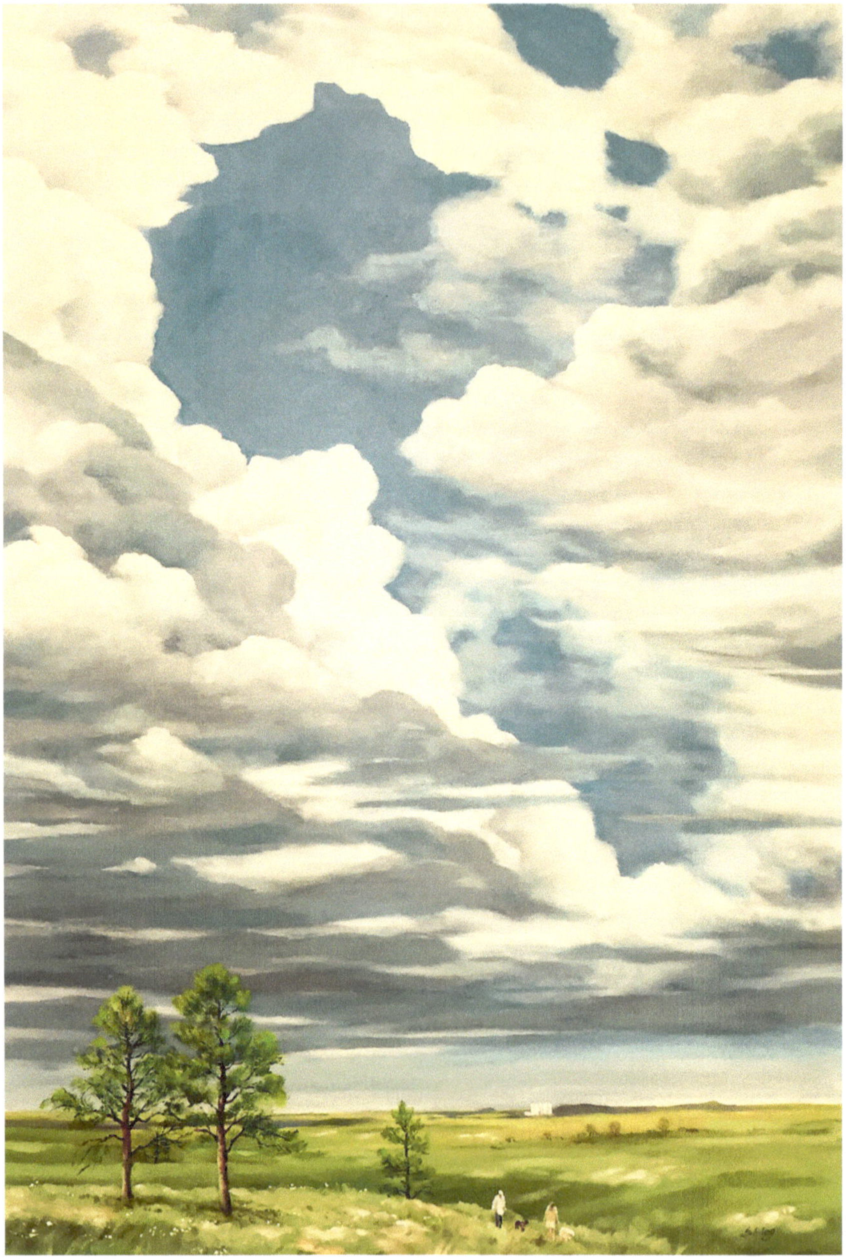

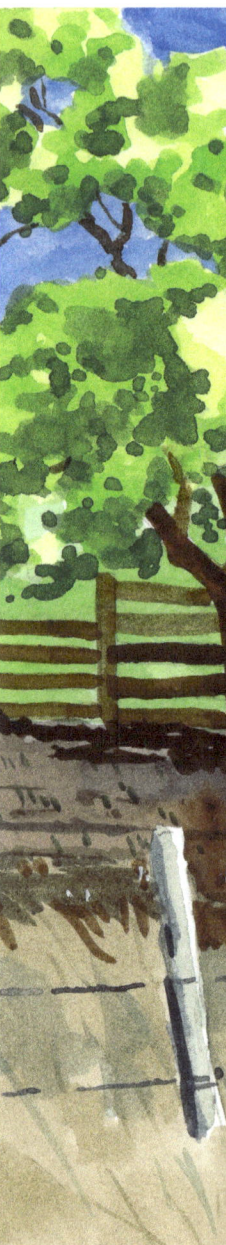

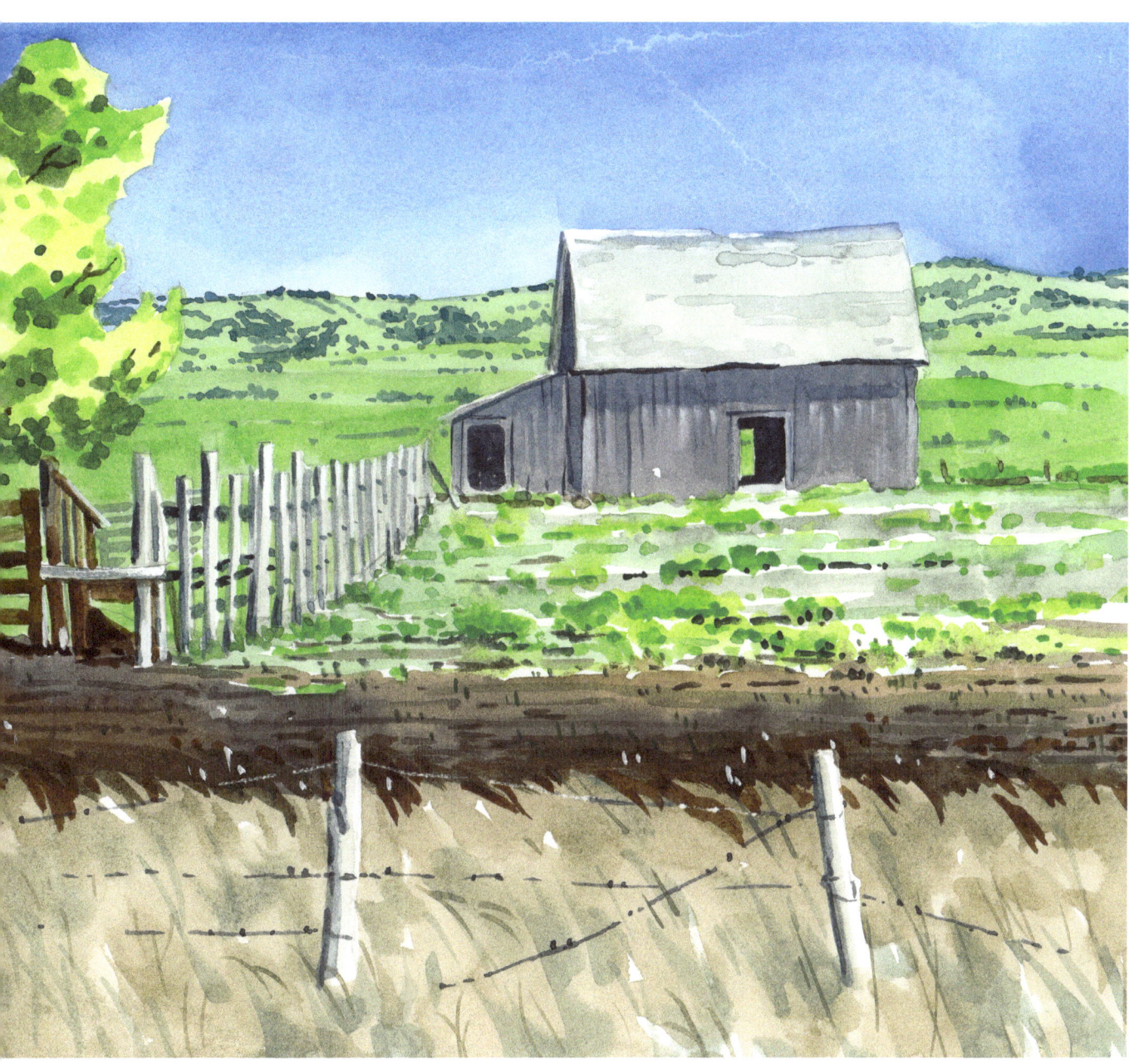

Nebraska Historical Marker
Mari Sandoz
1896-1966

This is the country of Mari Sandoz—historian, novelist, teacher—who brought its history and its people to life in her many books, articles, and stories. She was born in Sheridan County, Nebraska. Although she lived much of her life in the east she is buried here in her own west.

Mari Sandoz was first famed for *Old Jules* (1935), the story of her father and other settlers who came to the upper Niobrara region in the late nineteenth century. Her greatest achievement is the series of six related books on life as it developed with Indian and white men in the trans-Missouri country: *The Beaver Men, Crazy Horse, Cheyenne Autumn, The Buffalo Hunters, The Cattlemen,* and *Old Jules*. In these and a dozen other volumes she presented the drama of man on the Great Plains more completely, accurately and vividly than anyone before her had done.

Mari Sandoz was internationally known as a chronicler of the west and as an expert on Indian history. Her own aim was to understand all of life by understanding this one part of it: how man shaped the Plains country, and how it shaped him.

—NEBRASKA CENTENNIAL COMMISSION,
HISTORICAL LAND MARK COUNCIL

> *"Her own aim was to understand all of life by understanding this one part of it: how man shaped the Plains country, and how it shaped him."*

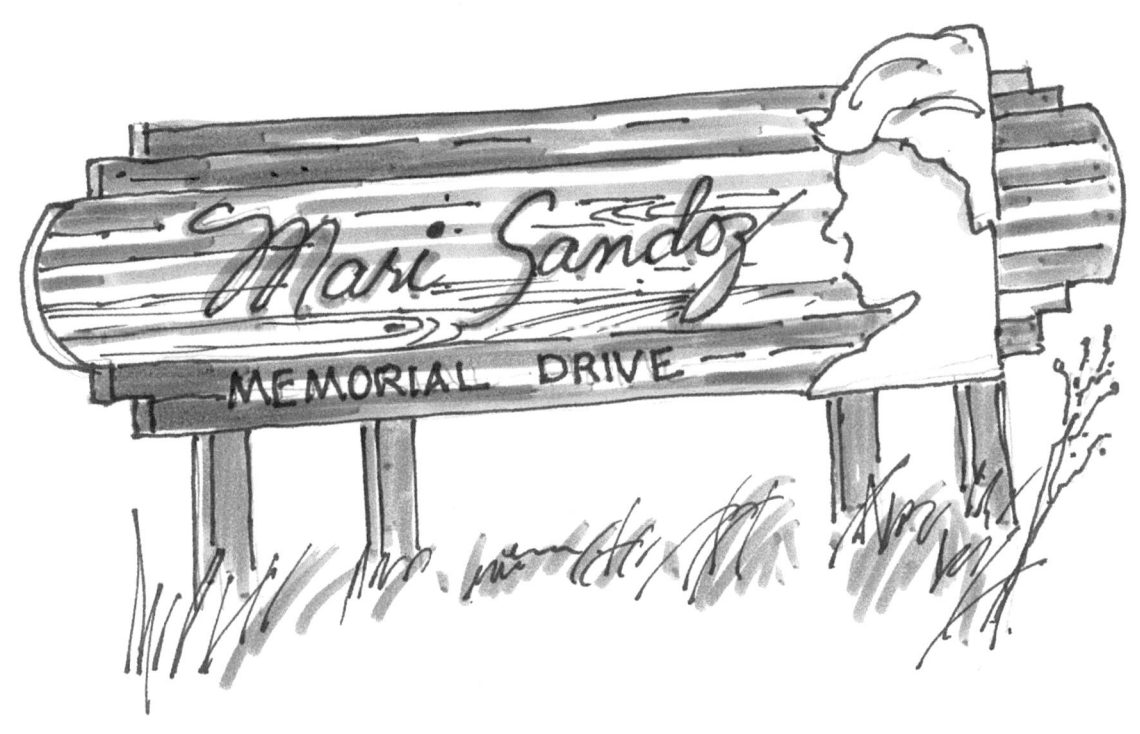

"An Idyllic Childhood"—Janet Larreau

Arnold, in Custer County, lies cloistered beneath high bluffs that provide a charming backdrop to this pleasant community. It lies on the southeastern edge of the Sandhills with an economy that bridges both agriculture and ranching. Nearby, the South Loup River waters the bucolic valley that is dotted with cattle. Poplars and cottonwoods shade modest homes that greet the visitor with happy faces; windowed with sparkling eyes, white porches that smile.

I found Janet Larreau, the editor of the *Arnold Sentinel*, in her office. She peered over the top of her office monitor and greeted me, one of few strangers seen in this little town. I explained the purpose of my visit. Janet warmed to my mission and immediately offered to give me a little tour of her town. She jumped in my car and we travelled north on Carol Street, past her childhood home. We continued up Judkin's Hill while Janet told me of her idyllic childhood.

"It was unsupervised fun. In the summer, we walked barefoot half a mile up this road to Elof's barn where we played with the kittens. We had total freedom; however we were expected to come home when the town siren blew at noon. In winter, we dragged our sleds all the way to the top and then slid back to town. Near the bottom, we had to duck beneath a barbed wire fence to continue the sled ride."

From the top of Judkin's Hill, we peered down into Devil's Den Canyon, where Janet said she and her friends often explored hidden niches in the bluff that provided substance for mysterious rumors that gave rise to its name.

"On cold winter days, mother would drive us down to the river to ice skate. We never thought it might be dangerous." "Did any of you ever get hurt or injured?" I asked. Janet pondered the question for a moment and replied, "No, I don't think so."

I asked Janet the BIG question: "What keeps you here?" "Freedom, family, friends and this beautiful land," was her answer.

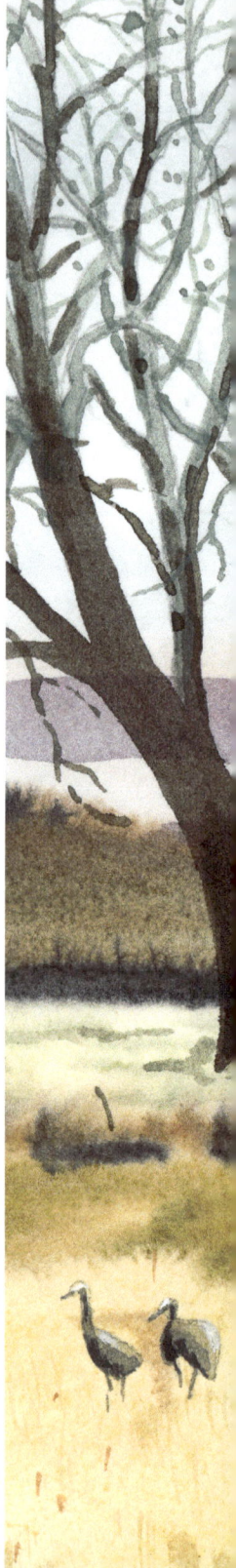

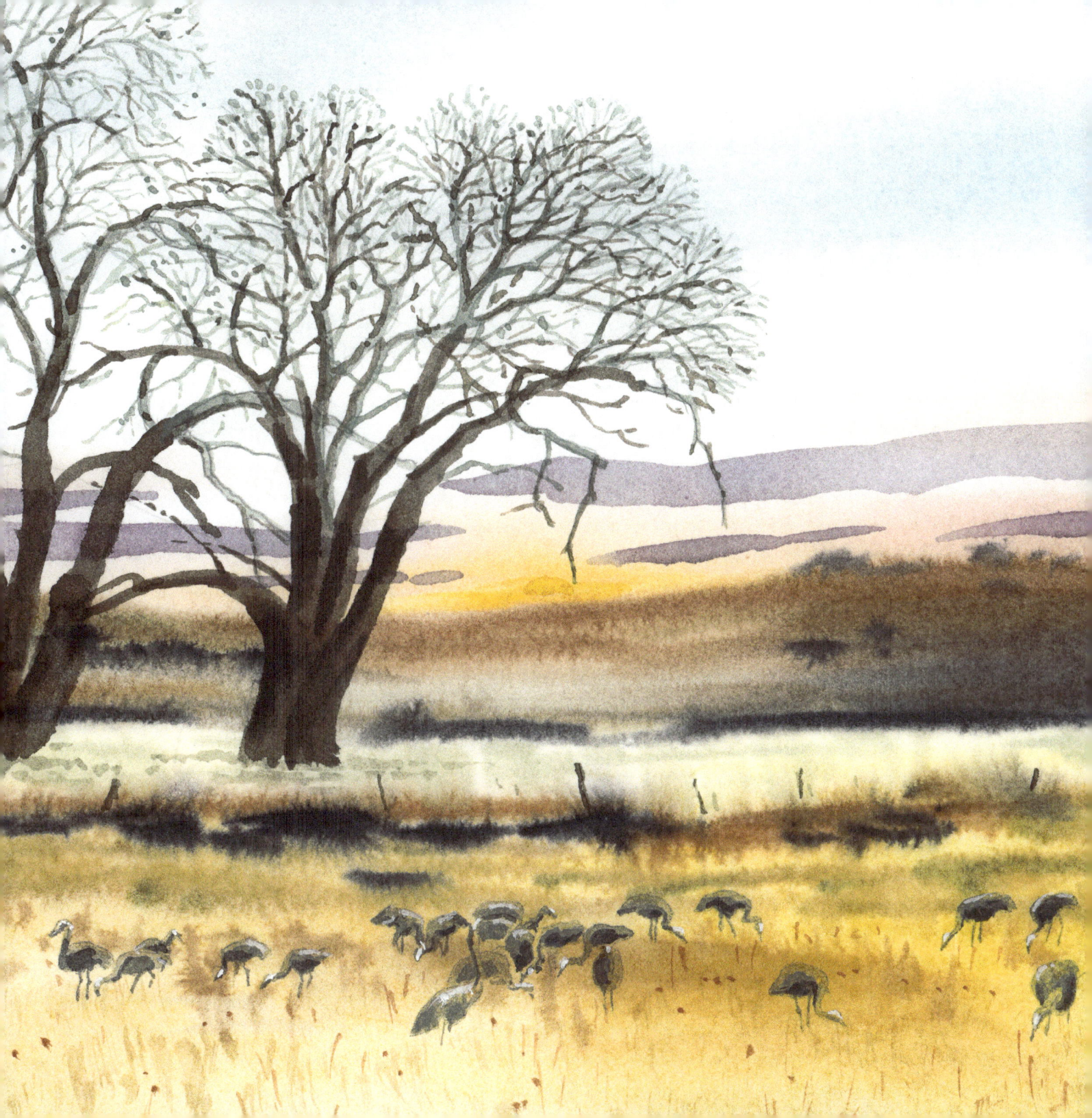

A Dark Night Adventure

An exciting time in the cold winter months was going with my Uncle Ray 'coon hunting. Uncle Ray's hobby and pleasure in life were his coonhounds. He would special order them from Missouri. He enjoyed stroking their heads as he sat under our big elm tree to rest after a hard day of work in the fields and milking cows. Uncle Ray would check the weather to know the right hunting night when there would be no wind and the temperature above freezing. He would put fresh hay in the back of his old pickup truck where Uncle Ray, the dogs, and I would ride. My dad was the driver. When we reached a certain chosen location, a cornfield, lake, or by deserted ranch buildings, we and the dogs would bail out of the truck and into the dark night with only a kerosene lantern carried by my uncle for light. Dad stayed in the truck and picked us up after the hunt. Upon unloading the dogs they immediately and excitedly began running around sniffing the ground. Within minutes they would either begin to bark "trail" or search farther afield for the scent. Their bark was different depending on how hot the trail was. Uncle Ray and I would follow them as fast as we could go. We would follow them for miles; raccoons are fast runners. Old "Drive" was usually the first hound to find the trail. We knew his bark and soon "Gouge" would chime in. When the dogs' long wailing barks became constant, and in a different pitch, we knew they were closing in. The dogs would bark "tree" or "hole" and we rushed faster to be there before the raccoon could get in a fight with the dogs. A raccoon would either run up a tree, duck into a badger hole, hide under a deserted building, crawl into a wood pile or climb a windmill. On one occasion, a 'coon mistakenly climbed up my dad's back which surprised them both. Raccoons could really injure a dog with their long claws and sharp teeth, so it was urgent we arrive quickly at the site of their catching. If it was in water, a raccoon could drown a dog by holding its head under water. Dad listened for the dogs' voices, to know the direction to drive on the country roads. He always ended up near our "catch" site. Uncle Ray knew his directions by looking at the stars, but sometimes we would have a distance to walk to the pickup carrying heavy raccoons slung over our shoulders. One night I carried a big lousy one. Mother wasn't too happy when I arrived home smelling like the dogs and my hair itching from lice.

–FRANCES GOTSCHALL LEIGHTON

> "A raccoon would either run up a tree, duck into a badger hole, hide under a deserted building, crawl into a wood pile or climb a windmill."

Broken Homes, Broken Dreams

If only dwellings could speak and walls had listened to those within, what stories they could tell. They might speak of dreams and plans for prosperity; of lives that began there, and possibly some whose toils came to an end there. The walls might speak of happiness; children laughing, playing, and at times quarreling. Or anger, frustration, and sadness when rains never came, or too much rain and hail came and destroyed a livelihood. They would tell of relentless winter storms, loss of cows and discouragement that followed.

The drought brought on the dust bowl with persistent winds stripping away precious top soil. Dirt found its way into homes through the smallest cracks and crevices. Women worked just to keep it out of clothing, cupboards, bedding, water, and food. Prices fell, crops failed, cattle found little grass for grazing, and loans were called. Misery bred heartbreak and depression. Many who came earlier to the Sandhills with dreams of land and wealth joined a reverse migration as the Great Depression dragged on.

Conditions improved in the forties, and the settlers that endured became successful farmers and ranchers. Today, there are new challenges to the family operations. Ninety percent of farms in the United States are still family managed. However, corporate farming is bringing about a change as farmers and ranchers age and retire. Their children are not always interested in continuing the ranching life. Small family farms and ranches are becoming larger family operations that later become part of larger corporations. Sadly, the small family operation lifestyle is vanishing. Farm and ranch children historically have learned the value of work; responsibilities of small chores, gathering eggs, raising and caring for animals.

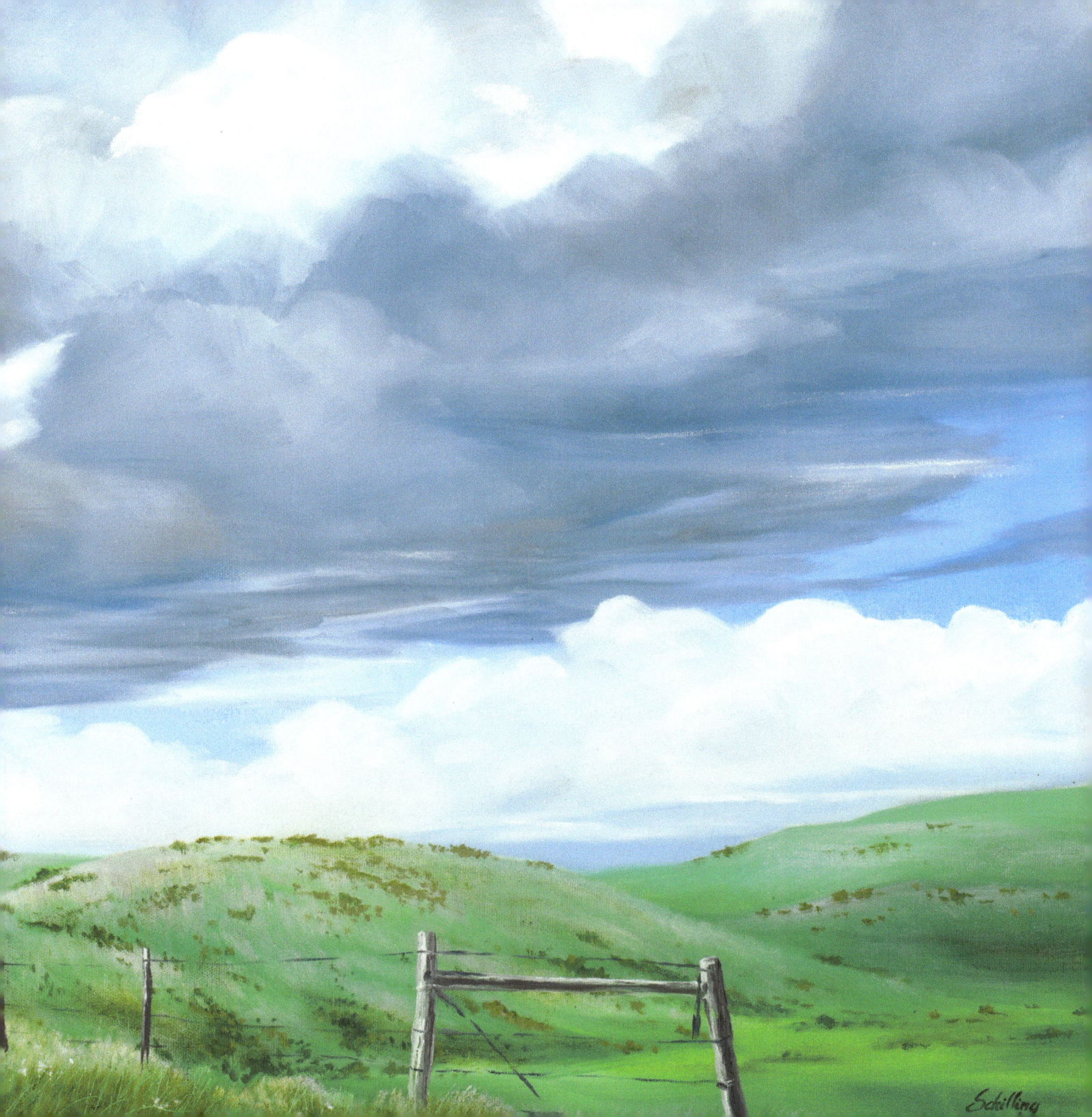

Pasture Grasses have a Story of their Own

Glenna Abbott is my new friend. She is a ninety-years-young, hard-working rancher who has a place south of Long Pine. As a young girl, Glenna was assigned chores, and every evening she walked or rode a pony to bring in the milk cows. It was then that she developed a love and respect for different grasses, especially the wild flowers. The adults often had "nicknames" for the plants. Glenna says that it was not until her eldest son took Agriculture in high school that she learned more about the plants in her pasture and their correct names. Much of her life has been devoted to teaching others to respect and enjoy the native grasses. Today, she continues to share her knowledge with young farmers and ranchers.

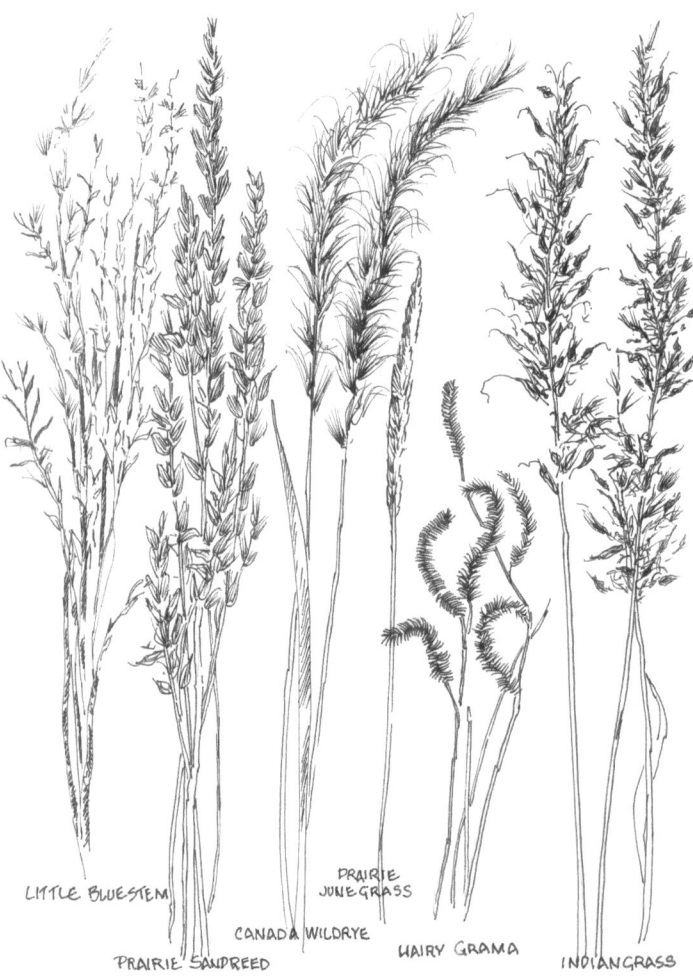

PASTURE GRASSES

There are three classes of plants: they are decreasers, increasers, and invaders. Their names rather describe their purposes. Decreasers are the most valuable for nutrition. They are the favorites of livestock and consequently they can be over-grazed if a pasture is not managed properly. Increasers provide less nutritional value but still have good forage value. Invaders may take over the other two types and make the pasture much less desirable. A well-managed range or meadow needs both decreasers and increasers. When more invaders creep into the pastures, it tells us we are lacking good management.

Hairy Grama is a short, warm seasonal grass and is a close cousin to Blue Grama. The difference can be seen in the seed head. Blue Grama has a spike at the end of the seed head and is blueish. Hairy Grama is rather hairy around the seed head and is greyish. It often is found where the soil is drier. Both are excellent food for late grazing if weather permits. They are a good "weight-gainer" for cattle; however the grass is short and cannot be used as a hay crop.

Prairie Sandreed is a warm-season perennial sod grass. It increases with underground rhizomes that creep horizontally. The sod makes good building blocks for homes and structures. It is considered a decreaser and grows as the weather becomes warm.

Big Blue Stem is another warm-season decreaser that grows in valleys where the soil is heavier and moister than on sandy hilltops. It is excellent in quality, quantity and palatability. It should not be over-grazed or mowed too often.

Canada Wildrye is a cool season, early grass. It is found along streams and shaded areas. It is a decreaser that gets coarse as the summer warms up.

Prairie June Grass is an early cool-season grass. It is good for forage and is very palatable. It is preferred by livestock and wildlife and can be easily over-grazed.

Indiangrass is a warm-season, perennial tall grass with short rhizomes. It grows rather dense and pretty. It is often found growing among bluegrass. It cuts heavy for hay and grazes well.

–GLENNA ABBOTT

I Want to Go Home

I want to go home to the prairie in spring
Oh, I want to go home.
Where meadowlarks on fence posts sing.
And sunburnt planters sweat and toil
In black fields of newly turned soil.
I want to hear the chatter of the cranes
Standing with thousands in fields of grain.

I want to go home to the prairie in summer.
Oh, I want to go home
To the fragrance of newly mown hay,
Where chicken is frying in the cookhouse,
And grandad's sitting on the porch swing
Telling tales of years gone by when
Work was hard, but life was good.

I want to go home to the prairie in autumn.
Sycamore, cottonwood trees red and gold.
We used to laugh and kick those leaves.
Wood smoke in the chimney when grandma calls
"Time you men come, 'cause there's pheasant
and apple pie's a-cooling just for you."
And that's the country I always knew.

I want to go home to the prairie in winter.
To sit by the fire, just mother and me,
Holding hands and Bibles on our knees.
The wind sings a soft hymn of praise,
Reminding us God blessed us all our days.
Oh, I want to go home, I want to go home,
I want to go home just one more time.

—RICHARD J. SCHILLING

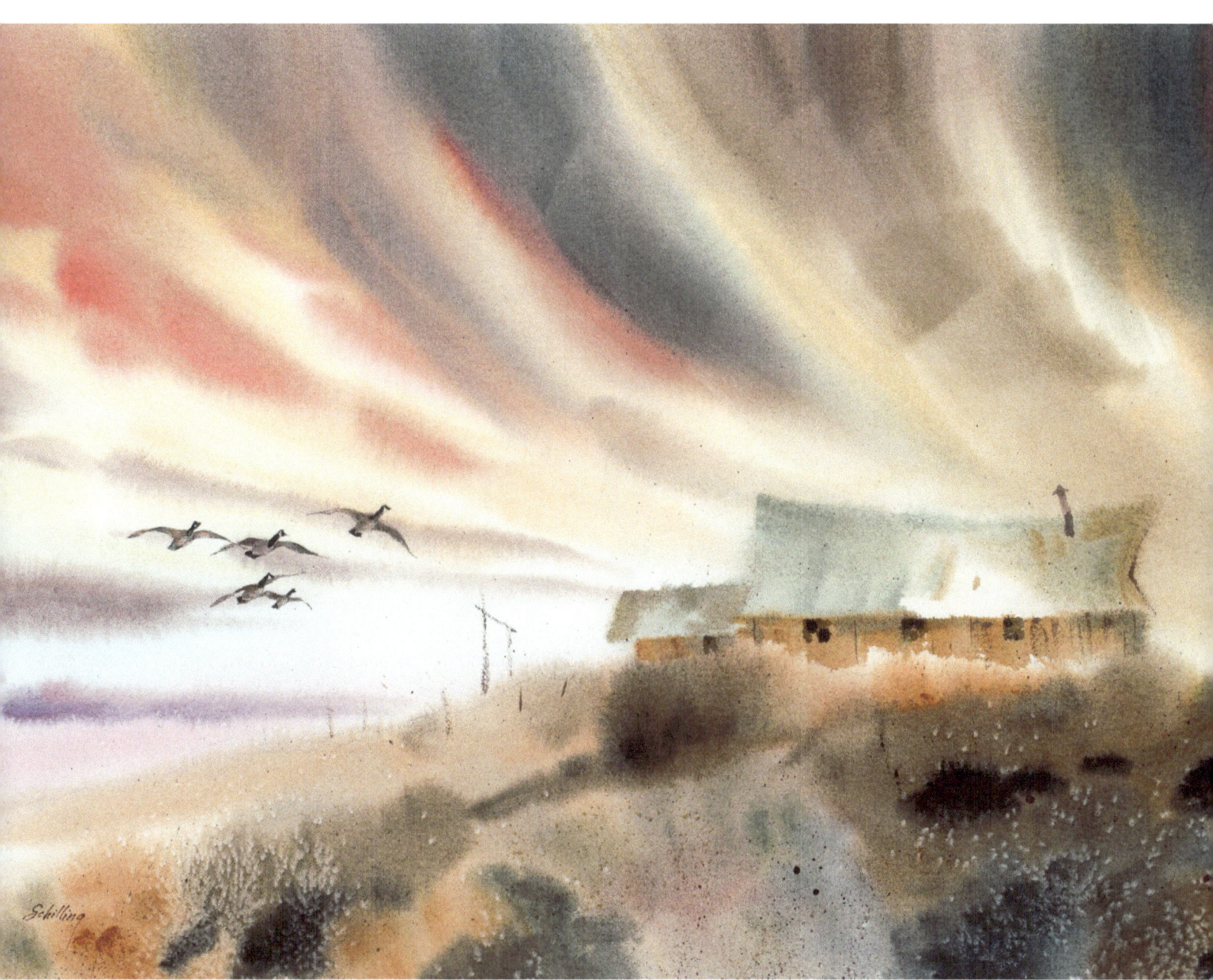

www.ingramcontent.com/pod-product-compliance
Lightning Source LLC
Chambersburg PA
CBHW051911210526
45473CB00006B/1973